RSF: The Russell Sage Foundation Journal of the Social Sciences

The Underground Gun Market: Implications for Regulation and Enforcement

VOLUME 3, NUMBER 5, OCTOBER 2017

RSF: The Russell Sage Foundation Journal of the Social Sciences   ISSN 2377-8261

The Russell Sage Foundation

The Russell Sage Foundation, one of the oldest of America's general purpose foundations, was established in 1907 by Mrs. Margaret Olivia Sage for "the improvement of social and living conditions in the United States." The foundation seeks to fulfill this mandate by fostering the development and dissemination of knowledge about the country's political, social, and economic problems. While the foundation endeavors to assure the accuracy and objectivity of each book it publishes, the conclusions and interpretations in Russell Sage Foundation publications are those of the authors and not of the foundation, its trustees, or its staff. Publication by Russell Sage, therefore, does not imply foundation endorsement.

Board of Trustees

Sara S. McLanahan, *Chair*

Larry M. Bartels
Karen S. Cook
W. Bowman Cutter III
Sheldon H. Danziger
Kathryn Edin
Michael Jones-Correa
Lawrence F. Katz

David Laibson
Nicholas Lemann
Martha Minow
Peter R. Orszag
Claude M. Steele
Shelley E. Taylor
Hirokazu Yoshikawa

Mission Statement

RSF: The Russell Sage Foundation Journal of the Social Sciences is a peer-reviewed, open-access journal of original empirical research articles by both established and emerging scholars. It is designed to promote cross-disciplinary collaborations on timely issues of interest to academics, policymakers, and the public at large. Each issue is thematic in nature and focuses on a specific research question or area of interest. The introduction to each issue will include an accessible, broad, and synthetic overview of the research question under consideration and the current thinking from the various social sciences.

RSF Journal Editorial Board

Elizabeth O. Ananat, Duke University
Karen S. Cook, Stanford University
Sheldon H. Danziger, Russell Sage Foundation
Mesmin Destin, Northwestern University
Janet C. Gornick, The CUNY Graduate Center
Jennifer Hochschild, Harvard University
Mary E. Pattillo, Northwestern University
Becky Pettit, University of Texas at Austin
James Sidanius, Harvard University
Miguel S. Urquiola, Columbia University
Mary C. Waters, Harvard University

Copyright © 2017 by Russell Sage Foundation. All rights reserved. Printed in the United States of America. No part of this publication may be reproduced, stored in a retrieval system, or transmitted in any form or by any means, electronic, mechanical, photocopying, recording, or otherwise, without the prior written permission of the publisher. Reproduction by the United States Government in whole or in part is permitted for any purpose.

Opinions expressed in this journal are not necessarily those of the editors, editorial board, trustees, or the Russell Sage Foundation.

We invite scholars to submit proposals for potential issues through the *RSF* application portal: https://rsfjournal.onlineapplicationportal.com/. Submissions should be addressed to Suzanne Nichols, Director of Publications.

To view the complete text and additional features online please go to **www.rsfjournal.org**.

Russell Sage Foundation
112 East 64th Street
New York, NY 10065

ISSN (print):   2377-8253
ISSN (electronic): 2377-8261
ISBN: 978-0-87154-742-2

The Underground Gun Market: Implications for Regulation and Enforcement

ISSUE EDITORS
Philip J. Cook, Duke University
Harold A. Pollack, University of Chicago

CONTENTS

Part I. Introduction

Reducing Access to Guns by Violent Offenders **2**
Philip J. Cook and Harold A. Pollack

Part II. The Primary Market

The Stock and Flow of U.S. Firearms: Results from the 2015 National Firearms Survey **38**
Deborah Azrael, Lisa Hepburn, David Hemenway, and Matthew Miller

Firearms Licensee Characteristics Associated with Sales of Crime-Involved Firearms and Denied Sales: Findings from the Firearms Licensee Survey **58**
Garen J. Wintemute

Part III. Response to Gun Regulation and Enforcement

Long-Term Trends in the Sources of Boston Crime Guns **76**
Anthony A. Braga

A Comparative Analysis of Crime Guns **96**
Megan E. Collins, Susan T. Parker, Thomas L. Scott, and Charles F. Wellford

The Initial Impact of Maryland's Firearm Safety Act of 2013 on the Supply of Crime Handguns in Baltimore **128**
Cassandra K. Crifasi, Shani A.L. Buggs, Seema Choksy, and Daniel W. Webster

Prohibited Possessors and the Law: How Inmates in Los Angeles Jails Understand Firearm and Ammunition Regulations **141**
Melissa Barragan, Kelsie Y. Chesnut, Jason Gravel, Natalie A. Pifer, Keramet Reiter, Nicole Sherman, and George Tita

PART I
Introduction

Reducing Access to Guns by Violent Offenders

PHILIP J. COOK AND HAROLD A. POLLACK

Since the massacre of children and educators in Newtown, Connecticut, in December 2012, public concern and mobilization around the issues of gun violence and regulation has surged, and not only in connection with mass shootings. President Obama called for universal background checks to limit access to guns by dangerous people, and gun control briefly rose to the top of the congressional agenda. The proper regulation of firearms was a prominent issue in the 2016 presidential campaign, both the Democratic primary and the general election. Many states have recently amended their firearms regulations, in some cases to make them more stringent, in others less. Law enforcement agencies, most prominently in Chicago and other cities where gun violence rates have increased since 2015, are seeking innovative methods to reduce the use of guns in criminal violence (Police Foundation and Major Cities Chiefs Association 2017).

Reducing gun violence deserves a prominent place on the political agenda. In part, it is a matter of social justice. The high gun-violence rate that afflicts many low-income neighborhoods is not merely a symptom of underlying poverty and joblessness; it also degrades the quality of life (Cook and Ludwig 2000). Further, violence contributes to a vicious cycle that exacerbates out-migration, loss of community cohesion, struggling schools, and withdrawal of employment and investment—setting the stage for more violence.

When the five-city Moving to Opportunity experiment recruited mothers living in public housing, by far the most common reason the mothers gave for signing up was fear of crime: 75 percent endorsed that reason (Ludwig et al. 2013). Further, the strongest finding was that moving to more prosperous neighborhoods reduced stress and improved adult mental health, apparently because crime rates were lower. Not only does crime disproportionately affect troubled neighborhoods, it also affects the most socially and economically vulnerable Americans as it widens racial and ethnic disparities in population health. Among males age fifteen to twenty-four in the United States, homicide is the fourth leading cause of death for non-Hispanic whites and the second for Hispanics. Among black males in this age group, it is the leading cause of death and

Philip J. Cook is ITT/Terry Sanford Professor of Public Policy and professor of economics and sociology at the Sanford School of Public Policy, Duke University. **Harold A. Pollack** is Helen Ross Professor at the School of Social Services Administration, University of Chicago.

© 2017 Russell Sage Foundation. Cook, Philip J., and Harold A. Pollack. 2017. "Reducing Access to Guns by Violent Offenders." *RSF: The Russell Sage Foundation Journal of the Social Sciences* 3(5): 1–36. DOI: 10.7758/RSF.2017.3.5.01. The authors thank Ted Alcorn, Joseph Blocher, Kristin Goss, Jens Ludwig, and Joel Wallman for their very helpful comments on an earlier draft. Direct correspondence to: Philip J. Cook at pcook@duke.edu, Sanford School of Public Policy, PO Box 90545, Duke University, Durham, NC 27708; and Harold A. Pollack at haroldp@uchicago.edu, University of Chicago, School of Social Service Administration, 969 East 60th St., Chicago, IL 60637.

claims more lives than the nine other leading causes *combined*.[1]

Criminal misuse of firearms is a problem over and above the general problem of criminal violence. Not only are guns far more lethal than knives and clubs, they also have the unique quality of killing indiscriminately and at a distance. In neighborhoods afflicted by gun violence, no place is safe; children are kept inside and the sound of gunshots spreads terror. Greater gun availability is one explanation for why even though overall rates of violent crime are similar between the United States and Europe, America's homicide rate is much higher (Zimring and Hawkins 1997). Reducing gun involvement in violence would reduce the lethality and social costs of crime, even if the overall volume of crime were unchanged.

In many cities, the promise of preventing gun crime motivates proactive police tactics that have the goal of getting guns off the street, where most shootings occur (Koper and Mayo-Wilson 2006). Although the goal is readily justified, the methods are sometimes controversial. One problematic tactic has been high-volume "stop, question, and frisk" encounters, which tend in practice to concentrate on African American and Latino young men. This approach has been successfully challenged in the courts as a violation of civil rights in Los Angeles, New York, and elsewhere (Meares 2015). Such tactics are a hallmark concern of Black Lives Matter and related efforts within minority communities. Commentators across the political spectrum are also ambivalent in light of the broader concern that more stringent gun policing might increase the flow of convicts into already overpopulated prisons and jails.

Public officials seek innovative approaches for disarming dangerous people, approaches that are less damaging to police-community relations, not to mention civil rights. One possibility is to supplement the effort to deter illicit gun carrying with an effort to stop the transactions that supply active offenders with guns in the first place. But designing an effective program of that sort is handicapped by our meager knowledge of the underground gun markets that supply a large share of these transactions. A better understanding of the workings of this underground market, and how it might respond to changes in regulation and enforcement, form the agenda for this volume.

Many commentators have asserted that it is not feasible to keep guns out of the hands of violent offenders in the United States given our permissive laws and abundance of guns. In the United States, every adult is constitutionally entitled to own guns except those relatively few explicitly disqualified on the basis of their criminal record, immigration status, or one of a handful of other criteria. Because an estimated 270 million guns are in private hands nationwide, effective control is said to be beyond reach (Azrael et al. 2017). But this "futility" claim is in our judgment based on a misunderstanding of how guns come to be used in criminal violence. Despite that the number of private guns is enough to arm every adult, the great majority of adults (78 percent) do not in fact own one. The main concern should be less about the current stock of guns in private hands and more about the flow of guns: the ease of obtaining one for criminal purposes.

It is an interesting thought experiment to ask what percentage of those who commit a gun robbery or assault today were in possession of the gun in the recent past—say, six months ago. Available evidence does not provide a precise answer but points to a general conclusion that guns used in crime have typically not been in the hands of the offender for long. For that reason, and because most firearms assaults and robberies are committed by those who are disqualified from legal gun ownership by federal or state law, it is reasonable to suppose that if law enforcement were somehow able to block all gun transactions that were arming youths, gang members, and other legally disqualified groups, the rate of gun violence would dwindle rapidly, and in six months be a fraction of its current level.[2] If correct, then it is fair to conclude that the *number* of

---

1. Computed from data available from the Centers for Disease Prevention utility WISQARS (https://webappa.cdc.gov/sasweb/ncipc/mortrate10_us.html, accessed October 1, 2017).

2. A recent study of people arrested for gun violence or gun-related offenses finds that 13 percent were disqualified by age (under age eighteen) and 63 percent of the remainder were disqualified by criminal record or other readily observable characteristic (Braga and Cook 2016).

guns in private hands is of less direct concern than the transactions involving those guns. Because most of those transactions are off the books and technically illegal for various reasons, we use the shorthand term *underground gun market*.

For those readers who took a microeconomics course at some point, the term *market* conjures up a diagram with supply and demand curves that intersect like an *X* to determine a single price and quantity of transactions per unit of time. If the underground gun market resembled the market for bushels of wheat, the simple diagram would provide a sound approach to the possibilities and limitations of suppressing this market.

Real-world markets tend to be a good deal messier than Economics 101 reveals, and underground markets particularly so. Surveys of prisoners and others who have been (or are) active offenders document a diverse terrain of transactions, only about half of which involve an instance in which cash or other items of value are exchanged for property rights to a gun. Loans, gifts, sharing arrangements, and thefts are also common. Even for transactions that are sales, relatively few involve purchase from a store, where federal rules require the clerk to conduct a background check and keep records. More common by far is purchase from a family member, an acquaintance, or a street source. Given that variety of transactions, it is not surprising that prices are far from uniform, even for the exact same make, model, and condition of gun (Hureau and Braga 2016). Furthermore, the money price is not the only or necessarily the most important cost to obtaining a gun outside the formal market. Other types of transactions costs are relevant, including the search time required for the buyer and seller to find each other, the payments to a broker or other intermediary, and the risk of arrest.

If gun regulation and enforcement is to be respectful of the commitment to preserve gun ownership as a convenient option for most adults while reducing gun use in crime, then it is worth assessing the prospects for reducing the flow of transactions that arm active offenders and other dangerous people by raising transactions costs for that group. A better understanding of the underground market should contribute not only to designing effective programs, but also and more fundamentally to judging whether this supply side approach is even feasible.

This article begins by describing trends and patterns of gun ownership and transactions in the population at large. The discussion is informed in part by another in this volume that reports the results of a new national survey (Azrael et al. 2017). This information sets the stage for an inquiry into the underground gun market, because the transactions that supply offenders involve guns that have at some point been diverted from the general commerce in guns. In particular, the guns that end up being used in crime, with few exceptions, were legally manufactured or imported and first sold at retail by a licensed dealer. (In this respect, the underground gun market is closer to the underground market for Vicodin than, say, the market for heroin.) The notable population-level trends are the decline in the prevalence of gun ownership, coupled with the "deepening" of ownership by those who do keep guns. The shift has been remarkable in the predominant motivation for buying and owning guns, from sporting uses to self-defense, as reflected by the types of firearms that are most popular (a shift from rifles and shotguns to handguns), by the overall decline in hunting, and by the near disappearance in the old rural-urban differences in gun ownership once one controls for other things.

Next, we review the social costs of gun misuse. The quest to reduce these costs is the ultimate motivation for our inquiry into underground markets. We acknowledge that guns provide a source of recreation or sense of security to millions of Americans and are sometimes instrumental in self-defense against criminal assault. But like so many useful commodities—motor vehicles, pharmaceuticals, pesticides—guns also cause extensive damage. For that reason, the design, distribution and uses of guns are widely regulated. Gun availability does not "cause" violence but does intensify it in the sense that when a gun rather than a knife is used in a violent encounter, the result is to greatly increase the chance that the victim will die rather than receive a nonfatal injury. Guns also give assailants the power to kill many people quickly, or to attack police and public officials. In neighborhoods where gun violence is concentrated, residents live in fear. The burden can be measured in terms of deleterious effects on public safety, health, economic development, and quality of life generally.

What can be done to reduce these burdens, and in particular to separate guns from violence? All levels of government regulate gun transactions, possession, and use. These regulations draw the line between legal and illegal gun transactions by imposing restrictions on weapon design, licensing of sellers, defining who is qualified to buy and possess, and mandating record keeping and reporting. To the extent that regulations have the effect of banning potentially profitable transactions, evasion becomes an attractive possibility. Thus the underground market is defined and motivated by regulation and partially undercuts regulatory effectiveness.

Turning to the heart of the matter, we next describe the underground gun market and assess the potential for additional regulation (or stronger enforcement of existing regulations) to reduce availability of guns to offenders. We report evidence suggesting that in some respects the underground market is sensitive to regulation. For example, when Virginia adopted a one gun per month maximum on handgun sales to any one customer, that state's prominence as a "source" state in trafficking to Massachusetts and other states with relatively stringent regulations dropped sharply (see Braga 2017). But the market tends to be quite adaptable, and it cannot be taken for granted that a regulation that distorts trafficking patterns achieves the ultimate goal of depriving dangerous people of guns.

A survey of promising results helps connect those dots. Several articles in this volume provide new descriptive information that helps us better understand the channels by which guns are diverted into the underground market (Wintemute 2017; Collins et al. 2017). Daniel Webster and his colleagues provide an impact evaluation of an important new set of regulations in Maryland; Melissa Barragan and her colleagues report survey results relevant to ascertaining whether ammunition regulations are likely to be effective (Barragan et al. 2017; Webster et al. 2017).

GUN OWNERSHIP: PRIVATE AND PUBLIC INTERESTS

Guns are versatile tools, useful in providing meat for the table, eliminating varmints and pests, providing entertainment for those who have learned to enjoy the sporting uses, and protecting life and property against criminal predators. Guns are a traditional feature of rural life, where wild animals provide both a threat and an opportunity for sport. As America has become more urban, however, the demand for guns has become increasingly motivated by the felt need for protection against other people.

Patterns of Gun Ownership

The annual General Social Survey, conducted by the National Opinion Research Center, has long included questions on gun ownership. In 2014, just 31 percent of American households included at least one firearm, down from 47 percent in 1980 (Smith and Son 2015). The drop in part reflects the trend in household composition during this period; households are less likely to include a gun because they have become smaller and, in particular, are less likely to include a man (Wright, Jasinski, and Lanier 2012). In most cases, guns (unlike, say, toasters) are owned by individuals rather than households, and it is meaningful to track individual ownership. As shown in figure 1, the General Social Survey reports a drop in the percentage of individual adults owning at least one gun from 28 percent (1980) to 22 percent (2014), confirming the household trend (Smith and Son 2015). The trend among women during this period is essentially flat (10 percent reported owning in 1980, and 12 percent in 2014), so that the downward trend is due to reduced ownership by men (50 percent in 1980, down to 35 percent in 2014) (Smith and Son 2015).

Figure 2 depicts the trend in the number of new guns shipped to U.S. retailers; the data in this case are based on federal tax records. Each year's total is the sum of manufactures and imports net of exports. Figure 2 documents the remarkable decade-long surge in the volume

Figure 1. Prevalence of Gun Ownership

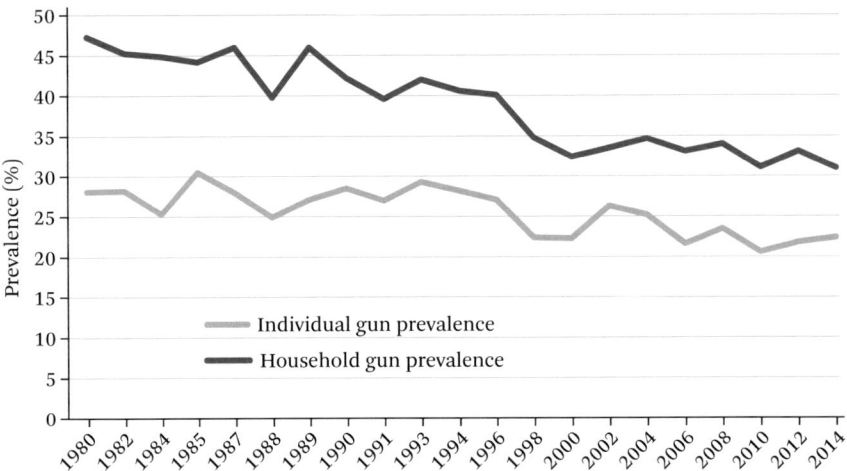

Source: Authors' tabulation based on Smith and Son 2015.

Figure 2. Trends in Shipments of New Guns

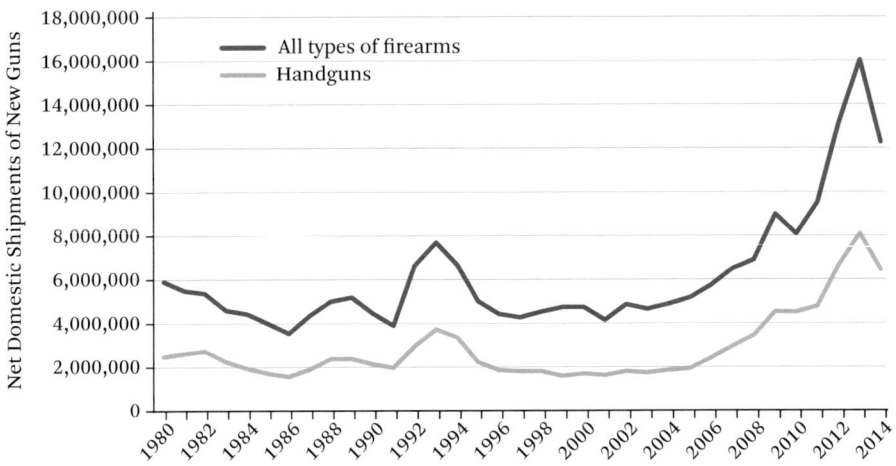

Source: Authors' tabulation based on ATF 2017.

of new guns beginning in 2003, and the growing relative importance of handguns (revolvers and pistols) as opposed to long guns (rifles and shotguns). In comparing the two figures, it is clear that if both are accurate, then the surge in new gun sales (increasing by a factor of 3.5) has been absorbed with no effect on the prevalence of gun ownership. The average number of guns kept by gun owners has been increasing.

The cumulative number of guns in private hands in the United States cannot be tracked from year to year, although a handful of surveys go beyond the usual questions on gun ownership to inquire about the *number* of guns in the home. The most recent national survey, the 2015 National Firearms Survey, found that gun-owning individuals average 4.9 guns in 2015, up substantially from the 1970s (Azrael et al. 2017). Administrative data on shipments of new guns to retailers tells us little about the net addition to the stock because the rate of disposal of existing guns through breakage, confiscation, and off-the-books imports and

Table 1. Correlates of Gun Ownership: Multivariate Logit Regression

Respondent	Coefficient	SE	Z-Ratio	P-Value
Female	−1.347***	0.132	−10.17	<.001
Race				
Non-Hispanic white	Referent (joint $p < .001$)			
Black	−1.107***	0.232	−4.76	<.001
Hispanic	−1.403***	0.261	−5.37	<.001
Other nonwhite	−0.433*	0.237	−1.83	.067
Income				
Less than $20k	−0.909***	0.234	−3.88	<.001
$20–40k	−0.308*	0.185	−1.66	.096
$40–75k	Referent (joint significance $p < .004$)			
$75k or more	−0.134	0.165	−0.81	.417
Income missing	−0.566**	0.228	−2.49	.013
Education				
Less than high school	−0.995***	0.360	−2.77	.006
High school graduate	Referent (joint significance $p < .002 \ldots$)			
Some college	−0.096	0.157	−0.61	.54
College graduate	−0.524***	0.154	−3.4	.001
Age				
Eighteen to thirty-four	−0.259	0.185	−1.40	.161
Thirty-five to forty-nine	Referent (joint significance $p < .04 \ldots$)			
Fifty to sixty-four	0.094	0.172	0.55	.583
Sixty-five or older	0.254	0.184	1.38	.168
Community				
Urban	Referent (joint significance $p < .28 \ldots$)			
Rural	0.338	0.241	1.4	.161
Suburban	−0.077	0.168	−0.46	.644
Region				
Midwest	Referent (joint significance $p < .001$)			
South	0.309**	0.156	1.97	.048
Northeast	−0.548***	0.197	−2.79	.005
West	0.145	0.182	0.8	.426
Constant	0.291	0.236	1.23	.218

Source: Authors' computation based on Pew Research Center 2015.
*$p < .1$; **$p < .05$; ***$p < .01$

exports is unknown (Cook 1993). As Azrael and colleagues explain in this volume, available survey data indicate a total U.S. gun stock of around 270 million guns (Azrael et al. 2017).

Qualitatively similar demographic patterns of gun ownership have persisted at least from the time it became possible to estimate them from survey data. A recent snapshot is provided by our analysis of Pew Research Center survey data for 2014; table 1 provides the results of a multivariate regression analysis of whether the respondent indicated that he or she personally owned a gun. This type of analysis answers the question of how each variable influences the likelihood of gun ownership when all other variables are held constant. What we learn is that, after adjusting for socioeconomic characteristics, men are much more likely to own a gun than women and whites are more likely than minorities (blacks and Hispanics). Low income and low education are both strongly and negatively related to gun ownership. A regional effect remains, the South at the high end and Northeast at the low end. Gun ownership by education peaks among those who graduated from high school but not from college. The biggest surprise is that after controlling for other factors, rural respondents do not display discernibly higher gun ownership rates than those living in urban or suburban areas.

Overall trends reflect the declining prevalence of hunting and rural traditions of gun sports. In 1940, 49 percent of teenagers were living in rural areas. By 2000, that proportion had dropped to 22 percent, and it continues to fall. Hunting is on the decline. Data from the General Social Survey indicate that the proportion of households with hunters fell from 32 percent in 1977 to 15 percent in 2014. The absolute number of hunting licenses issued in 2015 (fifteen million) was less than in 1970 (sixteen million), although the U.S. population had grown from 205 to 320 million people (U.S. Fish and Wildlife Service 2015).

Increasingly, people buy guns not to shoot animals or targets, but rather to prepare for a time when they might need to shoot or at least threaten another person. Although the prevalence of gun ownership is not increasing, those who do own guns are buying more of them and have an increasing preference for handguns over rifles and shotguns. Half of gun owners say that self-protection is the reason or primary reason they own a gun, compared with just a quarter of owners who gave that response as recently as 1999 (Pew Research Center 2013).[3]

The Virtues of Gun Ownership

Most private citizens who possess a handgun do so at least partly for defense against crime. Self-defense, particularly the defense of one's home and family, is viewed as a traditional duty of the head of a household and a natural extension to the collective purpose of public safety. In *Heller v. District of Columbia* (2008), the majority of the U.S. Supreme Court announced a Second Amendment right that overturned the near ban on private possession of handguns in the District of Columbia on the specific grounds that handguns were widely viewed as an appropriate weapon for protecting the home. Self-protection and the protection of the home may thus be viewed as having a public virtue and priority that goes beyond the usual arguments for consumer sovereignty.

A related, contested tradition regards gun ownership as a virtuous check on government authority. In this view, private arms serve as a bulwark against public tyranny. The belief in a right to insurrection is sometimes based on an interpretation of the Second Amendment, and is an important subtext in debates over the proper limits of government power in firearm registration, background checks, and computer databases containing information regarding firearms possession and sale (Horwitz and Anderson 2009; Bogus 2008; Henigan 2009).

Regardless of public perceptions and ideology, a question remains of whether guns are in fact effective in self-defense (let alone in combating tyranny), and whether it is prudent to keep one for that purpose. Research on self-defense covers a number of specific issues: the frequency and success with which guns are used in self-defense, the hazards of keeping a gun in the home, and the deterrent effect of increasing the number of potential victims who are armed. It comes as no surprise that on each of these issues disagreement is considerable in the scholarly literature, as well as among advocacy groups. Here we limit the discussion to evidence regarding deterrence, but interested readers should refer to more comprehensive treatments (Kleck 1997; Cook and Goss 2014; Hemenway 2004).

The strongest claim in support of the public virtue of widespread gun possession (and the perversity of regulations that curtail guns) is that guns in private hands generate a general deterrent effect on crime. Early arguments along these lines speculated about the effect on residential burglary, and especially "hot" burglaries of occupied homes (Kleck 1997;

---

3. The Pew Research Center poll reported 26 percent in 1999 and 48 percent in 2013 responding that the reason they own is self-protection.

Kopel 2001). The first systematic analysis of this issue demonstrated by use of the geocoded National Crime Victimization Survey data that the individual likelihood of residential burglary or hot burglary is not reduced by living in a county with high gun prevalence (Cook and Ludwig 2003). In fact, greater gun prevalence was associated with an *increase* in the residential burglary rate. One reason may be that more prevalent gun ownership increases the profitability of burglary, because stolen guns are readily fenced for good prices. The fraction of burglaries that are "hot" is not affected by the prevalence of gun ownership.

The most prominent research findings on the general deterrence issue were based on an evaluation of changes in state laws governing concealed carrying of handguns. Over the 1980s and 1990s, a number of states eased restrictions on concealed carry, adopting a regulation that required local authorities to issue permits to all applicants who met minimum conditions. These "shall issue" laws replaced "may issue" laws (which gave the authorities discretion) or outright bans on concealed carry. The economists John Lott and David Mustard published the first evaluation of these shall-issue laws, finding that they were associated with a reduction in homicide and some other types of crime (Lott and Mustard 1997). Lott went on to publish *More Guns, Less Crime* to report these results and variations on them (2000). He reached differing conclusions about the effect on property crime depending on the details of the statistical analysis (Cook, Moore, and Braga 2002). In every econometric specification, however, he found that ending restrictive gun-carrying laws reduced homicide rates (Lott 2000, 90).

In the finest scientific tradition, a number of analysts have sought to replicate Lott's findings and confirm or disconfirm them (Donohue 2003; Ludwig 1998; Black and Nagin 1998). The importance of this academic debate is indicated by the fact that an expert panel of eighteen scholars was created by the National Academy of Sciences to review the conflicting research. Panelists were chosen because they were expert on the relevant methods and had not been directly involved in research related to gun control. Among other things, this panel reanalyzed Lott's data, and, with one dissent, judged his findings to be unreliable (Wellford, Pepper, and Petrie 2004). The economist John Donohue and his co-authors have published several evaluations of the shall-issue laws, taking advantage of additional years of data and exploring alternative specifications, statistical techniques, and time periods (Ayres and Donohue 2009; Aneja, Donohue, and Zhang 2012). The most recent is the most comprehensive and reports consistent results using a variety of statistical techniques: deregulation of concealed carry has had the net effect of increasing criminal violence (Donohue, Aneja, and Weber 2017).

The scientific process has worked quite well in this case because replication based on extended experience has challenged dubious findings. Given the most recent evidence, we conclude with considerable confidence that deregulation of gun carrying over the last four decades has undermined public safety—which is to say that restricting concealed carry is one gun regulation that appears to be effective.[4]

THE SOCIAL BURDEN OF GUN VIOLENCE

As with motor vehicles and prescription painkilling medications, the widespread distribution and use of firearms creates both social costs and benefits. The benefits are primarily in the form of recreation and of a sense of security from criminal predation. The social burden comes from the misuse of guns to perpetrate deadly assaults and robberies, cause accidents, and translate passing thoughts of suicide into spontaneous and deadly action.

Gun violence is an important detriment to the standard of living in the United States, and is markedly more prevalent in the United States than in any other wealthy democracy. Gunshot injuries and deaths have a noticeable effect on life expectancy and contribute to health disparities across race and gender. Guns

---

4. Charles Manski and John Pepper conclude that considerable uncertainty remains about this conclusion (2015). But their analysis is based on a questionable specification regarding the year that Virginia adopted shall-issue licensing for concealed carry.

and gunfire terrorize some low-income communities and degrade community life. The choice of weapons appears to have a profound effect on the patterns and outcomes of criminal assault, and have a strong causal effect on the likelihood of death in a suicide attempt.[5] In a word, guns *intensify* violence.

It is common place for commentators to assert that gun violence is a "public health problem" (Hemenway and Miller 2013). Given the tens of thousands of deaths and injuries from gunshots annually, that claim seems uncontroversial, and serves as a useful connection to the methods (epidemiology and evidence-based policy design) and preferred styles of intervention (non-punitive, community-engaged) that characterize other public health interventions to address threats to population health (Moore 1993). This designation also underscores the basic normative judgment that all lives are valuable.

We embrace this perspective, but add that the social harms associated with gun violence go well beyond the number of firearms-related injuries or its effect on life expectancy. Gun violence is a public health problem, but it is also a crime problem, an economic development problem, and a burden on everyday quality of life for heavily affected communities. All of these perspectives are relevant to setting public priorities and crafting effective programs and policies to ameliorate gun violence.

Victimization

Approximately one million Americans have died from gunshot wounds in homicides, accidents, and suicides since 1986. In 2015, the most recent year for which the National Center for Health Statistics has provided final tabulations on injury deaths, the total was 36,252 firearm deaths, including 12,979 homicides, 22,018 suicides, and 489 unintentional killings (CDC 2017).[6] As a point of reference, in 2015 there were about as many gun deaths as motor vehicle deaths. Another point of reference is the years of potential life lost before age sixty-five: guns account for one of every fifteen years lost to early death from all causes.

Of the 17,793 criminal homicides reported in 2015, 73 percent were by gunshot. It is also true that half of all suicides are committed with firearms. (Gun suicide is a distinctive and severe public health problem beyond the scope of this volume.) Of course, not all gunshot injuries are fatal. Emergency rooms treated 84,997 nonfatal gunshot injuries in 2015, including 62,896 nonfatal injuries from criminal assaults. And the police recorded more than three hundred thousand assaults and robberies in that year in which the perpetrator used a gun, in most cases to threaten the victim.[7]

Most of the firearms used against people are handguns—revolvers or, more commonly in recent decades, pistols. Specifically, about 70 percent to 80 percent of firearm homicides and 90 percent of nonfatal firearm victimizations were committed with a handgun from 1993 to 2011 (Zawitz 1995; Planty and Truman 2013). The predominance of handguns in criminal misuse occurs despite the fact that the majority of guns in private hands are rifles and shotguns—that is to say, long guns. But handguns are more convenient to conceal and carry in public, where much of the crime occurs.

Gun violence contributes to racial and ethnic disparities in mortality. Focusing just on males age fifteen to thirty-four, homicide victimization rates in 2015 (consistent with earlier years) were seventeen times as high for blacks as for non-Hispanic whites. Homicide is the

---

5. Widespread gun-carrying may also make police more wary during encounters with the public, engendering more aggressive procedures that could result in unnecessary violence.

6. These and subsequent statistics in this paragraph are taken from the Centers for Disease Control public-use website WISQARS (https://www.cdc.gov/injury/wisqars/fatal.html, accessed June 21, 2017). The classification of gunshot deaths as "unintentional" in the Vital Statistics Registry is unreliable. Catherine Barber and David Hemenway demonstrate the numerous false positives and false negatives in this classification, and that to some extent they balance out (2011).

7. The FBI reports 764,449 aggravated assaults known to the police, of which 24.2 percent were with a gun, and 327,374 robberies, of which 40.8 percent were with a gun (2015). The implied number of nonfatal gun crimes is 318,566.

leading cause of death for blacks in this age group, and the second leading cause of death for Hispanic males. For all men in this age range, most (86 percent) homicides are committed with guns.

Guns are the weapons of choice for assassins and cop killers. Fourteen of the fifteen direct assaults against presidents, presidents-elect, and presidential candidates in United States history were perpetrated with firearms, including the five resulting in death (Kaiser 2008). (The one exception of the fifteen, a failed attack with a hand grenade against President George W. Bush, occurred overseas.) In the decade from 2006 to 2015, 521 law enforcement officers were shot dead, against just twelve who were stabbed to death and thirteen who were victims of a terrorist attack (NLEOMF 2017).

The most prominent cases of firearms victimization in recent decades have been the mass shootings at campuses, workplaces, movie theaters, and other public places. Some of these infamous events have become grim touchstones, including Columbine, Virginia Tech, Aurora, Newtown, San Bernardino, Orlando, and the attack on Representative Steve Scalise and others in Alexandria, Virginia. The estimate of the rate at which such events occur of course depends on the definition of *mass shooting*. Using a relatively broad definition of at least four people shot in a single incident, more than one thousand such incidents, that included 1,300 deaths, occurred between 2013 and 2015; by the most stringent definition in widespread use, at least six people shot and killed in a single incident, "just" eleven occurred during those three years, seven in 2015 alone (Klarevas 2016).

Despite the prominence of the mass shootings in the public discourse on gun violence, the overall number of victims in such incidents remains less than 3 percent of total gun homicides. The weapons and motivations—and corresponding policy challenges—behind such mass shooting incidents also differ from most gun homicides. Fortunately, the homicide rate (both gun and nongun) has dropped in recent years, declining from twentieth-century highs in 1980 and 1991 of more than ten per hundred thousand to just five in 2014. The persistent characteristic of American homicide through these ups and downs is the high involvement of guns, particularly handguns, which account for the bulk of gun homicides (Zimring and Hawkins 1997). Overall violence rates in the United States are also above average, though not to nearly the same extent: one comparison of the United States with other high-income countries found that the U.S. firearm homicide rate was almost twenty times as high, but that the nongun homicide rate was "just" 2.9 times as high as the average of the other countries (Richardson and Hemenway 2011).

How and Why the Type of Weapon Matters

A popular slogan admonishes, "Guns don't kill people, people kill people."[8] The bumper sticker is right that depriving "people" of guns does not automatically remove the impulse to kill. Yet the argument overlooks something else: without a gun, the *capacity* to kill is greatly diminished. As one wag suggested, "Guns don't kill people, they just make it real easy."

Bumper stickers aside, the true causal role of guns in homicide remains a fundamental issue in gun-violence research and evidence-based policymaking. The type of weapon obviously matters in some circumstances. The number of drive-by knifings, or people killed accidentally by stray fists, is remarkably low. When well-protected people are murdered, it is almost always with a gun; as mentioned, more than 90 percent of lethal attacks on law enforcement officers are with firearms, and all assassinations of U.S. presidents have been by firearm. When lone assailants set out to kill as many people as they can in a business office, movie theater, public park, or college campus, the most readily available weapon that will do the job is a gun.

But what about the more mundane attacks that make up the vast bulk of violent crime? The first piece of evidence is that robberies and assaults committed with guns are more likely to result in the victim's death than similar violent crimes committed with other weapons are.

---

8. This was a popular bumper strip in the 1970s and prominently endorsed by the Republican presidential candidates as recently as 2016.

In public health jargon, case-fatality rates differ by weapon type. Take the case of robbery, a crime that includes holdups, muggings, and other violent confrontations motivated by theft, regardless of whether they result in serious injury. The case-fatality rate for gun robbery is three times as high as for robberies with knives, and ten times as high as for robberies with other weapons (Cook 1987).

For aggravated (serious) assault it is more difficult to come up with a meaningful case-fatality estimate because the crime itself is in part *defined* by the type of weapon used. (In the FBI's Uniform Crime Reports, a threat delivered at gunpoint is likely to be classified as an aggravated assault, but the same threat delivered while shaking a fist would be classified as a simple assault.) We do know that for assaults from which the victim sustains an injury, the case-fatality rate is closely linked to the type of weapon (Zimring 1968, 1972; Kleck and McElrath 1991), as is also the case for family and intimate assaults (Saltzman, Mercy, and Rhodes 1992). For all victims who sustain an injury in a robbery or criminal assault serious enough to be treated in a hospital emergency department, the death rate for gunshot cases is more than twelve times as high as for knife attacks.[9]

Case-fatality rates do not by themselves prove that the type of weapon has an independent causal effect on the probability of death. The type of weapon might provide an indicator of the assailant's intent—and that it is the intent, rather than the weapon, that determines whether the victim lives or dies. This was offered as a reasonable possibility by the revered criminologist Marvin Wolfgang, who in his seminal study of homicide in Philadelphia stated that "it is the contention of this observer that few homicides due to shooting could be avoided merely if a firearm were not immediately present, and that the offender would select some other weapon to achieve the same destructive goal" (1958, 83). James Wright, Peter Rossi, and Kathleen Daly and others offer the same theme: the gun makes the killing easier and is hence the obvious choice if the assailant indeed intends to kill (1983). If no gun were available, this argument asserts, most would-be killers would still find a way to kill. In this view, fatal and nonfatal attacks form two distinct sets of events with little overlap, at least with respect to the assailant's intent.

This speculation that the intent is all that matters seems to contradict much of what we know about human behavior. When a tool is available to make a difficult task (such as killing another person) much easier, then we expect that the task will be undertaken with greater frequency and likelihood of success.

The first systematic research (as opposed to speculation) on this matter was conducted by Franklin Zimring, who demonstrated the significant overlap between fatal and nonfatal attacks with respect to circumstances and apparent motivation (1968, 1972). Even in the case of earnest and potentially deadly attacks, assailants commonly lack a clear or sustained intent to kill. Zimring notes that in many cases the assailant is drunk or enraged, unlikely to be acting in a calculating fashion. Whether the victim lives or dies then depends on the lethality of the weapon with which the assailant strikes the initial blow.

Zimring's studies of wounds inflicted in gun and knife assaults suggest that the difference between life and death is often a matter of chance, determined by whether the bullet or blade punctures a vital organ. It is relatively rare for assailants to administer the coup de grâce that would ensure their victim's demise. For every homicide inflicted with a single bullet wound to the chest are two survivors of a bullet wound to the chest that are indistinguishable with respect to intent. It is largely because guns are intrinsically more lethal than knives that gunshot injuries are more likely to result in death than sustained attacks with a knife to vital areas of the body (Zimring 1968). Zimring's second study provides still more compelling evidence by comparing case-fatality rates for gunshot wounds with different calibers—a wound inflicted by a larger caliber

---

9. Using data from WISQARS data on violent deaths and nonfatal injuries for 2013, we find a case fatality rate of 1.20 percent for knife assaults causing serious injury, and a case-fatality rate of 15.26 percent for gun attacks causing serious injury. The ratio is 12.7.

gun was more likely to prove lethal than a wound inflicted by a smaller caliber gun. Assuming that the caliber of gun is not correlated with the intent of the assailant, the clear suggestion is that the type of weapon has a causal effect on outcome.

Zimring's argument in a nutshell is that robbery murder is a close relative of robbery and that homicide is a close relative of armed assault; death is effectively a probabilistic by-product of violent crime. Thus, though the law determines the seriousness of the crime by whether the victim lives or dies, that outcome is not a reliable guide to the assailant's intent or state of mind.

One logical implication is that the overall volume of violent crimes and the number of murders should be closely linked, moderated by the type of weapons used. Where Zimring provides a detailed description of cases as the basis for his conclusion, tests based on aggregate data are also potentially informative. One such study demonstrates that robbery murder trends in forty-three large cities (for which data were available) behaved as we would expect, displaying a tight connection between variation in robbery and in robbery murder. An increase of one thousand gun robberies is associated with three times as many additional murders as an increase of one thousand nongun robberies (Cook 1987). *Instrumentality* provides a natural explanation for these patterns.

Three decades after his pioneering research on instrumentality, Zimring and a colleague published *Crime Is Not the Problem,* presenting the case that violent-crime rates in American cities are not particularly high relative to their counterparts across the developed world—except for homicide and gun-related crimes generally (Zimring and Hawkins 1997). American "exceptionalism" is the result of the unparalleled prevalence of firearms in assaults and robberies in the United States. In this view, American perpetrators are not more vicious than those in Canada, Western Europe, and Australia—they are just better armed. Furthermore, the trend in guns used in crime, as for guns sold to the public, over the last generation has been toward larger caliber pistols with more power and larger capacity to fire multiple rounds without reloading—as Anthony Braga documents in this volume (2017).

The case-fatality rate in violent encounters is not the only outcome in violent crime that is affected by weapon type. Other instrumentality effects have been documented for the crime of robbery (Cook 1980b, 1991). Assuming that robbers are generally in it for the money, then their goals are to choose lucrative victims, control them, and make good the escape. Use of a gun enhances the robber's power, making it possible to successfully rob hard-to-control but relatively lucrative victims (groups of individuals, businesses).

Based on this reasoning, we might expect gun robberies to be more likely to be successful than other robberies, and to involve more loot when they do succeed. Further, robbers with guns should be able to control the situation by use of the potent threat of the gun, rather than by physical attack (as with a strong-arm robbery or mugging).

As it turns out, these patterns are indeed evident in victim survey data. Robbers bearing guns are 12.5 percentage points more likely to succeed than their knife-wielding counterparts are, and the average value of offender's "take" almost doubles when robberies by firearm do succeed (Cook 2009; Kleck and McElrath 1991). Further, the likelihood of injury to the victim depends on the type of weapon, and gun robberies are the least likely to involve injury. Of course, when the robber does fire his gun, it is quite likely that the victim will die, making gun robberies (as noted) by far the most lethal type of robbery (Cook 1980b).

In sum, the type of weapon deployed in violent confrontations is not just an incidental detail; it matters in several ways. Because guns provide the power to kill quickly, at a distance, and often without much skill or strength, they also provide the power to intimidate other people and gain control of a violent situation without an actual attack. When a physical attack happens, the type of weapon is an important determinant of whether the victim survives; and guns are far more lethal than other commonly used weapons. Notably, the handguns available on the market and used by offenders have become more deadly over the last generation: the prevalence of large-capacity magazines, larger caliber, and greater power has increased (see Braga 2017).

The most important implication of this instrumentality perspective is that policies that are effective in reducing gun use in violent crime would reduce the murder rate even if the volume of violent crime were unaffected. As it turns out, about half of the states have incorporated sentencing enhancements for use of a gun in crime (Vernick and Hepburn 2003). These enhancements, most of which were adopted in the 1970s and 1980s, were intended to reduce gun use in violence; systematic evaluations offer some indication that they have been effective (Loftin and McDowall 1981, 1984; Abrams 2012).[10] In any event, the widespread adoption of sentencing enhancements for using a gun in robbery is a clear indication of the commonsense recognition of the instrumentality effect.

That gun robberies are so much more lucrative than robberies with other weapons raises a related question: why are most robberies committed without a gun? One possibility is that many robbers lack ready access to a gun, which would suggest that the underground gun market has high transactions costs for some offenders. But it is also possible that some robbers are deterred from firearm possession, carrying, or use in crime by the threat of severe punishment.

Social Costs of Gun Violence

A comprehensive account of the societal impact of gun violence requires imagining all the ways in which it affects the quality of life. The elevated rate of homicide, as important as it is, provides just the beginning in this calculation. It is useful to establish a ballpark estimate of the magnitude of this problem in terms that could be compared with other problems of health, safety, and urban development.

The traditional approach for valuing disease and injury is the cost-of-illness (COI) method, which misses most of what is important about gun violence. In essence, the cost-of-illness approach values people the way a farmer would value his livestock (Schelling 1968), based on their productivity and market value together with the cost of their medical care and other maintenance. The alternative approach, which is almost universally favored by economists, values the reduction in risk of injury according to the effect on the subjective quality of life. In short, the difference is between whether safety should be valued on the basis of how the lives saved contribute to gross domestic product (the COI approach), or rather by the value that people place on living in a safer environment.

In the latter perspective, violence, particularly gun violence, is a neighborhood disamenity, akin to pollution, traffic, and poor schools. Anyone living in a neighborhood where gunshots are commonly heard is likely to be negatively affected. The possibility of being shot, or of a loved one's being shot, engenders fear and costly efforts at avoidance and self-protection—as when mothers keep their children from playing outside for fear of stray bullets (Cook and Ludwig 2002). Property values fall as people with sufficient means move to safer neighborhoods; by one estimate, every homicide in Chicago results in seventy people moving out of the city (Cook and Ludwig 2000). Business suffers as customers gravitate to shopping districts where they feel safe. Neighborhood educational quality suffers through multiple pathways, including the impact of neighborhood dislocation on children's mental health and school readiness (Stein et al. 2003). Tax revenues are diverted to cover the financial costs of medically treating gunshot victims, usually at public expense (Cook et al. 1999).

Data from a randomized trial of Chicago Head Start interventions provided a particularly poignant illustration of the associated mental health challenges. When children happened to be assessed within a week of a homicide—almost always gun homicide—that occurred near their homes, they exhibited lower

---

10. Philip Cook and Daniel Nagin document the influence of weapon use in a case on prosecutorial and judicial discretion (1979). That study finds that defendants who used weapons were more likely to be convicted and sentenced to prison in the District of Columbia in 1974, but that there was little distinction between guns and other types of weapons in that court. Marcy Rasmussen Podkopacz and Barry C. Feld document the importance of weapon use as an influence on the decision to waive juveniles to adult courts (1996).

levels of attention and impulse control and lower pre-academic skills. Researchers also found strong effects of local violence on parental distress, which appears to be a key pathway through which local violence affects the well-being of young children (Sharkey et al. 2012). Gun violence has similarly detrimental impacts on educational attainment. Research conducted in Chicago indicates that student performance on standardized tests declines in the immediate aftermath of a local shooting (Sharkey 2010).

The costs of fear, suffering, and avoidance are largely subjective. One challenge in assessing the social burden of violence is to place a monetary value on these subjective effects, and in particular to estimate how much households would be willing to pay to reduce the perceived risks. One approach is to analyze property values, comparing neighborhoods with differing rates of gun violence while controlling for other factors that may be relevant in that market. That approach is bound to be incomplete (because at best it can capture only the local place-related effects of gun violence) and poses an almost insurmountable analytical challenge (because other neighborhood disamenities that also affect property values are highly correlated with gun violence).

An alternative approach, the contingent-valuation (CV) method, provides a comprehensive cost estimate in monetary terms, and without the challenge of extracting the value of safety from real-estate transactions data. Economists have used CV widely in valuing different aspects of the environment, but the first application to crime was specifically in the context of gun violence (Cook and Ludwig 2000; Thaler 1978).

To perform the CV estimate, a series of questions on a national survey that asked whether respondents would be willing to vote for a measure that would reduce gun violence in their community by 30 percent if it were going to cost them a specified amount (randomly varied across respondents). The pattern of answers was interesting. Perhaps surprisingly, given the unfamiliar nature of the questions for many respondents, the pattern of answers was also reasonable. For example, respondents with children at home were more willing to pay than those without. The overall estimate was that such a reduction would be worth $24 billion (Cook and Ludwig 2000; Ludwig and Cook 2001). Multiplying up to a hypothetical 100 percent reduction, we could estimate that interpersonal gun violence was at the time an $80 billion problem, and that the subjective costs were by no means confined to the people and communities that were at highest risk of injury—indeed, the willingness-to-pay for this reduction actually increased with income.

Regardless of the empirical method, it is surely informative to view gun violence as a neighborhood disamenity such as pollution. Translating the burden of this disamenity into monetary terms requires going well beyond valuing the lives and medical costs of actual victims. The costs of prevention, avoidance, and fear loom large in any comprehensive accounting of the value of safety.

One particularly important difference in practice between the CV and COI approaches is in the distinction between gun suicide and criminal assault. Because the annual toll of gun deaths includes twice as many suicides as homicides, the COI valuation tends to attribute the bulk of the burden of gun violence to suicide. But that ignores the difference in the costs of avoidance, prevention, and fear, which greatly elevate the relative importance of criminal gun assault in affecting the community's standard of living.[11] A similar set of distinctions might be made between mass shootings and

---

11. *Mother Jones* recently published an ambitious analysis of the costs of gun violence, working closely with the analyst Ted Miller of the Pacific Institute for Research and Evaluation. Miller estimated a total annual cost of $229 billion using a modern variant of the COI method that values life on the basis not only of lost earnings but also of the monetized value of "quality of life." The latter is typically based on wrongful death lawsuit settlements, and in this case averaged more than $6 million per life. The result was that lost quality of life made up 74 percent of the total cost. This variation on COI is still valuing lives (ex post) rather than attempting to value safety and take account on avoidance and mitigation. Further, the dollar value of a life takes no account of the actual circumstances of the victims. The result is that suicides dominate the social cost.

everyday homicides; the seemingly random mass attacks, often with military-related weaponry, on schoolchildren and other entirely innocent victims in normally safe places have the effect of creating nationwide anxiety, with a cost out of all proportion to the actual number of victims.

REGULATIONS GOVERNING FIREARMS TRANSACTIONS AND POSSESSION

The crack-fueled epidemic of violence that began in 1984 crested in the early 1990s and then subsided. Despite the fact that some cities experienced sharp increases in 2015 and 2016, the 2016 homicide rate of roughly five per hundred thousand population is half of the peak value and comparable to the low rates circa 1960. Robbery and assault rates have dropped in proportion. Virtually every large city has shared in this trend and is now safer, with all the attendant benefits, than it was a generation ago (Levitt 2004).

Gun violence has trended downward at close to the same rate as nongun violence.[12] The obvious conclusion is that the general reduction in violence, whatever its causes (and those have been extensively debated), had the effect of greatly reducing gun violence (Blumstein and Wallman 2006; Cook and Laub 2002; Levitt 2004). Any systematic discussion of the problem of gun violence should include the possibility offered by programs that are potentially effective against violence generally—cognitive-behavioral therapy for school-age youth and juvenile offenders, youth summer employment, higher alcohol taxes, and others (Cook, Ludwig, and McCrary 2011; Gelber, Isen, and Kessler 2014; Heller 2014; Heller et al. 2017).

Despite the crime drop, rates of criminal violence are unacceptably high and thus a leading problem in many communities across the country. Gun violence remains a particular problem because—as noted—gun use in violence intensifies that violence, terrorizing neighborhoods and greatly increasing the likelihood that assault victims will die. For that reason, reducing gun use is a worthy goal. Reducing the proportion of assaults and robberies committed with guns is thus what is known as a harm-reduction strategy. It has the potential to reduce the harm caused by violent crime without reducing the overall volume of violent crime.

Current law and practice incorporate diverse mechanisms for reducing the misuse of guns. Criminal law enforcement is coupled with regulations on gun commerce ("gun control") and other programs intended to reduce careless or criminal use (safety training, public education, improved safety devices). Here we focus primarily on regulation of gun commerce. Among other things, federal and state regulations have the effect of defining which transactions are legal. For the most part, the transactions that arm active offenders violate existing regulations, and constitute what we refer to as the "underground gun market." We offer a brief history of federal regulation (see table 2), and characterize trends in state regulation as well. We then characterize the various channels by which offenders can and do circumvent these regulations. (compare Zimring 1991; Cook and Ludwig 2006; Wintemute 2006).

Federal Regulation

Compared with other high-income nations, the United States is lax in regulating firearms. It does nonetheless impose nontrivial regulation of their design, possession, transfer, and uses. A teenager shooting squirrels with a sawed-off shotgun in New York's Central Park would be in violation of a number of local, state, and federal laws.

Actually the first federal law regulating guns, the Uniform Militia Act, was intended to *increase* the prevalence of gun ownership. Enacted by Congress in 1792, it required that every "free able-bodied white male citizen" between the ages of eighteen and forty-five equip himself with a rifle or musket and ammunition in preparation of being called to serve with his state's militia (Whitney 2012). The vision of a citizen's militia in each state was held out as the alternative to a standing national army. It soon gave way to the realistic requirements of defending the new nation. In the twentieth

---

12. A comparison of rates in 2014 with the peak year of 1991 indicates a decline in the gun homicide rate of 48 percent and a decline in the nongun homicide rate of 59 percent.

century, Congress came to recognize that the widespread private ownership of guns (which incidentally had become much cheaper and more deadly than in 1792, and of lower military value) was generating negative consequences that required federal regulation.

Table 2 summarizes the sequence of prominent federal laws and litigation, coupled with comments on contemporaneous trends in criminal violence. Congress first got into this arena during the Prohibition Era because of its associated gang violence. The federal excise tax on guns was imposed in 1919 primarily for revenue purposes, although the sumptuary aspects were noted in the congressional debate. In 1927, well into the Roaring Twenties, a ban was imposed on the use of the U.S. mail to ship handguns. The focus on particular types of guns continued with the National Firearms Act of 1934 (NFA), which required owners of fully automatic weapons (machine guns), sawed-off shotguns, and other gangster weapons to register these weapons with the federal authorities. All transfers of these weapons were subjected to a tax of $200, which at the time was prohibitive. It was not until 1986 that Congress banned the manufacture of NFA weapons for civilian use. Some indications are that this law has been effective—the use of fully automatic weapons in crime, even in domestic terrorism, appears to be rare in modern times, for example.

Comprehensive federal legislation was not enacted until 1968, following a surge in crime, urban riots, and political assassinations (Zimring 1975). Building on the precedent of the Federal Firearms Act of 1938, the Gun Control Act (GCA) strengthened federal licensing of firearms dealers and limited interstate shipments of guns to licensees. Such legislation sought to protect states that opted for tighter regulation against inflows of guns from lax-regulation states. (As Anthony Braga observes in this volume, this remains a challenging task for America's highly decentralized firearm policies.)

In particular, the GCA banned mail order shipments across state lines of the sort that supplied Lee Harvey Oswald with the gun he used to assassinate President Kennedy. The GCA also expanded federal prohibition on possession by certain categories of people deemed dangerous because of their criminal record, substance use or psychiatric disorder, or youth. "Felon in possession" thus became a federal offense, which facilitated partnership between local prosecutors and U.S. attorneys in combating violent crime. The GCA's recordkeeping requirements assisted law enforcement agencies in tracing guns to their first retail sale, which has proven quite useful in some murder investigations. Finally, the GCA banned the import of foreign-made handguns that were small or low quality and hence did not meet a "sporting purposes" test.

The agency created to do the regulatory enforcement and criminal investigation of gun trafficking is the Bureau of Alcohol, Tobacco, Firearms and Explosives (ATF). It has been something of a political football since its creation. In 1986, the Firearm Owners Protection Act placed limits on ATF's ability to inspect dealers and keep records that would help identify suspicious purchasing patterns. But with the surge of violence during the 1980s associated with the introduction of crack cocaine, and a shift in the political winds in favor of the Democrats, it became politically possible to strengthen the federal regulatory scheme.

The Brady Handgun Violence Prevention Act, which went into effect in 1994, required that every purchase from a federally licensed dealer be preceded by a background check and eventually established a federal "instant check" system that dealers could access. Also in that year, Congress imposed a ban on the manufacture or import of assault weapons for civilian use, as well as large-capacity magazines. (That ban was allowed to sunset ten years later, although some states have enacted a version of it.) In 1996, the Lautenberg Amendment expanded the list of people proscribed from possessing a firearm to those who had been convicted of misdemeanor crimes of domestic violence.

In recent years, the primary federal forum has shifted from Congress to the courts. Following the success of the state attorneys general in suing the tobacco industry (resulting in the Master Settlement Agreement of 1998), a number of cities filed suit against the gun industry. These suits proposed different theories

Table 2. Time Line of Federal Gun Policy

Era	Crime Patterns	Federal Crime Policy Innovations
1920s	Prohibition-related gang violence Tommy gun era	1919 Federal excise tax on handguns (10 percent) and long guns (11 percent) 1927 Handgun shipments banned from U.S. Mail

1930s	End of Prohibition in 1933
	Declining violence rates
		1934 National Firearms Act
		    Requires registration and high transfer tax on fully automatic weapons and other gangster weapons
		1938 Federal Firearms Act
		    Requires anyone in the business of shipping and selling guns to obtain a federal license and record names of purchasers

1960s	Crime begins steep climb in 1963 with Vietnam era & heroin epidemic
	Assassinations
	Urban riots
		1968 Gun Control Act
		    Bans mail-order shipments except between federally licensed dealers (FFLs) and strengthens licensing and recordkeeping requirements
		    Limits purchases to in-state or neighboring-state residents
		    Defines categories of people (felons, children) who are banned from possession
		    Bans import of Saturday Night Specials

1970s	Violence rates peak in 1975 (heroin) and again in 1980 (powder cocaine era)	1972 Bureau of Alcohol, Tobacco and Firearms created and located in the U.S. Department of Treasury (ATF)

1980s	Epidemic of youth violence begins (roughly) in 1984 with introduction of crack	1986 Firearm Owners Protection Act
		    Eases restrictions on in-person purchases of firearms by people from out of state
		    Limits FFL inspections by ATF, and bans the maintenance of some databases on gun transfers
		    Ends manufacture of NFA weapons for civilian use

1990s	Violence rates peak in early 1990s, begin to subside School rampage shootings	1994 Brady Handgun Violence Prevention Act Requires licensed dealers to perform a criminal background check on each customer before transferring a firearm. 1994 Partial ban on manufacture of assault weapons and large magazines for civilian use 1996 Congress bans the Centers for Disease Control (CDC) from promoting gun control, and effectively stops CDC from funding research on gun violence 1996 Lautenberg Amendment bans possession by those convicted of misdemeanor domestic violence
2000s	Crime and violence continue to decline	2004 Assault weapons ban is allowed to sunset 2005 Congress immunizes firearms industry against civil suits in cases where a gun was used in crime 2008 *Heller v. District of Columbia* for the first time establishes personal right under the Second Amendment

Source: Cook 2013.

of mass tort, but had the common goal of using the courts to do what the legislatures would not when it came to regulating the design and marketing of firearms (Lytton 2005). In 2005, Congress intervened to stop this litigation by taking the rather extraordinary step of immunizing the gun industry from lawsuits where the damages had resulted from misuse of a gun (Protection of Lawful Commerce in Arms Act, PL 109–92).

In a different way, the courts nonetheless become an important arena for the fight over gun control. With the *Heller v. District of Columbia* decision in 2008, the U.S. Supreme Court for the first time discovered in the Second Amendment a personal right to keep a handgun in the home for self-protection, suggesting that this personal right might also bar other sorts of regulations. Two years later, in *McDonald v. City of Chicago*, the Court ruled that the constitutional restriction also applied to states and local governments beyond the federal district. Gun rights advocates have now brought a flood of litigation challenging nearly every sort of restriction on gun design, possession, transactions, and use. The courts of appeal after *Heller* have been nearly uniform in giving the government substantial deference with regard to firearms regulation. Nearly 95 percent of post-*Heller* Second Amendment claims have failed. At this writing, we still have no clear indication of what the Supreme Court will end up doing to resolve all of the open questions about the newfound freedom created by *Heller* and *McDonald* (Cook, Ludwig, and Samaha 2011; Rosenthal and Winkler 2013; Blocher and Miller 2016).

Trends in State-Level Regulation

Much of the action in gun control has been at the state and local level (Blocher 2013). Cities have traditionally regulated the place and manner of gun carrying and discharge. States have imposed a variety of requirements or bans on transfers, possession, and carrying, focusing in particular on handguns. For example, New York State's Sullivan Act of 1911 mandated a license for anyone wishing to possess or carry a handgun; North Carolina in 1919 required that anyone seeking to acquire a handgun obtain a pistol permit after satisfying local officials of the buyer's good moral character and need for a handgun for defense of home or self-protection.

In recent years, the National Rifle Association and its allies have been highly effective in persuading the great majority of states to relax their regulations. Most states have now adopted preemption laws (banning local governments from imposing regulations that go beyond the state law), and have eased or erased restrictions on carrying concealed firearms. On another front, about half the states have adopted some version of the Stand Your Ground law, which allows people to use deadly force to defend themselves if they feel threatened, even if they are in a public place and have a realistic option to retreat (McClellan and Tekin 2012; Cheng and Hoekstra 2012).

Thus the gun rights movement has made broad gains in erasing the modest level of control on gun carrying and use that had traditionally been applied by state and local governments. So far, however, federal regulations on gun design and transactions, and on who can legally be in possession, have remained in place, and some states have strengthened their regulations in those areas. Data systems for background checks remain imperfect. Yet these systems have been improved since the Brady Act was first put in place, so that would-be buyers with a serious criminal record or a disqualifying history of sufficiently serious mental illness are more likely to be blocked from buying a gun from a dealer.[13] That said, such individuals may well be able to pick up a gun in the underground market.

TRANSACTIONS THAT ARM DANGEROUS OFFENDERS

The 270 million guns in private circulation are owned by fifty-five million adults. Some of those current owners will end up using their guns in crime, but in a sense the greater threat to public safety comes from the fact that these guns form a reservoir that supplies guns to fu-

---

13. Nationwide, the number of states that do not submit mental health records has fallen from nearly half in 2010 to just four as of 2015 (see Everytown for Gun Safety 2015).

ture delinquents, gang members, convicted felons, and other offenders. Criminal careers tend to be quite brief—by one estimate, an average of five years for those who begin committing property and violent crimes as youths (Blumstein, Cohen, and Hsieh 1982)—and each new crime cohort must acquire their guns if they are to be armed. Some evidence suggests that the elapsed time between the acquisition of a particular gun and use of that gun in crime is typically a matter of weeks or months.[14] That evidence suggests that the *transactions* that arm offenders should be a critical focus of policy and law enforcement concern. If these transactions could be successfully interdicted, the rate of gun crime would dwindle rapidly. That observation motivates our interest in the markets in which the relevant transactions take place.

As we have seen, American regulations on firearms transactions and possession are intended to reduce the social cost of misuse but to preserve ready access to guns for the great majority of the adult public. Felons, illegal aliens, and other groups deemed to be dangerous are banned from possession, and some types of weapons—such as Tommy guns and sawed-off shotguns—are very closely regulated. Interstate shipments are limited to federally licensed dealers (FFLs), and licensed dealers are required to run background checks on buyers and to keep records of transactions that can be checked by law enforcement. Some states supplement these federal regulations but preserve the principle of general access. It is intrinsically difficult to prevent disqualified people from obtaining the guns they want when most Americans are entitled to possess all they want. But that the regulations can be and are widely circumvented does not imply that they are entirely ineffective. Indeed, evidence indicates that some existing regulations curtail gun use in crime.

About fifteen million new firearms are sold each year for private use (see figure 2), and several million more transactions involve used firearms. Most of these transactions are legal. Illegal sales and transfers include thefts, transfers to people who are disqualified because of their youth or criminal record, and transactions that are in technical violation of firearms regulations (for example, a state regulation requiring that the buyer have a permit). The available evidence (meager though it is) suggests that a large percentage of the transactions that arm dangerous offenders are illegal under current law (Braga and Cook 2016).

Also relevant is whether the transaction is in the primary market—a documented sale by a licensed dealer—or in the informal secondary market. Figure 3 attempts to represent these distinctions and locate the underground transactions that arm dangerous offenders. To the extent that illegal transactions play a prominent role in arming youths, gang members, and violent criminals, enforcement of existing gun regulations appears to offer an opportunity to reduce gun violence.

Firearms are quite durable, and the retail market for used guns is active. Some resales occur through a licensed gun dealer, which must follow the same federal rules that apply to transactions involving new guns. Resales between unlicensed individuals (often called private transactions) are only loosely regulated by federal law, with one exception—a gun cannot be shipped directly to an out-of-state purchaser unless that person has a retail license.[15] Federal law also bans knowingly transferring a gun to someone who is disqualified because of their criminal record or other factor. Nineteen states currently require that private transactions involving handguns (or in some states all types of guns) be subjected to a background check, either through a licensed dealer, or through a permit or licensing requirement.

Figure 4 presents a schematic representation of one gun's possible transaction history. It illustrates that guns may change hands several times following the first federal firearms license (FFL) sale, and that some of those subsequent transactions, though typically not documented, may be legal (depending on state and local regulations). Those secondary transactions may include private sales (possibly at a gun show or through the Internet), gifts to fam-

---

14. An Illinois survey of Chicago offenders conducted by the authors included questions about the gun they used in the current crime. More than half of the guns were acquired within nine weeks of the crime.

15. In so-called Internet sales of guns, the physical transaction is typically arranged through a licensed dealer.

Figure 3. Transactions: Illegal Versus Dangerous

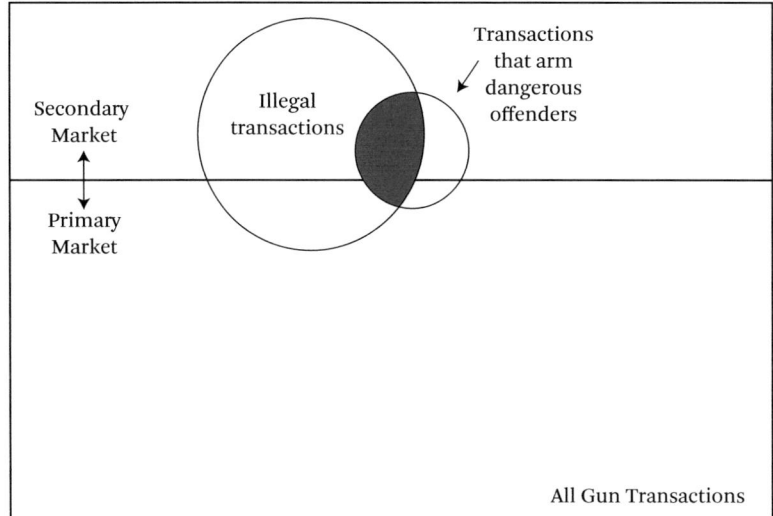

Source: Authors' tabulation.

Figure 4. Supply Chain of Guns Used in Crime

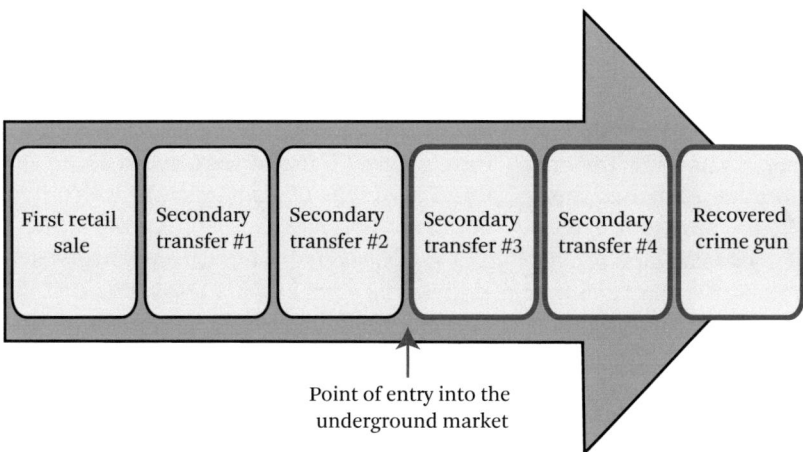

Source: Cook, Parker, and Pollack 2015.[16]

ily members, a consignment sale through an FFL, or an agreement between friends to share in the use of a weapon. At some point, a transaction—possibly a theft or a sale—may transfer the gun to the hands of someone who is proscribed from gun possession on the basis of criminal record or youth. Subsequent transactions may then move the gun among other offenders until it is ultimately discarded or confiscated by the police. Of course, most every pattern is possible and found to some extent in practice, including cases in which the offender buys directly from a licensed dealer or through a straw purchaser.

Survey evidence provides strong evidence that the gun market is sharply differentiated

---

16. Reprinted from *Preventive Medicine* 79 (October), Philip J. Cook, Susan T. Parker, and Harold A. Pollack, "Sources of Guns to Dangerous People: What We Learn by Asking Them," 28–36, 2015, with permission from Elsevier.

Table 3. Sources of Guns Used in Current Crime

Source	SISCF State Prisoners n=438 2004[a]	SIFCF Federal Prisoners n=155 2004[a]	SILJ Jail Inmates n=145 2002
Gun store or pawn shop	10.1	12.9	18.8
Flea market or gun show	1.1	2.6	1.7
Friend or family	36.8	31.6	45.4
Fence, street, drug dealer	31.4	22.8	24.2
From victim, burglary	2.7	1.4	2.7
Other	8.2	14.2	7.3
Refused, don't know, blank	5.3	11.6	—
Total	100.0	100.0	100.0

Source: Authors' compilation based on NACJD 2004. Reprinted from Cook, Parker, and Pollack 2015 (see footnote 16).
Note: All numbers in percentages.
[a]Sample restricted to males age eighteen to forty who are in first two years of their prison term and who admit in the survey interview that they had a gun at the time of crime. For the state and federal prison surveys, the results are based only on those respondents who were sentenced in 2002 or 2003, who used or possessed a weapon when the offense occurred, and whose weapon was a gun. All results weighted by the final sample weight for males. For the jail survey, the same definitions applied: used or possessed a gun.

by the characteristics of the individual seeking a gun. Adults entitled to possess a gun are more likely than not to buy from an FFL, that is, a retail dealer. (Later in this issue, Deborah Azrael and her colleagues find that three-quarters of all purchases are from a retail dealer.) For individuals who can pass the requisite background checks, FFLs are a simple and inexpensive channel to purchase a gun of known quality and not associated with a previous crime.

Disqualified purchasers sometimes directly obtain guns from FFLs. Some FFLs are particularly likely to encounter such prohibited possessors or to sell guns later recovered in crimes. Later in this issue, Garen Wintemute provides further information regarding such flows and the characteristics of FFLs likely to become sources for guns recovered in crimes (2017).

Yet prohibited possessors are most likely to obtain their guns in off-the-books transactions, often from social connections such as family and acquaintances, or from street sources such as illicit brokers or drug dealers. Some of these illicit transactions are purchases, but they also take a variety of other forms.

The U.S. Department of Justice has conducted several nationally representative surveys of inmates of state and federal prisons and jails, the most recent of which are from 2004. Gun-involved inmates were asked about the source and type of transaction by which they obtained their most recent gun (see tables 3 and 4). The state prisoner survey is largest and is the focus here, but it is reassuring that the results from the other two surveys are similar (Cook, Parker, and Pollack 2015).

It is rare for offenders to obtain their guns directly from the formal market: only 10 percent of recently incarcerated state prison inmates who carried a gun indicate that they purchased that gun from a licensed dealer (gun store or pawnbroker). Rather, most of the transactions (70 percent) are with social connections (friends and family) or street sources. The latter may include fences, drug dealers, brokers who sell guns, and gangs. Street sources are not necessarily strangers—the survey questionnaire does not ask. And though it is fair to suppose that most of these transactions were illegal for some reason (including the criminal record of the recipient), they are not necessarily so.

Cash purchases and trades constitute about

Table 4. Type of Transaction, Guns Used in Current Crime

Source	SISCF State Prisoners n=438 2004[a]	SIFCF Federal Prisoners n=155 2004[a]	SILJ Jail Inmates n=145 2002
Purchase or trade	51.9	49.0	50.4
Theft	4.3	1.3	4.0
Rent, borrow, hold it for someone	15.8	16.8	18.9
Gift	12.1	9.0	9.0
Other	8.8	16.1	14.4
Refused, don't know, blank	7.1	7.8	—
Total	100.0	100.0	100.0

Source: Authors' compilation based on NACJD 2004. Reprinted from Cook, Parker, and Pollack 2015 (see footnote 16).
Note: SISCF = Survey of Inmates in State Correctional Facilities SILJ = Survey of Inmates in Local Jails.
[a]Sample restricted to males age eighteen to forty who are in first two years of their prison term, and who admit in the survey interview that they had a gun at the time of crime. For the state and federal prison surveys, the results are based only on those respondents who were sentenced in 2002 or 2003, who used or possessed a weapon when the offense occurred, and whose weapon was a gun. All results weighted by the final sample weight for males. For the jail survey, the same definitions applied: used or possessed a gun.

half of all transactions. About one in six are temporary arrangements involving a gun owned by someone else, and take the form of borrowing, renting, or holding the gun. Perhaps surprisingly, one in ten guns are gifts—but gifting of guns is also quite common in the population at large.

Finally, the respondent admits to having directly stolen the gun in only a small fraction of cases, so it appears that theft is of scant importance as an immediate source of guns to offenders. Of course, theft may also play a role at an earlier stage of moving guns from the licit to the illicit sector.

The results from this national survey receive qualitative support from the results of a recent survey of inmates of Cook County Jail (Cook, Parker, and Pollack 2015). The gun transactions in which the respondents were involved were typically with family and acquaintances, illustrating the importance of social network as the source of guns (Papachristos, Wildeman, and Roberto 2015; Papachristos 2009; Braga, Papachristos, and Hureau 2010; Papachristos and Wildeman 2013). Relatedly, guns do not change hands in the equivalent of open-air drug markets; buyers and sellers are likely to know each other, or at least to have an acquaintance in common who can vouch for them. The logical implication is that the underground gun market is thin and balkanized, characterized by great variability in price and other transactions costs.

Thus, within the same city, some individuals may have ready access to guns and others no idea how to find one (Cook et al. 2007). That observation may explain the disagreement among observers as to whether guns are readily available in a particular jurisdiction—the right answer may be that guns are readily available to some criminal offenders and not to others. Furthermore, for those buyers who are "connected" and can access the underground market, the economist's famous law of one price does not apply; similar guns sell at a wide range of prices (Hureau and Braga 2016).

Surveys of offenders provide information on the last transaction in the supply chain illustrated in figure 4. The first link in the chain—the sale of the gun when new by a licensed dealer—can be documented in some cities based on ATF trace data on guns confiscated by the police. ATF traces guns by using the serial number to link to a manufacturer or importer, which then provide the distributor and finally the retail dealer. The last stop, for better or worse, is the record kept by that dealer (Cook and Braga 2001).

For the small percentage of crime guns in which the offender purchased the gun directly from a licensed dealer, the trace provides the whole story. Yet for most guns used in crime, the trace only provides information on the original source of the gun. That information is useful in determining the age of the gun and the location of its first sale, and provides one basis for assessing the workings of the underground market.

Evidence That Gun Availability Influences Criminal Misuse

Given the widespread skepticism about whether the gun-rich environment of the United States allows feasible measures to limit offenders' access, it may be useful to provide a sort of proof of concept. Actually, the evidence we have in mind falls short of a proof but remains compelling.

A variety of empirical research suggests that the availability of guns in a community affects the likelihood that a firearm will be used in assaults and robberies. Indeed, rates of gun ownership differ widely across regions, states, and localities—from 13 percent in Massachusetts to 60 percent in Mississippi, according to one set of estimates (Azrael, Cook, and Miller 2004). Current gun ownership influences the use of guns in crime directly—a gun in the home increases the chance that violent domestic relationships will end up involving gunplay and result in death (Campbell et al. 2003). But the prevalence of guns may also affect the availability of guns to active offenders. Burglaries and thefts from vehicles are more likely to include a gun as part of the loot (Cook and Ludwig 2003). In a community in which guns are prevalent, it is more likely that an offender who is seeking a gun will know someone, or know someone who knows someone, who would be willing to lend, sell, or share a gun. Regardless of the scenario, violent crimes in gun-rich communities are more likely to involve guns than in other communities.

A test of the hypothesis that greater gun prevalence induces greater criminal gun use requires a measure of the prevalence of gun possession, a measure that is valid for comparing jurisdictions at a point in time and tracking movements over time. It turns out that in many respects the best index is the percentage of suicides with guns (Azrael, Cook, and Miller 2004; Kleck 2004). Several studies have investigated the effect of gun prevalence, measured by this proxy of firearm suicide divided by suicide, and homicide rates across counties (see, for example, Miller, Azrael, and Hemenway 2002; Cook and Ludwig 2002).

The interpretation of such results is in some doubt. It is difficult to isolate a causal mechanism from analysis of cross-sectional data. Gun-rich jurisdictions, such as Mississippi, systematically differ from those with relatively few guns, such as Massachusetts. The usual approach for addressing this apples and oranges problem has been to statistically control for other characteristics, such as population density, poverty, and the age and racial composition of the population. But these variables never explain very much of the cross-sectional variation in crime rates, suggesting that the list of available control variables is inadequate to the task (Glaeser, Sacerdote, and Scheinkman 1996). Also unclear is whether widespread gun ownership is the cause or effect of an area's crime problem, given that high crime rates may induce residents to buy guns for self-protection. These same concerns are arguably even more severe with cross-national comparisons at any point in time.

Some of the problems with cross-sectional studies can be overcome by using panel data (repeated cross-sections of city, county, or state data measured at multiple times) to compare changes in gun ownership with changes in crime. Compared with Massachusetts, Mississippi may have much higher homicide rates year after year for reasons that cannot be fully explained from existing data sources. But, by comparing changes rather than levels, we implicitly control for many unmeasured differences across states that are relatively fixed over time, such as a "Southern culture of violence" (see Butterfield 1997; Loftin and McDowall 2003). The best available panel-data evidence suggests that more guns lead to more homicides, a result driven entirely by a relationship between gun prevalence and homicides committed with firearms; association of gun prevalence with nongun homicides or other types of crimes is scant (Duggan 2001; Cook and Ludwig 2006).

It is worth emphasizing that the conclusion from this line of research is not "more guns, more crime." Gun prevalence is unrelated to the rates of assault and robbery (Cook 1979; Cook and Ludwig 2006; see also Kleck and Patterson 1993). The strong finding that emerges from this research is that gun use *intensifies violence*, making it more likely that the victim of an assault or robbery will die. The positive effect is on the murder rate, not on the overall violent-crime rate.

These findings raise a basic question. Are there feasible methods for reducing overall gun prevalence? Some jurisdictions have adopted regulations intended to reduce overall handgun prevalence, either through a near ban on acquiring such guns (Chicago, District of Columbia) or by restrictive licensing (New York City, Massachusetts). As noted, handgun bans were ruled unconstitutional by the U.S. Supreme Court in *McDonald v. Chicago* (2010), which extended the Second Amendment ruling in *District of Columbia v. Heller* to states and localities. In any event, it is not clear whether the ban in either Chicago or the District of Columbia was effective in reducing overall prevalence (Cook and Ludwig 2006). Both jurisdictions border states where guns are largely unregulated.

Finally, both government and nonprofit groups have shown enthusiasm for reducing availability through gun buy-back programs. Research on these programs, which are typically short-duration offers of cash or goods in exchange for guns, has suggested that these approaches are not effective at reducing gun violence (Kennedy, Piehl, and Braga 1996; Romero, Wintemute, and Vernick 1998; Rosenfeld 1996). Yet a note of caution is in order. The effects of a gun buy-back will likely depend on the circumstances.

Australia's 1997 buy-back of semiautomatic rifles is often cited as one that reduced gun violence. Yet that effort bore little resemblance to the usual American-style buy-back. The Australian buy-back was a prelude to a near-comprehensive ban on private ownership of these weapons. Thus owners could not exploit the buy-back to exchange their old gun for a new one, nor were the sellers to the buy-back limited to those who had no further use for the weapon. Some evidence suggests that, in this extreme case, the buy-back saved lives (Reuter and Mouzos 2003). Most striking, Australia, which averaged about one mass shooting a year before its buy-back, has had none since then (Davey 2016).

In the American context, the relevance of the gun-prevalence studies is not so much to program design as it is to demonstrating that gun availability influences weapon choice by some violent offenders. That conclusion is strengthened by survey evidence, including surveys of arrestees who say they would like to have a gun but do not know how to obtain one (Cook et al. 2007). Oft-heard claims—that guns are not scarce and that in any event criminals will do whatever is necessary to get their guns—appear to be exaggerated. The next question is whether it is possible that regulations targeted at depriving a select group from obtaining guns can be effective if overall availability is not reduced.

Evidence of Effective Regulation

As we have seen, current regulations are effective in keeping offenders from buying their guns at retail dealers, and in influencing interstate trafficking patterns and other aspects of the underground gun market. One consistent pattern is that guns recovered in states that have relatively tight regulations are more likely to come from out of state, and in particular from states with lax regulations (Knight 2013). For example, 85 to 90 percent of the guns recovered in New York City were first sold in another state, and for the most part were first sold in lax states along the eastern seaboard (the I-95 corridor) such as Virginia, Georgia, and Florida (Smith 2016).

Interstate gun flows change in response to a change in regulations. A notable example is the dramatic change in sources of crime guns to Chicago following the adoption of the Brady Act in 1994; the percentage coming from the Deep South states, where gun stores for the first time were required to run background checks, dropped abruptly by 15 points, replaced by in-state sales (Cook and Braga 2001). Other examples have also been well documented (Braga et al. 2012). In this volume, Anthony Braga uses 1981–2015 Boston data to strengthen these analyses (2017). The likelihood that a Boston handgun would be traced to a Virginia FFL nearly doubled after Virginia repealed its law limiting consumers to one handgun per month. Such evidence helps document the importance of systematic trafficking into jurisdictions with tight controls, though, as noted, the trafficking is not generally on a large scale.

The question is whether regulatory effects on transaction patterns translate into reduced gun violence. A noteworthy example is the Brady Act, which required FFLs to conduct background checks of would-be buyers. Since it was fully implemented in 1998, three million transactions have been blocked as a result of these background checks, for the most part because the customer had a felony conviction. According to one evaluation, however, the direct effect of the Brady Act on homicide rates was statistically negligible (Ludwig and Cook 2000). Closing the secondary market or private sale loophole may be a necessary precondition for effective screening (Cook and Ludwig 2013).

As of this writing, nineteen states require a background check for most private sales of handguns (and in some cases long guns); these checks are accomplished either by requiring buyers to obtain a permit from local government authorities, or by mandating that the transaction be processed by a licensed dealer (Wintemute 2013). This sort of universal background check requirement was proposed by the Obama administration following the Sandy Hook massacre of schoolchildren in 2012 but was narrowly defeated through filibuster in the U.S. Senate.

The strongest evidence that a permit system can be effective comes from an evaluation of the *repeal* of the Missouri law requiring that all handgun buyers obtain a permit from the sheriff. After the law, changes were measureable in the transaction channels that were arming criminals, as, more importantly, was a spike in firearms violence (but no change in nonfirearms violence) unique to Missouri (Webster, Crifasi, and Vernick 2014). The involvement of local authorities in the Missouri law may have been key to its effectiveness—so far none of the laws that simply require private transactions to be channeled through FFLs have been shown to be effective in reducing gun violence. Additional evidence on effectiveness of a universal background check comes from an evaluation of Connecticut's 1995 pistol permit law by Kara Rudolph and her colleagues (2015). These authors report a large drop in gun violence, based on a statistical technique that uses "synthetic" controls.

Strong evidence suggests that expansions in the categories of people disqualified from owning guns could save lives. In 1991, California implemented legislation that disqualified those convicted of violent crimes at the misdemeanor level. A causal analysis by Wintemute and his colleagues finds a substantial reduction in violent recidivism by those convicted of misdemeanor violence after the gun ban than immediately before (2001). Similarly, in 1996 the Gun Control Act was amended to expand the federal ban on felons to include those convicted of misdemeanor-level domestic violence. The ban was implemented at different times in different jurisdictions due to legal challenges, which created a natural experiment for evaluating its effectiveness. Using this source of variation, Kerri Raissian finds that the ban reduced domestic murders involving guns, with no effect on nongun murders (2016).

Another area of gun regulation that has been in flux is the disqualification of those who are mentally ill or incapacitated. The Gun Control Act bans gun possession by those who have been "adjudicated as a mental defective," an unfortunate and antiquated phrase that among other things refers to individuals who have at some point been involuntarily committed to a mental institution. The background checks conducted by gun dealers tap into several data bases kept by federal authorities, but most states have not provided the necessary information on a consistent basis. One exception has been Connecticut, which in 2007 began reporting relevant records of mental illness to the federal National Instant Criminal Background Check System (NICS). One analysis found that disqualified individuals were less likely to be arrested after the data transfer made their history accessible as part of the NICS check (Swanson et al. 2013).

Some commentators have argued for measures that would temporarily prohibit individuals from purchasing or possessing firearms after a short-term involuntary hospitalization, or by individuals whose behavior presents known risk factors for violence. Jeffrey Swanson and his collaborators suggest that such temporary firearm prohibitions might apply to individuals convicted of a violent misdemeanor, those subject to a temporary domestic violence restraining order, and those convicted of certain drug- and alcohol-related offenses. These authors suggest that focusing on known and identifiable risk factors rather than psychiatric diagnoses and treatment histories would more effectively identify people who pose a danger to themselves or others. Preliminary evidence is now emerging regarding the likely impact of such policies (Swanson et al. 2015).

In sum, gun regulations have in various instances been carefully evaluated and shown effective at reducing criminal misuse of firearms. The lesson is not that all such regulations are effective, but rather that regulation can be effective and should not automatically be written off as futile given the alleged efficiency of the underground market. But there is no such thing as a free lunch when it comes to regulatory effectiveness, and in particular jurisdictions that adopt regulations but do not enforce them will be disappointed (Braga and Hureau 2015).

Enforcement Options

Interdicting transfers within the illicit sector has been a low-priority mission for most police departments. Because experience with local investigations directed at stopping the redistribution of guns among offenders is so scant, it is not clear what can be accomplished in this arena.

In particular, drug enforcement experience provides few lessons and sometimes a misleading guide. Compared with markets for cocaine and heroin, transactions in guns are relatively few (Koper and Reuter 1996). Organized crime groups cannot monopolize the distribution of guns to offenders because many offenders can source them from acquaintances or relatives who have legal access to the primary market.

Indeed, a better analogy might be the market for underage beer sales; the potential sources of beer to teenagers include almost every adult, and the actual source in any one transaction is likely to be a family member or friend who does not charge much, if anything, for the service. More opportunity exists for underground brokers or traffickers in tightly regulated jurisdictions, but even in cities such as Boston, New York, and Chicago, evidence of individuals who are making a living solely by servicing the gun market is minimal. Supplying guns tends to be a sideline.

To the extent that the underground market does have many small suppliers and little structure, it is an unappealing target for law enforcement, where investigators and prosecutors are looking for clear villains and big cases (Braga et al. 2012). Still, some law enforcement tactics may provide valuable leverage in reducing supply to dangerous people.

Regulatory Enforcement Against Licensed Dealers

Federally licensed dealers are authorized to receive interstate shipments of guns. They are also clearly in a position to serve as an important source of illicit supply if they are inclined to ignore regulations governing transactions and record keeping. Without a doubt, some of the sixty thousand licensed dealers are scofflaws, some of them in a big way. ATF's investigations have turned up cases where a dealer is a major direct source of guns to criminal organizations (Braga et al. 2012). In several cases specific dealers have been shut down or "reformed" by investigations and lawsuits brought by cities (Webster et al. 2006; Webster, Vernick, and Bulzacchelli 2006). Several studies have documented the willingness of clerks and gun store owners to help callers who indicate they are disqualified or intend to use guns in crime (Sorenson and Vittes 2003; Wintemute 2010). Garen Wintemute's article in this issue, however, provides evidence that even well-meaning dealers may end up with a relatively high percentage of sales ending up as crime guns, with the percentage being sensitive to their mix of customers (2017).

ATF has the lead responsibility in the regulatory enforcement of licensed dealers, but is limited by law and by an intentionally constrained budget from taking effective action. In some jurisdictions, state or local agencies also have regulatory authority over dealers. Violations appear to be widespread, but whether a stepped-up enforcement regime would ultimately reduce gun crime has not been demonstrated directly.

As reported, surveys suggest that gun stores are not an immediate source of guns to more than say, 10 percent of offenders, although straw-purchase arrangements appear quite common (Cook et al. 2015). But scofflaw dealers may well play a more important role several steps back in the supply chain, providing guns to traffickers and other go-betweens.

Internet Sales and Gun Shows
A large volume of gun transactions flows through gun shows (akin to flea markets for guns), and the Internet is increasingly connecting buyers and sellers on sites such as ArmsList and GunBroker.com. Gun shows are more closely regulated in some states than others, with a marked difference in the prevalence of suspect transactions. Online sites are largely unregulated in practice and do support illicit transactions.[17] Despite the apparent advantage to disqualified buyers, gun shows and the Internet scarcely figure in offenders' self-reports of where they obtain their guns. But it is reasonable to believe that some trafficking pipelines exploit gun shows. Internet sales have also played some role in the provision of guns to perpetrators of mass homicides. These perpetrators may be legally entitled to purchase firearms, but may be more readily identified and thwarted were they forced to pursue in-person transactions.

Interstate Traffickers and Local Brokers
In tightly controlled jurisdictions, out-of-state sources are important to the local underground gun market. ATF takes the lead in trafficking investigations, sometimes working in conjunction with local law enforcement. Because trafficking is typically conducted by individuals and small partnerships, developing cases with enough heft to be of interest to U.S. attorneys may be a challenge. The same analysis applies to local brokers who serve to connect buyers and sellers in tight-control jurisdictions (Cook et al. 2007). These small businesses are unlikely to attract much interest or attention from the police and prosecutors. In particular, buy and bust programs are rare.

Straw Purchasers and Diffuse Private Transactions
Most offenders avoid purchasing directly from gun stores, presumably because they are disqualified and not prepared to use false identification—or simply do not want a record kept of the sale. One alternative that preserves the convenience of shopping at a store is to enlist someone who is qualified to make the purchase on a disqualified person's behalf.

If that arrangement is worked out in advance, then the straw purchaser has committed a crime by signing the form that indicates that he is buying the gun for himself. But this is a minor crime, difficult to prove, and rarely prosecuted. One indication of how common it is comes from a recent study of trace data from guns recovered by the Chicago Police. Fully 15 percent of the newer guns (less than two years since first sale) recovered from gang-involved offenders were originally purchased by a woman and then recovered from a man (Cook et al. 2015). Although that does not prove that the woman was acting as the man's agent, it is a plausible scenario.

Some straw purchases could be stopped by vigilant clerks (if the true buyer were actually in the store with the straw buyer), and it is possible that regulatory pressure, including requirements such as the mandatory videotaping of gun sales, may help encourage that sort of vigilance. In many cases, however, the true buyer will not be evident at the time of the purchase, and the second transfer (from straw purchaser to the true buyer) becomes just one of millions of private transactions that are generally unregulated.

---

17. Everytown for Gun Safety's "The Wild Wild Web" documents the prevalence of disqualified buyers for internet sales in Nevada (https://everytownresearch.org/reports/the-wild-wild-web/, accessed July 7, 2017).

We believe that diffuse transactions and small-time brokers and traffickers are suitable targets for concerted enforcement. In suggesting more effective enforcement measures, we are mindful of concerns that enhanced gun enforcement might aggravate America's mass incarceration problem. Overly punitive policies, particularly in the domain of illicit drugs, have undermined community trust and public legitimacy of any policy that might increase incarceration. That is a fact of American life and casts some shadow over every criminal justice proposal to tougher enforcement, even those that could credibly reduce violent crime.

These tensions are real but can be sensibly managed in the domain of gun policy. A voluminous criminology literature suggests the likelihood of apprehension and punishment are more powerful levers than the severity of punishment itself in deterring crime (Cook 1980a; Nagin 2013). What is required are policies that puncture the sense of impunity among participants in underground gun markets. More effective enforcement policies may not require many actual convictions of gun sources to send a message that these gun transfers are criminal and do carry some salient legal risks.

Interestingly, our interviews with inmates of Cook County Jail uncovered a widespread perception that police agents were making undercover buys and that selling to a stranger without careful vetting was a mistake (Cook, Parker, and Pollack 2015). The reality is that the Chicago Police Department rarely buys guns undercover. So it appears that even a small effort will make gun sellers more careful not to move outside their social network—a good thing if the goal is to stop the proliferation of guns across networks.

Measures implemented in other policy domains suggest other strategies and infrastructures that might help identify scofflaw dealers, straw purchasers, and other individuals at high-risk of low-level offending. Prescription drug monitoring programs (PDMPs) have identified hundreds of thousands of high-risk patients, thousands of high-risk prescribing medical professionals, and significant numbers of scofflaw medical facilities and pharmacies that contribute to the underground market for prescription opioid medications. PDMPs are associated with reduced prescription opioid diversion and misuse yet impose manageable burdens on legitimate patients and prescribers (Bao et al. 2016). A similar program in the gun area would require a registry of gun sales that exists only in California and a handful of other states.

But, in principle, any jurisdiction could proactively seek to identify the sources of guns to armed offenders who are arrested. The quid pro quo for gaining the defendants' cooperation may be a bargain to reduce the sentence, which may be difficult to justify unless creating a legal liability for gun sources were viewed as a high priority.

LOOKING AHEAD

Fifteen million new guns are sold each year, together with many millions of used guns that are also sold or otherwise change hands. Some unknown number of those transactions are illegal because of regulatory violations or because the "transaction" is a theft. Although these illegal transactions likely represent a small fraction of overall gun sales, they make up a large share of the transactions that end up arming delinquents, gang members, and other dangerous offenders. Even though regulations on gun transactions are widely violated, they are not necessarily ineffective. Evidence is compelling of their (partial) effectiveness in particular cases and in particular ways.

There has been some confusion about just what we can hope to accomplish through gun regulation and enforcement. It is often said that guns cause violence. Although that may be true in particular instances, it is not true that changes in gun availability will have a discernible effect on the rates of assault, robbery, and rape. The primary consequence of an assailant's using a gun rather than a knife or club is the likelihood that the attack will be fatal. Guns *intensify* violence. In that sense, separating guns from violence can be viewed as a mitigation strategy. The cost of any given volume of violence is keenly sensitive to the types of weapons used.

This volume seeks to develop a better understanding of how dangerous people obtain their guns. It explores programs and policies designed to make gun access by this group more difficult. The focus on gun transactions to dangerous people concentrates attention on just one part of the problem of gun violence. We are very much aware that a significant share of gun crime is committed by people who are not obviously or actionably "dangerous," and thus not disqualified from owning a gun. We also are aware that suicide makes up a large share of the gun-violence problem, and that overlap between suicide and the underground gun market is negligible. Even if illegal transactions were somehow eliminated, the problem of gun violence would remain—but it would be greatly diminished.

Even those who endorse the goal of keeping guns out of the hands of youths, gang members, and active offenders may despair, believing that the large inventory of guns in private hands, combined with lax regulations, has the effect that as a practical matter guns are readily available to all. From the evidence, however, we conclude that the truth is more nuanced. The United States is remarkably differentiated when it comes to the prevalence of gun ownership, and weapon choice by criminals is correlated with ownership prevalence; a natural interpretation is that robbers and other violent criminals find it more difficult to obtain a gun in Massachusetts than New Orleans. Furthermore, fine-grained studies within a single jurisdiction suggest that some criminals are more closely connected to gun sources than others, and have lower costs of finding and obtaining one. Those who take it as a matter of faith that markets operate efficiently to bring together buyers and sellers may be surprised by the reality of the underground gun market in Boston or Chicago, where an offender who is not well connected may have a difficult time obtaining an affordable gun and as a result go unarmed some of the time. Finally, evidence from impact evaluations is compelling that some firearms regulations have been effective in reducing gun violence.

To be effective, regulations must be enforced. If a gang member's friend can earn $50 making an illegal straw purchase for him, why not do it? The answer may depend on whether the friend believes that the police will take an interest in tracking down the source of the gun if the gang member is arrested for a robbery or assault. Even occasional enforcement actions may be helpful in sending a message that such gun sources are not immune from legal consequences.

Empirical research is essential if myths about the gun market are to be confronted by good evidence. The articles in this issue are offered in that spirit.

REFERENCES

Abrams, David S. 2012. "Estimating the Deterrent Effect of Incarceration Using Sentencing Enhancements." *American Economic Journal: Applied Economics* 4(4): 32–56.

Aneja, Abhay, John J. Donohue, and Alexandria Zhang. 2012. "The Impact of Right to Carry Laws and the NRC Report: The Latest Lessons for the Empirical Evaluation of Law and Policy." *NBER* working paper no. 18294. Cambridge, Mass.: National Bureau of Economic Research.

Ayres, Ian, and John J. Donohue. 2009. "More Guns, Less Crime Fails Again: The Latest Evidence from 1977–2006." *Econ Journal Watch* 6(2): 218–38.

Azrael, Deborah, Philip J. Cook, and Matthew Miller. 2004. "State and Local Prevalence of Firearms Ownership: Measurement, Structure, and Trends." *Journal of Quantitative Criminology* 20(1): 43–62.

Azrael, Deborah, Lisa Hepburn, David Hemenway, and Matthew Miller. 2017. "The Stock and Flow of U.S. Firearms: Results from the 2015 National Firearms Survey." *RSF: The Russell Sage Foundation Journal of the Social Sciences* 3(5): 38–57. DOI: 10.7758/RSF.2017.3.5.02.

Bao, Yuhua, Yijun Pan, Aryn Taylor, Sharmini Radakrishnan, Feijun Luo, Harold Alan Pincus, and Bruce R. Schackman. 2016. "Prescription Drug Monitoring Programs Are Associated with Sustained Reductions in Opioid Prescribing by Physicians." *Health Affairs* 35(6): 1045–51. DOI: 10.1377/hlthaff.2015.1673.

Barber, Catherine, and David Hemenway. 2011. "Too Many or Too Few Unintentional Firearm Deaths in Official U.S. Mortality Data?" *Accident Analysis and Prevention* 43(3): 724–31.

Barragan, Melissa, Kelsie Y. Chesnut, Jason Gravel, Natalie A. Pifer, Keramet Reiter, Nicole Sherman, and George Tita. 2017. "Prohibited Possessors and the Law: How Inmates in Los Angeles Jails

Understand Firearm and Ammunition Regulations." *RSF: The Russell Sage Foundation Journal of the Social Sciences* 3(5): 141–63. DOI: 10.7758/RSF.2017.3.5.07.

Black, Dan A., and Daniel S. Nagin. 1998. "Do Right-to-Carry Laws Deter Violent Crime?" *Journal of Legal Studies* 27(1): 209–19.

Blocher, Joseph. 2013. "Firearm Localism." *Yale Law Journal* 123(1): 82–146.

Blocher, Joseph, and Darrell A. H. Miller. 2016. "Lethality, Public Carry, and Adequate Alternatives." *Harvard Journal on Legislation* 53(1): 279–301.

Blumstein, Alfred, Jacqueline Cohen, and Paul Hsieh. 1982. "Duration of Adult Criminal Careers—Final Report." National Criminal Justice Reference Service (NCJRS) Report No. 89569. Washington: U.S. Department of Justice, Office of Justice Programs.

Blumstein, Alfred, and Joel Wallman. 2006. *The Crime Drop in America*, rev. ed. New York: Cambridge University Press.

Bogus, Carl T. 2008. "Heller and Insurrectionism." *Syracuse Law Review* 59: 253–66.

Braga, Anthony A. 2017. "Long-Term Trends in the Sources of Boston Crime Guns." *RSF: The Russell Sage Foundation Journal of the Social Sciences* 3(5): 76–95. DOI: 10.7758/RSF.2017.3.5.04.

Braga, Anthony A., and Philip J. Cook. 2016. "The Criminal Records of Gun Offenders." *Georgetown Journal of Law and Public Policy* 14(1): 1–16.

Braga, Anthony A., and David Hureau. 2015. "Strong Gun Laws Are Not Enough; The Need for Improved Enforcement of Secondhand Gun Transfer Laws in Massachusetts." *Preventive Medicine* 79 (October): 27–42.

Braga, Anthony A., Andrew V. Papachristos, and David M. Hureau. 2010. "The Concentration and Stability of Gun Violence at Micro Places in Boston, 1980–2008." *Journal of Quantitative Criminology* 26(1): 33–53.

Braga, Anthony A., Garen J. Wintemute, Glenn L. Pierce, Philip J. Cook, and Greg Ridgeway. 2012. "Interpreting the Empirical Evidence on Illegal Gun Market Dynamics." *Journal of Urban Health* 89(5): 779–93.

Bureau of Alcohol, Tobacco, Firearms and Explosives (ATF). 2017. "Firearms Commerce in the United States: Annual Statistical Update 2017." Accessed August 10, 2017. https://www.atf.gov/resource-center/docs/undefined/firearms-commerce-united-states-annual-statistical-update-2017/download.

Butterfield, Fox. 1997. *All God's Children: The Bosket Family and the American Tradition of Violence*. New York: Alfred A. Knopf.

Campbell, Jacquelyn C., Daniel Webster, Jane Koziol-McLain, Carolyn Block, Doris Campbell, Mary Ann Curry, Faye Gary, Nancy Glass, Judith McFarlane, Carolyn Sachs, Phyllis Sharps, Yvonne Ulrich, Susan A. Wilt, Jennifer Manganello, Xiao Xu, Janet Schollenberger, Victoria Frye, and Kathryn Laughon. 2003. "Risk Factors for Femicide in Abusive Relationships: Results from a Multisite Case Control Study." *American Journal of Public Health* 93(7): 1089–97.

Centers for Disease Control and Prevention (CDC). 2017. "Injury Prevention and Control." Web-based Injury Statistics Query and Reporting System (WISQARS). Atlanta, Ga.: Centers for Disease Control and Prevention, National Center for Injury Prevention and Control. Accessed July 3, 2017. https://www.cdc.gov/injury/wisqars/index.html.

Cheng, Cheng, and Mark Hoekstra. 2012. "Does Strengthening Self-Defense Law Deter Crime or Escalate Violence? Evidence from Castle Doctrine." *NBER* working paper no. 18134. Cambridge, Mass.: National Bureau of Economic Research.

Collins, Megan E., Susan T. Parker, Thomas L. Scott, and Charles F. Wellford. 2017. "A Comparative Analysis of Crime Guns." *RSF: The Russell Sage Foundation Journal of the Social Sciences* 3(5): 96–127. DOI: 10.7758/RSF.2017.3.5.05.

Cook, Philip J. 1979. "The Effect of Gun Availability on Robbery and Robbery Murder: A Cross Section Study of Fifty Cities." *Policy Studies Review Annual* 3: 743–81.

———. 1980a. "Research in Criminal Deterrence: Laying the Groundwork for the Second Decade." In *Crime and Justice: An Annual Review of Research*, edited by Norval Morris and Michael Tonry. Chicago: University of Chicago Press.

———. 1980b. "Reducing Injury and Death Rates in Robbery." *Policy Analysis* 6(1): 21–45.

———. 1987. "Robbery Violence." *Journal of Criminal Law and Criminology* 78(2): 357–76.

———. 1991. "The Technology of Personal Violence." *Crime and Justice: An Annual Review of Research* 14:1–71. DOI: 10.2307/1147458.

———. 1993. "Notes on the Availability and Prevalence of Firearms." *American Journal of Preventive Medicine* 9(S3): 33–38.

———. 2009. "Crime Control in the City: A Research-Based Briefing on Public and Private Measures." *Cityscape* 11(1): 53–79. DOI: 10.2307/20868690.

———. 2013. "The Great American Gun War: Notes from Four Decades in the Trenches." *Crime and Justice* 42(1): 19–73.

Cook, Philip J., and Anthony A. Braga. 2001. "Comprehensive Firearms Tracing: Strategic and Investigative Uses of New Data on Firearms Markets." *Arizona Law Review* 43(2): 277–309.

Cook, Philip J., and Kristin A. Goss. 2014. *The Gun Debate: What Everyone Needs to Know*. Oxford: Oxford University Press.

Cook, Philip J., Richard J. Harris, Jens Ludwig, and Harold A. Pollack. 2015. "Some Sources of Crime Guns in Chicago: Dirty Dealers, Straw Purchasers, and Traffickers." *Journal of Criminal Law and Criminology* 104(4): 717–59.

Cook, Philip J., and John H. Laub. 2002. "After the Epidemic: Recent Trends in Youth Violence in the United States." *Crime and Justice* 29(1): 1–37.

Cook, Philip J., Bruce A. Lawrence, Jens Ludwig, and Ted R. Miller. 1999. "The Medical Costs of Gunshot Injuries in the United States." *Journal of the American Medical Association* 282(5): 447–54.

Cook, Philip J., and Jens Ludwig. 2000. *Gun Violence: The Real Costs*. New York: Oxford University Press.

———. 2002. "The Costs of Gun Violence Against Children." *The Future of Children* 12(2): 87–99. DOI: 10.2307/1602740.

———. 2003. "The Effects of Gun Prevalence on Burglary: Deterrence vs Inducement." In *Evaluating Gun Policy*, edited by Jens Ludwig and Philip J. Cook. Washington, D.C.: Brookings Institution Press.

———. 2006. "Aiming for Evidence-Based Gun Policy." *Journal of Policy Analysis and Management* 25(3): 691–736. DOI: 10.2307/30162752.

———. 2013. "The Limited Impact of the Brady Act: Evaluation and Implications." In *Reducing Gun Violence in America*, edited by Daniel W. Webster and Jon S. Vernick. Baltimore, Md.: Johns Hopkins University Press.

Cook, Philip J., Jens Ludwig, and Justin McCrary, eds. 2011. *Controlling Crime: Strategies and Tradeoffs*. National Bureau of Economic Research Conference Report. Chicago: University of Chicago Press.

Cook, Philip J., Jens Ludwig, and Adam M. Samaha. 2011. "Gun Control After Heller: Litigating Against Regulation." In *Regulation versus Litigation*, edited by Daniel Kessler. Chicago: University of Chicago Press.

Cook, Philip J., Jens Ludwig, Sudhir Venkatesh, and Anthony A. Braga. 2007. "Underground Gun Markets." *Economic Journal* 117(524): 588–618. DOI: 10.2307/4625574.

Cook, Philip J., Mark H. Moore, and Anthony A. Braga. 2002. "Gun Control." In *Crime: Public Policies for Crime Control*, edited by James Q. Wilson and Joan Petersilia. Oakland, Calif.: ICS Press.

Cook, Philip J., and Daniel S. Nagin. 1979. *Does the Weapon Matter? An Evaluation of a Weapons-emphasis Policy in the Prosecution of Violent Offenders*. Washington, D.C.: Institute for Law and Social Research.

Cook, Philip J., Susan T. Parker, and Harold A. Pollack. 2015. "Sources of Guns to Dangerous People: What We Learn by Asking Them." *Preventive Medicine* 79 (October): 28–36.

Crifasi, Cassandra K., Shani A.L. Buggs, Seema Choksy, and Daniel W. Webster. 2017. "The Initial Impact of Maryland's Firearm Safety Act of 2013 on the Supply of Crime Handguns in Baltimore." *RSF: The Russell Sage Foundation Journal of the Social Sciences* 3(5): 128–40.

Davey, Melissa. 2016. "Australia's Gun Laws Stopped Mass Shootings and Reduced Homicides, Study Finds." *Guardian*, June 23. Accessed June 28, 2017. https://www.theguardian.com/world/2016/jun/23/australias-gun-laws-stopped-mass-shootings-and-reduced-homicides-study-finds.

Donohue, John J. 2003. "The Impact of Concealed-Carry Laws." In *Evaluating Gun Policy: Effects on Crime and Violence*, edited by Jens Ludwig and Philip J. Cook. Washington, D.C.: Brookings Institution Press.

Donohue, John J., Abhay Aneja, and Kyle D. Weber. 2017. "Right-to-Carry Laws and Violent Crime: A Comprehensive Assessment Using Panel Data and a State-Level Synthetic Controls Analysis." Cambridge, Mass.: National Bureau of Economic Research.

Duggan, Mark. 2001. "More Guns, More Crime." *Journal of Political Economy* 109(5): 1086–14. DOI: 10.1086/322833.

Everytown for Gun Safety. 2015. "Closing the Gaps: Strengthening the Background Check System to

Keep Guns Away from the Dangerously Mentally Ill." New York: Everytown for Gun Safety Support Fund. Accessed Jun 28, 2017. http://everytown research.org/reports/closing-the-gaps.

FBI. 2015. "Crime in the United States: 2015." Washington, D.C.: Federal Bureau of Investigation. Accessed June 26, 2017. https://ucr.fbi.gov/crime-in-the-u.s/2015/crime-in-the-u.s.-2015/offenses-known-to-law-enforcement/.

Gelber, Alexander, Adam Isen, and Judd B. Kessler. 2014. "The Effects of Youth Employment: Evidence from New York City Summer Youth Employment Program Lotteries." Cambridge, Mass.: National Bureau of Economic Research.

Glaeser, Edward L., Bruce Sacerdote, and Jose A. Scheinkman. 1996. "Crime and Social Interactions." *Quarterly Journal of Economics* 111(2): 507–48.

Heller, Sara B. 2014. "Summer Jobs Reduce Violence Among Disadvantaged Youth." *Science* 346(6214): 1219–23.

Heller, Sara B., Anuj K. Shah, Jonathan Guryan, Jens Ludwig, Sendhil Mullainathan, and Harold A. Pollack. 2017. "Thinking, Fast and Slow? Some Field Experiments to Reduce Crime and Dropout in Chicago." *Quarterly Journal of Economics* 132(1): 1–54.

Hemenway, David. 2004. *Private Guns, Public Health*. Ann Arbor: University of Michigan Press.

Hemenway, David, and Matthew Miller. 2013. "Public Health Approach to the Prevention of Gun Violence." *New England Journal of Medicine* 368(21): 2033–35.

Henigan, Dennis A. 2009. *Lethal Logic: Exploding the Myths that Paralyze American Gun Policy*: Washington, D.C.: Potomac Books.

Horwitz, Joshua, and Casey Anderson. 2009. *Guns, Democracy, and the Insurrectionist Idea*. Ann Arbor: University of Michigan Press.

Hureau, David, and Anthony A. Braga. 2016. "The Illicit Entry of Guns into High-Risk Networks." Unpublished manuscript. State University of New York at Albany: Department of Criminology.

Kaiser, Frederick M. 2008. "CRS Reports to Congress: Direct Assaults Against Presidents, Presidents-Elect, and Candidates." *CRS Report* no. RS20821. Washington, D.C.: Government Printing Office. Accessed January 10, 2017. https://fas.org/sgp/crs/misc/RS20821.pdf.

Kennedy, David M., Anne M. Piehl, and Anthony A. Braga. 1996. "Youth Violence in Boston: Gun Markets, Serious Youth Offenders, and a Use-Reduction Strategy." *Law and Contemporary Problems* 59(1): 147–96.

Klarevas, Louis. 2016. *Rampage Nation: Securing America from Mass Shootings*. Amherst, N.Y.: Prometheus Books.

Kleck, Gary. 1997. *Targeting Guns: Firearms and Their Control*. Hawthorne, N.Y.: Aldine de Gruyter.

———. 2004. "Measure of Gun Ownership for Macro-Level Crime and Violence Research." *Journal of Research in Crime & Delinquency* 41(1): 3–36.

Kleck, Gary, and Karen McElrath. 1991. "The Effects of Weaponry on Human Violence." *Social Forces* 69(3): 669–92.

Kleck, Gary, and E. Britt Patterson. 1993. "The Impact of Gun Control and Gun Ownership Levels on Violence Rates." *Journal of Quantitative Criminology* 9(3): 249–87.

Knight, Brian. 2013. "State Gun Policy and Cross-State Externalities: Evidence from Crime Gun Tracing." *American Economic Journal: Economic Policy* 5(4): 200–29.

Kopel, David B. 2001. "Laywers, Guns, and Burglars." *Arizona Law Review* 43(2): 345–68.

Koper, Christopher S., and Evan Mayo-Wilson. 2006. "Police Crackdowns on Illegal Gun Carrying: a Systematic Review of Their Impact on Gun Crime." *Journal of Experimental Criminology* 2(2): 227–61.

Koper, Christopher S., and Peter Reuter. 1996. "Suppressing Illegal Gun Markets: Lessons from Drug Enforcement." *Law and Contemporary Problems* 59(1): 119–46.

Levitt, Steven D. 2004. "Understanding Why Crime Fell in the 1990s: Four Factors That Explain the Decline and Six That Do Not." *Journal of Economic Perspectives* 18(1): 163–90.

Loftin, Colin, and David McDowall. 1981. "'One With a Gun Gets You Two': Mandatory Sentencing and Firearms Violence in Detroit." *Annals of the American Academy of Political and Social Science* 455(1): 150–67.

———. 1984. "The Deterrent Effects of the Florida Felony Firearm Law." *Journal of Criminal Law and Criminology* 75(1): 250–59.

———. 2003. "Regional Culture and Patterns of Homicide." *Homicide Studies* 7(4): 353–67.

Lott, John R. 2000. *More Guns, Less Crime*, 2nd ed. Chicago: University of Chicago Press.

Lott, John R., and David B. Mustard. 1997. "Crime,

Deterrence, and Right-to-Carry Concealed Handguns." *Journal of Legal Studies* 26(1): 1–68.

Ludwig, Jens. 1998. "Concealed-Gun-Carrying Laws and Violent Crime: Evidence from State Panel Data." *International Review of Law and Economics* 18(3): 239–54.

Ludwig, Jens, and Philip J. Cook. 2000. "Homicide and Suicide Rates Associated with Implementation of the Brady Handgun Violence Prevention Act." *Journal of the American Medical Association* 284(5): 585–91.

———. 2001. "The Benefits of Reducing Gun Violence: Evidence from Contingent-Valuation Survey Data." *Journal of Risk and Uncertainty* 22(3): 207–26.

Ludwig, Jens, Greg J. Duncan, Lisa A. Gennetian, Lawrence F. Katz, Ronald C. Kessler, Jeffrey R. Kling, and Lisa Sanbonmatsu. 2013. "Long-Term Neighborhood Effects on Low-Income Families: Evidence from Moving to Opportunity." *American Economic Review* 103(3): 226–31.

Lytton, Timothy. 2005. *Suing the Gun Industry: A Battle at the Crossroads of Gun Control and Mass Torts*. Ann Arbor: University of Michigan Press.

Manski, Charles F., and John V. Pepper. 2015. "How Do Right-to-Carry Laws Affect Crime Rates? Coping with Ambiguity Using Bounded-Variation Assumptions." *NBER* working paper no. 21701. Cambridge, Mass.: National Bureau of Economic Research.

McClellan, Chandler B., and Erdal Tekin. 2012. "Stand Your Ground Laws and Homicides." *NBER* working paper no. 18187. Cambridge, Mass.: National Bureau of Economic Research.

Meares, Tracey L. 2015. "Programming Errors: Understanding the Constitutionality of Stop and Frisk as a Program, Not an Incident." *University of Chicago Law Review* 82: 159–79.

Miller, Matthew, Deborah Azrael, and David Hemenway. 2002. "Rates of Household Firearm Ownership and Homicide Across U.S. Regions and States, 1988–1997." *American Journal of Public Health* 92(12): 1988–93.

Moore, Mark H. 1993. "Justice Or Public Health? Perspective: Violence Prevention: Criminal Justice or Public Health?" *Health Affairs* 12(4): 34–45.

Nagin, Daniel S. 2013. "Deterrence: A Review of the Evidence by a Criminologist for Economists." *Annual Review of Economics* 5(1): 83–105. DOI: 10.1146/annurev-economics-072412-131310.

National Archive of Criminal Justice Data (NACJD). 2004. "Survey of Inmates in State and Federal Correctional Facilities, 2004 (ICPSR 4572)." Accessed July 12, 2017. http://www.icpsr.umich.edu/icpsrweb/NACJD/studies/4572?q=ICPSR+4572.

National Law Enforcement Officers Memorial Fund (NLEOMF). 2017. "Facts and Figures: Causes of Law Enforcement Deaths." Washington, D.C.: NLEOMF. Accessed February 24, 2017. http://www.nleomf.org/facts/officer-fatalities-data/causes.html.

Papachristos, Andrew V. 2009. "Murder by Structure: Dominance Relations and the Social Structure of Gang Homicide." *American Journal of Sociology* 115(1): 74–128.

Papachristos, Andrew V., and Christopher Wildeman. 2013. "Network Exposure and Homicide Victimization in an African American Community." *American Journal of Public Health* 104(1): 143–50.

Papachristos, Andrew V., Christopher Wildeman, and Elizabeth Roberto. 2015. "Tragic, but Not Random: The Social Contagion of Nonfatal Gunshot Injuries." *Social Science & Medicine* 125 (January): 139–50.

Pew Research Center. 2013. "Why Own a Gun? Protection Is Now Top Reason Perspectives of Gun Owners, Non-Owner." *U.S. Politics & Policy*, March 12, 2013. Accessed June 28, 2017. http://www.people-press.org/2013/03/12/why-own-a-gun-protection-is-now-top-reason/.

———. 2015. "July 2015 Political Survey." *U.S. Politics & Policy*, July 2015. Accessed July 13, 2017. http://people-press.org/category/datasets/.

Planty, Michael, and Jennifer L. Truman. 2013. "Firearms Violence 1993–2011." NCJ 24170. Washington: U.S. Department of Justice, Office of Justice Programs, Bureau of Justice Statistics.

Podkopacz, Marcy Rasmussen, and Barry C Feld. 1996. "The End of the Line: An Empirical Study of Judicial Waiver." *The Journal of Criminal Law and Criminology* 86(2): 449–92.

Police Foundation and Major Cities Chiefs Association. 2017. "Reducing Violent Crime in American Cities: An Opportunity to Lead." Washington, D.C.: Police Foundation. Accessed February 24, 2017. https://www.policefoundation.org/publication/reducing-violent-crime-in-american-cities-an-opportunity-to-lead-full-report/.

Raissian, Kerri. 1996. "Hold Your Fire: Did the 1996 Federal Gun Control Act Expansion Reduce Domestic Homicides?" *Journal of Policy Analysis and Management* 35(1): 67–93.

Reuter, Peter, and Jenny Mouzos. 2003. "Australia: A Massive Buyback of Low-Risk Guns." In *Evaluating Gun Policy*, edited by Jens Ludwig and Philip J. Cook. Washington, D.C.: Brookings Institution Press.

Richardson, Erin G., and David Hemenway. 2011. "Homicide, Suicide, and Unintentional Firearm Fatality: Comparing the United States with Other High-Income Countries, 2003." *Journal of Trauma and Acute Care Surgery* 70(1): 238–43.

Romero, Michael P., Garen J. Wintemute, and Jon S. Vernick. 1998. "Characteristics of a Gun Exchange Program, and an Assessment of Potential Benefits." *Injury Prevention* 4(3): 206–10.

Rosenfeld, Richard. 1996. "Crime Prevention or Community Mobilization? The Dilemma of the Gun Buy-Back Program." In *Under Fire: Gun Buy-Backs, Exchanges and Amnesty Programs*, edited by Martha Plotkin. Washington, D.C.: Police Executive Research Forum.

Rosenthal, Lawrence E., and Adam Winkler. 2013. "The Scope of Regulatory Authority under the Second Amendment." In *Reducing Gun Violence in America*, edited by Daniel W. Webster and Jon S. Vernick. Baltimore, Md.: Johns Hopkins University Press.

Rudolph, Kara E., Elizabeth A. Stuart, Jon S. Vernick, and Daniel W. Webster. 2015. "Association Between Connecticut's Permit-to-Purchase Handgun Law and Homicides." *American Journal of Public Health* 105(8): e49–e54.

Saltzman, Linda E., James A. Mercy, and Philip H. Rhodes. 1992. "Identification of Nonfatal Family and Intimate Assault Incidents in Police Data." *American Journal of Public Health* 82(7): 1018–20.

Schelling, Thomas C. 1968. "The Life You Save May Be Your Own." In *Problems in Public Expenditure and Analysis*, edited by Samuel B. Chase. Washington, D.C.: Brookings Institution Press.

Sharkey, Patrick T. 2010. "The Acute Effect of Local Homicides on Children's Cognitive Performance." *Proceedings of the National Academy of Sciences* 107(26): 11733–38.

Sharkey, Patrick T., Nicole Tirado-Strayer, Andrew V. Papachristos, and C. Cebele Raver. 2012. "The Effect of Local Violence on Children's Attention and Impulse Control." *American Journal of Public Health* 102(12): 2287–93.

Smith, Aaron. 2016. "How the Iron Pipeline Funnels Guns into Cities with Tough Gun Laws." CNN, January 19. Accessed June 28, 2017. http://money.cnn.com/2016/01/19/news/iron-pipeline-gun-control.

Smith, Tom W., and Jaesok Son. 2015. "General Social Survey: Trends in Gun Ownership in the United States, 1972–2014." Chicago: National Opinion Research Center at the University of Chicago. Accessed June 28, 2017. http://www.norc.org/PDFs/GSS%20Reports/GSS_Trends%20in%20Gun%20Ownership_US_1972-2014.pdf.

Sorenson, Susan B, and Katherine A Vittes. 2003. "Buying a Handgun for Someone Else: Firearm Dealer Willingness to Sell." *Injury Prevention* 9(2): 147–50.

Stein, Bradley D., Lisa H. Jaycox, Sheryl H. Kataoka, Marleen Wong, Wenli Tu, Marc N. Elliott, and Arlene Fink. 2003. "A Mental Health Intervention for Schoolchildren Exposed to Violence: A Randomized Controlled Trial." *Journal of the American Medical Association* 290(5): 603–11. DOI: 10.1001/jama.290.5.603.

Swanson, Jeffrey W., Allison Gilbert-Robertson, Linda K. Frisman, Michael A. Norko, Hsiu-Ju Lin Lin, Marvin S. Swartz, and Philip J. Cook. 2013. "Preventing Gun Violence Involving People with Serious Mental Illness." In *Reducing Gun Violence in America: Informing Policy with Evidence and Analysis*, edited by Daniel W. Webster and Jon S. Vernick. Baltimore, Md.: Johns Hopkins University Press.

Swanson, Jeffrey W., E. Elizabeth McGinty, Seena Fazel, and Vickie M. Mays. 2015. "Mental Illness and Reduction of Gun Violence and Suicide: Bringing Epidemiologic Research to Policy." *Annals of Epidemiology* 25(5): 366–76. DOI: 10.1016/j.annepidem.2014.03.004.

Thaler, Richard. 1978. "A Note on the Value of Crime Control: Evidence from the Property Market." *Journal of Urban Economics* 5(1): 137–45.

U.S. Fish and Wildlife Service. 2015. "Historical Hunting License Data." U.S. Fish and Wildlife Service, Wildlife and Sport Fish Restoration Program. Last modified September 22, 2015. Accessed June 28, 2017. https://wsfrprograms.fws.gov/Subpages/LicenseInfo/Hunting.htm.

Vernick, Jon S., and Lisa M. Hepburn. 2003. "State and Federal Gun Laws: Trends for 1970–99." In

Evaluating Gun Policy: Effects on Crime and Violence, edited by Jens Ludwig and Philip J. Cook. Washington, D.C.: Brookings Institution Press.

Webster, Daniel W., Maria T. Bulzacchelli, April M. Zeoli, and Jon S. Vernick. 2006. "Effects of Undercover Police Stings of Gun Dealers on the Supply of New Guns to Criminals." *Injury Prevention* 12(4): 225–30.

Webster, Daniel W., Cassandra K. Crifasi, and Jon S. Vernick. 2014. "Effects of the Repeal of Missouri's Handgun Purchaser Licensing Law on Homicides." *Journal of Urban Health* 91(3): 293–302.

Webster, Daniel W., Jon S. Vernick, and Maria T. Bulzacchelli. 2006. "Effects of a Gun Dealer's Change in Sales Practices on the Supply of Guns to Criminals." *Journal of Urban Health* 83(5): 778–87.

Wellford, Charles F., John V. Pepper, and Carol V. Petrie, eds. 2004. *Firearms and Violence: A Critical Review*. Washington, D.C.: National Academies Press.

Whitney, Craig. 2012. *Living with Guns: A Liberal's Case for the Second Amendment*. New York: Public Affairs.

Wintemute, Garen J. 2006. "Guns and Gun Violence." In *The Crime Drop in America*, rev. ed., edited by Alfred Blumstein and Joel Wallman. New York: Cambridge University Press.

———. 2010. "Firearm Retailers' Willingness to Participate in an Illegal Gun Purchase." *Journal of Urban Health* 87(5): 865–78.

———. 2013. "Comprehensive Background Checks for Firearm Sales: Evidence from Gun Shows." In *Reducing Gun Violence in America*, edited by Daniel W. Webster and Jon S. Vernick. Baltimore, Md.: Johns Hopkins University Press.

———. 2017. "Firearms Licensee Characteristics Associated with Sales of Crime-Involved Firearms and Denied Sales: Findings from the Firearms Licensee Survey." *RSF: The Russell Sage Foundation Journal of the Social Sciences* 3(5): 58–74. DOI: 10.7758/RSF.2017.3.5.03.

Wintemute, Garen J., Mona Wright, C. M. Drake, and J. J. Beaumont. 2001. "Subsequent Criminal Activity Among Violent Misdemeanants Who Seek to Purchase Handguns." *Journal of the American Medical Association* 265(8): 1019–26.

Wolfgang, Marvin E. 1958. *Patterns of Criminal Homicide*. Philadelphia: University of Pennsylvania Press.

Wright, James D., Jana L. Jasinski, and Drew N. Lanier. 2012. "Crime, Punishment, and Social Disorder: Crime Rates and Trends in Public Opinion over More Than Three Decades." In *Social Trends in American Life: Findings from the General Social Survey Since 1972*, edited by Peter V. Marsden. Princeton, N.J.: Princeton University Press.

Wright, James D., Peter Henry Rossi, and Kathleen Daly. 1983. *Under the Gun: Weapons, Crime, and Violence in America*. New York: Aldine de Gruyter.

Zawitz, Marianne W. 1995. "Guns Used in Crime." NCJ-148201. Washington: U.S. Department of Justice, Bureau of Justice Statistics. Accessed June 28, 2017. https://www.bjs.gov/content/pub/pdf/GUIC.PDF.

Zimring, Franklin E. 1968. "Is Gun Control Likely to Reduce Violent Killings?" *The University of Chicago Law Review* 35(4): 721–37.

———. 1972. "The Medium Is the Message: Firearm Caliber as a Determinant of Death from Assault." *Journal of Legal Studies* 1(1): 97–123.

———. 1975. "Firearms and Federal Law: The Gun Control Act of 1968." *Journal of Legal Studies* 4(1): 133–97.

———. 1991. "Firearms, Violence and Public Policy." *Scientific American* 265(5): 48–54.

Zimring, Franklin E., and Gordon Hawkins. 1997. *Crime Is Not the Problem: Lethal Violence in America*. New York: Oxford University Press.

PART II
The Primary Market

The Stock and Flow of U.S. Firearms: Results from the 2015 National Firearms Survey

DEBORAH AZRAEL, LISA HEPBURN, DAVID HEMENWAY, AND MATTHEW MILLER

Since the mid-1990s, the U.S. civilian gun stock has grown from approximately 192 million (65 million handguns) to approximately 265 million (113 million handguns). In 2015, gun owners owned more weapons and were more likely to own both handguns and long guns than in 1994. As in 1994, ownership in 2015 was highly concentrated: the median owner owned two, but the 8 percent of all owners who owned ten or more accounted for 39 percent of the stock. Approximately seventy million firearms changed hands within the past five years (from 2011 to 2015); most were purchased. Two and a half percent of Americans had guns stolen within the past five years, accounting for an estimated five hundred thousand guns per year.

Keywords: firearms, guns, gun stock, handguns

In 2015, 36,252 people died of a firearm-related injury in the United States, approximately the same number of deaths as occurred in motor vehicle crashes. The same year, more than eighty thousand people were nonfatally injured (CDC 2017). The distribution of firearm deaths in 2015 is typical of the distribution over the past several decades: the majority of firearm deaths were suicides (22,018), followed by homicides (13,463) and then unintentional firearm injuries (fewer than one thousand). By contrast, of the more than eighty thousand nonfatal firearm injuries, 60,470 were assault related, 15,928 were unintentional (self or

---

Deborah Azrael is research scientist at the Harvard School of Public Health and director of research for the Harvard Injury Control Research Center. **Lisa Hepburn** is adjunct research associate at the Harvard Injury Control Research Center. **David Hemenway** is professor of health policy at the Harvard School of Public Health and co-director of the Harvard Injury Control Research Center. **Matthew Miller** is professor of health sciences and epidemiology at Northeastern University, adjunct professor of epidemiology at the Harvard School of Public Health, and co-director of the Harvard Injury Control Research Center.

© 2017 Russell Sage Foundation. Azrael, Deborah, Lisa Hepburn, David Hemenway, and Matthew Miller. 2017. "The Stock and Flow of U.S. Firearms: Results from the 2015 National Firearms Survey." *RSF: The Russell Sage Foundation Journal of the Social Sciences* 3(5): 38–57. DOI: 10.7758/RSF.2017.3.5.02. This research was supported by grants from the Fund for a Safer Future (New Venture Fund/Fund for a Safer Future: 03272014) and the Joyce Foundation (16-37317). The authors wish to acknowledge our research assistants Joanna Cohen and Vincent Storie, both of whom took the project on with the very highest level of intelligence, curiosity, and care. The survey would have been poorer if not for the GfK's collaboration and professional input. Direct correspondence to: Deborah Azrael at azrael@hsph.harvard.edu, Harvard Injury Control Research Center, Harvard School of Public Health, 677 Huntington Ave., Boston, MA 02115; Lisa Hepburn at lhepburn@gmail.com, Harvard Injury Control Research Center, Harvard School of Public Health, 677 Huntington Ave., Boston, MA 02115; David Hemenway at hemenway@hsph.harvard.edu, Harvard Injury Control Research Center, Harvard School of Public Health, 677 Huntington Ave., Boston, MA 02115; and Matthew Miller at ma.miller@neu.edu, Northeastern University, Bouvé College of Health Sciences, Room 316 Robinson Hall, 360 Huntington Ave., Boston, MA 02115.

other) injuries, and fewer than 3,320 were acts of deliberate self-harm that proved nonlethal.

The firearms involved in these injuries, and the millions more not involved in any injuries, all start out as legally manufactured or imported guns introduced into the primary market through federally licensed dealers. Subsequently, these firearms may exchange hands through private sales, some of which involve federally licensed dealers, or through gifts, inheritance, or nonpurchase transfers such as theft or borrowing, arrangements that characterize the underground gun market (as Cook and Pollack describe in the introduction).

Beyond that, little more is known about these guns than that they are owned by roughly one in five U.S. adults and can be found in approximately one of three U.S. households. In fact, the most recent peer-reviewed nationally representative survey that focused on details about firearms other than these two basic measures of exposure was conducted in 2004 (Hepburn et al. 2007). Between 2004 and today, we know that the proportion of adults who personally own firearms (and the proportion who live in households with guns) has continued to decline, modestly but steadily, largely because of a decline in personal gun ownership by men. In 2014, for example, the National Opinion Research Center's General Social Survey, an annual survey that every other year or so includes the same two questions (about personal and household firearm ownership) estimated that 22 percent of U.S. adults personally owned a firearm (35 percent of men and 12 percent of women) and that 31 percent of American households included at least one firearm, compared with 28 percent of U.S. adults (50 percent of men and 10 percent of women) and 47 percent of U.S. households in 1980 (Smith and Son 2015).

Although the National Opinion Research Center's General Social Survey and other surveys have asked respondents whether they personally own a firearm or live in a home with firearms, few have asked about the *number* of guns respondents own, let alone more detailed information about these firearms and the people who own them, such as reasons for firearm ownership, where firearms were acquired, how much firearms cost, whether they are carried in public, and how they are stored at home (Smith and Son 2015; Gallup 2016; Morin 2014). Because of this, the best and most widely cited estimates of the number of firearms in civilian hands are derived from two national surveys dedicated to producing detailed, disaggregated, estimates of the U.S. gun stock, one conducted in 1994, the other in 2004 (Cook and Ludwig 1997, 1996; Hepburn et al. 2007). In the 1994 survey, sponsored by the National Institute of Justice, Philip Cook and Jens Ludwig estimated that American civilians owned approximately 192 million firearms, approximately one-third of which (sixty-five million) were handguns. In 2004, using a random-digit dial survey toward the end of an era when most Americans had land lines and answered their telephones, we estimated that U.S. adults owned approximately 283 million firearms (more than four per owner), 40 percent of which were handguns. These two surveys, taken together, suggested several important trends in firearm ownership between 1994 and 2004: a steady increase in the number of firearms in civilian hands, a growing proportion of the U.S. gun stock represented by handguns, and concentration of firearms among fewer gun owners.

Less is known about the movement of firearms between people than about the gun stock. Firearm manufacturing data provide one measure of the annual number of new guns available to be purchased (flow of new guns into the market); other data collected by the Bureau of Alcohol, Tobacco, Firearms and Explosives (ATF) provide a related, but overlapping measure: the annual number of adults who undergo a background check before acquiring (or attempting to acquire) one or more guns. Other movements of firearms, such as dispositions by the police and military, are not centrally recorded (Wright, Rossi, and Daly 1983; Cook and Ludwig 1996). The National Crime Victimization Survey (NCVS) collects information on firearm theft (Langton 2012; Rand 1994). Recent estimates suggest that between 2005 and 2010 approximately 250,000 guns were stolen annually (Langton 2012). No single source provides an estimate of the flow of guns, however. In consequence, as with the gun stock, the best available evidence to date regarding the frequency of gun transfers and the number of guns transferred comes from the 1994 and 2004 surveys.

To learn more about private ownership and use of firearms in the United States today, as well as to characterize where and the extent to which new and used firearms have exchanged hands over the past five years, we conducted the first nationally representative survey of firearm ownership and use in more than a decade—the 2015 National Firearms Survey (NFS). In this article, we focus on features related to the gun stock (such as its size, composition, and distribution and the reasons for private gun ownership) and on salient aspects of firearm transfers between parties, such as where current firearm owners acquired their most recent firearm, by type of gun and recency of acquisition.

METHODS

Data for this study come from the NFS, a national web-based survey (N=3949) designed by the authors and conducted in January 2015 by the survey research firm Growth for Knowledge (GfK). Respondents were drawn from GfK's KnowledgePanel (KP), an online panel that includes approximately fifty-five thousand U.S. adults.[1] The KP panel is selected on an ongoing basis, using an equal probability of selection design, to provide samples, after minor adjustments for deviations from equal probability selection (base weights), that are representative of the U.S. population. Prior to selection of a study sample, GfK adjusts panel base weights to account for any discrepancies between panel composition and the distribution of key demographic characteristics of the U.S. population as reflected in the most recent Current Population Survey (GfK 2013).[2]

KP panel members complete an initial demographic survey and then periodic subsequent surveys, answers to which allow efficient panel sampling and weighting for future surveys. For the NFS, the study target population comprised adults eighteen years or older who fell into one of three groups: gun owners, non–gun owners living in a gun-owning household, or non–gun owners living in a non–gun-owning household, ascertained from the demographic surveys. An additional target population was veterans, who could fall into any of the three groups. To sample this population, GfK targeted respondents who met the criteria in GfK profile surveys and reconfirmed their gun ownership and veteran status within the survey. The final study weights provided by GfK combined pre-sample weights with a set of study-specific poststratification weights accounting for oversampling and for survey nonresponse.[3]

For this survey, 7,318 KP panel members received an invitation to participate. Of these,

1. As discussed at greater length later, historically, most estimates of gun ownership come from either random-digit dial telephone surveys or, in the case of the General Social Survey, in-person interviews of respondents. Online panels such as KP have been used increasingly in the social science literature to overcome the cost and response rate limitations of these survey modalities.

2. GfK structures recruitment for the KP with the goal of having the resulting panel represent the adult population of the United States with respect to a broad set of geodemographic distributions including particular subgroups of hard-to-reach adults (for example, those without a landline telephone or those who primarily speak Spanish). Panel members are randomly recruited through probability-based sampling, and participating households are provided with access to the Internet and hardware if needed. GfK recruits panel members by using address-based sampling (previously, GfK relied on random-digit dialing methods). For selection of general population samples from KP, GfK uses an equal probability of selection method design by weighting the entire KP to the benchmarks from the latest March supplement of the U.S. Census Current Population Survey. The geo-demographic dimensions used for weighting the entire KP typically include sex, age, race, ethnicity, education, census region, household income, home ownership status, metropolitan area, and Internet access. Using these weights as the measure of size for each panel member, in the next step a probability proportional to size procedure is used to select study specific samples. Application of the proportional to size procedure methodology with the above measure of size values produces fully self-weighing samples from KP, for which each sample member can carry a design weight of unity.

3. After the study sample was selected and fielded and all of the survey data were edited and made final, design weights were adjusted for any survey nonresponse (to the initial and to the supplemental survey) as well as for

3,949 completed the survey, yielding a survey completion rate of 54.6 percent.[4] In contrast, nonprobability, opt-in, online panels typically achieve a survey completion rate between 2 percent and 16 percent (Callegaro and DiSogra 2008). All panel members except those serving in the U.S. armed forces at the time were eligible to participate. Invitations to participate were sent by email; one reminder email was sent to nonresponders three days later. Participants were not given any specific incentive to complete this survey, although GfK has a point-based program through which participants accrue points for completing surveys and can later redeem them for cash, merchandise, or participation in sweepstakes. The final sample consisted of gun owners (n=2,072), non–gun owners in gun households (n=861), and non–gun owners (n=1,016). The sample also included 1,044 veterans, distributed across the three gun ownership groups.

Following earlier work, our estimates of the magnitude and distribution of the U.S. gun stock, as well as gun transfers and theft, come from the reports of those who personally own guns (Cook and Ludwig 1997; Hepburn et al. 2007). Gun owners were identified through two questions: "Do you or does anyone else you live with currently own any type of guns?" followed by, among all respondents who answered in the affirmative, "Do you personally own a gun?" Gun owners were then asked about the types of guns they owned (handguns, divided into pistols and revolvers), long guns, and other guns) and the number of each type. Respondents were also asked about the main reasons they owned guns, as well as about their most recent firearm acquisition, including whether they bought the gun or acquired it in some other way (such as an inheritance), and whether, and if so how many, guns had been stolen from them in the past five years.[5] Data for this article come from respondents who personally own guns.

---

any under- or overcoverage imposed by the study-specific sample design. For this study, the following strata of gun ownership from weighted KP data and veteran status from the 2014 veteran supplemental survey of the census Current Population Survey were used for the raking adjustment of weights: gender by age (eighteen to twenty-nine, thirty to forty-four, forty-five to fifty-nine, sixty to sixty-nine, or seventy and older); census region (Northeast, Midwest, South, West) by metropolitan area (yes or no); gender by veteran status (yes or no); age (eighteen to twenty-nine, thirty to forty-four, forty-five to fifty-nine, sixty to sixty-nine, or seventy and older) by veteran status (yes or no); race-Hispanic ethnicity (white or non-Hispanic, black or non-Hispanic, other or non-Hispanic, two or more races and non-Hispanic, Hispanic) by veteran status (yes or no); census region (Northeast, Midwest, South, West) by veteran status (yes or no); metropolitan area (yes or no) by veteran status (yes or no); education (less than high school or high school, some college, bachelor's or greater) by veteran status (yes or no); household income (less than $25,000, $25,000 to less than $50,000, $50,000 to less than $75,000, $75,000 or more) by veteran status (yes or no); Internet access (yes or no) by veteran status (yes or no); veteran serving year (less than two years, two to three years, four to nine years, or ten or more years); armed services branch (Air Force, Army, Coast Guard or Marines or other, Navy). An iterative proportional fitting (raking) procedure was used to produce final weights aligned with respect to all strata simultaneously. In the final step, calculated weights were examined to identify and, if necessary, trim outliers at the extreme upper and lower tails of the weight distribution. The resulting weights were then scaled to the sum of the total sample size of all eligible respondents.

4. The 55 percent participation rate, according to GfK, is within the expected range for its surveys and does not signal that recruitment for this survey was particularly difficult. We did not add incentives because the participation rate was unexceptional. In surveys of this sort the participation rate can be artificially inflated by waiting a longer time for eligible parties to respond or contacting eligible members of the panel with reminders. We did not need to do so as we hit our target number of participants within a short period.

5. Each gun-owning respondent was asked separately for handguns and long guns: "What are the main reasons you own . . . ?" Response categories were as follows: "1) For protection against strangers; 2) For protection against people I know; 3) For protection against animals; 4) For hunting; 5) For other sporting use; 6) For a collection; 7) For some other reason." Respondents could check multiple responses and provide a free text answer if they indicated that a main reason for owning guns was "other." Respondents who reported that they owned other guns were asked to indicate a single primary reason they owned these guns.

A supplement to our survey was conducted by GfK in November 2015. For the supplement, all gun owners from the original survey (n=2072) who were still in the KP panel (n=1880) were invited to answer an additional set of questions about the timing of their most recent gun acquisition, the number of guns they had acquired in the previous five years, and the number of guns stolen from them in the previous five years.[6]

Of those eligible for the survey (n=1,880), 1,613 responded (86 percent). The respondents to the supplemental survey did not differ from respondents to the original survey with respect to age, gender, race, type of gun most recently acquired, or acquisition patterns. Nonresponders (n=267) were more likely than responders to be younger and female and to have acquired their most recent firearm as a gift or inheritance than by purchase. Respondents to the original survey who were no longer in the GfK panel (n=192) were more likely to be younger and have refused to describe the type of gun they most recently acquired than those in the original sample. They were also less likely to have purchased their most recent firearm. These differences did not affect the overall similarities between the supplemental and original samples. We use a supplemental survey weight provided by GfK for analyses using the supplemental survey.

The Northeastern University Institutional Review Board approved this study.

RESULTS

Results from the NFS detail the U.S. gun stock, including its size, distribution, and reasons for gun ownership, as well as gun transfers, including sales and theft.

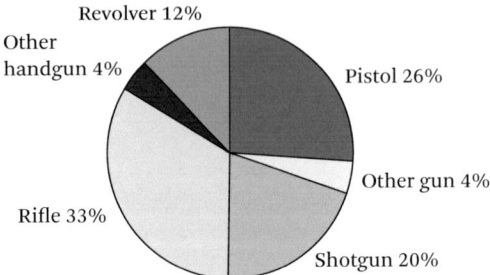

Figure 1. U.S. Gun Stock by Gun Type

Source: Authors' tabulations based on the National Firearms Survey.

The Gun Stock

Twenty-two (22) percent of our sample reported that they personally owned a gun. Extrapolating to the U.S. population of adults age eighteen and older (245,157,000 in 2014) (Colby and Ortman 2015), we estimate approximately 54.7 million gun owners in the United States (CI: 50.7–58.8). Sixty respondents who said that they owned guns did not answer our questions about how many guns they owned. We use results from the 2012 respondents who did provide an answer to estimate the mean number of guns owned by gun owners: 4.8 (CI: 4.37–5.32), yielding a gun stock of 265 million (CI: 245 million to 285 million).[7]

Number and Types of Guns in U.S. Gun Stock
Of the estimated 265 million guns in civilian hands in the United States, approximately four in ten (42 percent) are handguns, the remainder primarily (53 percent) long guns (4 percent are "other" guns).[8] Among handguns, the majority are semiautomatic pistols (62 percent) and revolvers (29 percent); the remainder are described by respondents as "other" hand-

---

6. Respondents were asked "When you completed the prior national firearms survey, sponsored by Northeastern University, in April 2015, you said that the gun you acquired most recently was a [insert type based on type noted in the April 2015 survey]. Thinking about this gun, approximately when did you acquire it?" Three options were offered: "1) Within the past two years; 2) Between two and five years ago; 3) More than five years ago." The second question was "What was the exact year that you acquired this gun?" Respondents were asked to specify the exact year or to report that they did not know what year.

7. Including or excluding those who reported being a gun owner but reported owning no guns, or calculating the mean number of guns per gun owner including those who reported owning no guns, does not materially change our estimates (21.8 percent personal gun ownership; mean number of guns, 4.7).

8. We did not ask respondents to specify what type of gun. Other guns might include single-shot "black powder" guns or machine guns.

Figure 2. Cumulative Distribution of Gun Stock

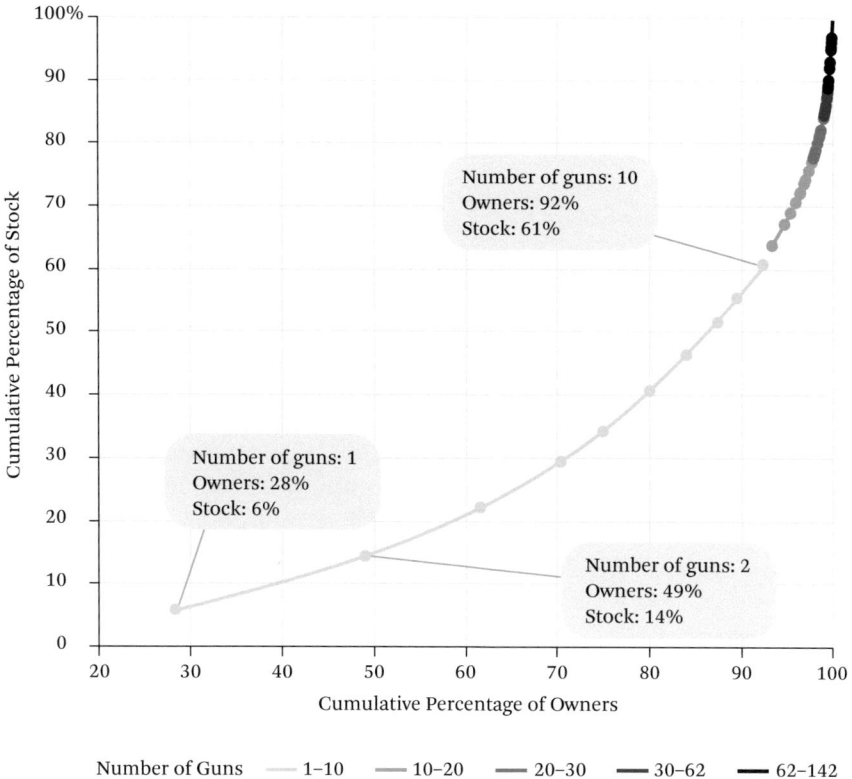

Source: Authors' tabulations based on the National Firearms Survey.

guns. Approximately six in ten long guns (62 percent) are rifles and four in ten (38 percent) are shotguns (see figure 1).

Distribution of Gun Ownership

Gun-owning respondents owned an average of 4.8 firearms (range: 1 to 140); the median gun owner reported owning approximately two guns. As seen in figure 2, approximately half (48 percent) of gun owners report owning one or two guns, accounting for 14 percent of the total U.S. gun stock, while those who own ten or more (8 percent), own 39 percent. Put another way, half of the gun stock (approximately 130 million guns) is owned by approximately 86 percent of gun owners, and the other half is owned by 14 percent (14 percent of gun owners equals 7.6 million adults, or 3 percent of the adult U.S. population).[9]

Distribution of Gun Ownership, by Gun Type

Although the majority of guns in the U.S. gun stock are long guns, in terms of the distribution of gun types, only one in five gun owners (21 percent) own long guns only, 25 percent of gun owners own handguns only (2 percent report own "other guns" only), and half of gun owners own both handguns and long guns (44 percent) or handguns, long guns, and other guns (6 percent). The remainder of gun owners (4 percent) reported owning either "other guns" along with handguns or long guns, or

9. About one quarter (22 percent) of gun owners reported that one of the primary reasons they owned a firearm was as part of a collection, although the large majority of those who cited owning guns for a collection also cited other reasons for owning (for example, 72 percent of collectors also said they owned guns for protection). Not surprisingly, gun collectors owned more guns than those who do not collect guns (ten versus three guns), and gun collectors accounted for most of the upper range of number of guns owned (noncollectors owned one to forty-three guns; collectors owned between one and 140).

Figure 3. U.S. Gun Ownership by Number and Type of Firearm

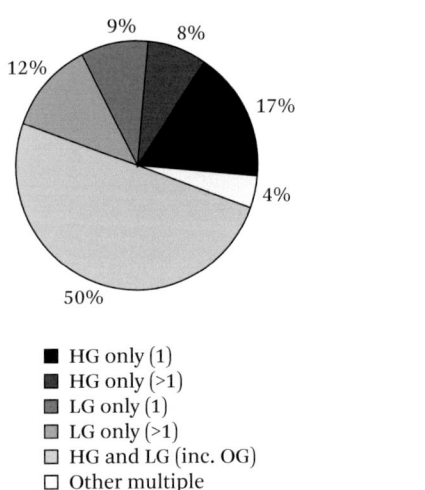

- HG only (1)
- HG only (>1)
- LG only (1)
- LG only (>1)
- HG and LG (inc. OG)
- Other multiple

Source: Authors' tabulations based on the National Firearms Survey.

did not specify.[10] Among those who own handguns only, two-thirds (67 percent) own one gun; for those owning long guns only, 43 percent own only a single gun (see figure 3).

Distribution of Gun Ownership by Gun Owner Demographics
Table 1 describes the demographic characteristics of respondents who own handguns only, long guns only, and both handguns and long guns (for simplicity of presentation, it does not include the small number of respondents (ninety-one) who are not in one of these three categories). The demographic characteristics of gun owners have been well established in multiple surveys. Consistent with these surveys, we find that gun owners overall are disproportionately male, white, older, non-urban, and from the South.

Differences among gun owners emerge, however, when those who own handguns only and those who own long guns only are compared with those who own both types. Handgun-only owners, in particular, appear to be a distinct group: they are more likely to be female, nonwhite, and living in urban areas, and are less likely to have grown up in a house with a gun compared to other gun owners. For example, whereas approximately 20 percent of long gun owners are female, among gun owners who own handguns only, 43 percent are women, versus 13 percent of long gun owners and 14 percent of those who own both.

Reasons for Gun Ownership
Almost two in three gun owners (63 percent) reported that one of the primary reasons they own their guns is for protection against people (not shown). Three-quarters of handgun owners (76 percent) reported that they owned one primarily for protection (not shown). Other reasons include hunting (40 percent), collecting (34 percent), sporting use (28 percent), protection against animals (20 percent), and some other reason (40 percent). Other reasons volunteered by respondents included gift or inheritance or the right to have them (see table 2).

Reasons for ownership varied significantly depending on the types of guns respondents owned (handguns only, long guns only, or both) and demographic characteristics. Overall, those who own only handguns or both handguns and long guns were similar to one another with respect to protection, whereas those who own only long guns and those who own both were similar with respect to hunting and sporting use. For example, almost 80 percent of people who own handguns cite protection against strangers as a reason for ownership, as do 72 percent of those who own both handguns and long guns, but only 31 percent of those who own only long guns do. Likewise, 2 percent of those who only own handguns report that hunting is a primary reason for gun ownership, while 57 percent of those who only own long guns and 55 percent of those who own handguns and long guns do.

Across demographic characteristics, female gun owners were more likely than their male counterparts to report owning any gun for protection and less likely to report owning a gun for any other reasons (see table 2). Reasons for ownership were relatively consistent across age groups, although owning a gun for protection was less common among older gun owners,

---

10. Other guns may include single-shot black powder guns or machine guns.

Table 1. Demographic Characteristics of Gun Owners

Demographic (Percent Total Survey Population)	Any Firearm	Handgun Only	Long Gun Only	Both
All respondents	22	6	5	11
Age				
Eighteen to twenty-nine (19.1)	13	3	4	6
Thirty to forty-four (23.5)	21	6	4	10
Forty-five to fifty-nine (28.2)	24	6	5	13
Sixty or older (29.2)	25	6	5	14
Sex				
Male (48.3)	32	7	8	18
Female (51.7)	12	5	2	5
Race				
White (70.5)	25	5	6	13
Hispanic (11.7)	16	6	3	7
Black (11.0)	14	8	1	5
Multiracial (1.4)	25	4	6	15
Other (5.5)	8	3	<1	5
Marital status				
Married (54.0)	26	6	6	14
Never married (23.6)	12	3	3	5
Divorced (9.2)	23	6	5	12
Living with partner (6.9)	19	6	4	9
Widowed (5.4)	21	5	4	12
Separated (1.0)	24	14	2	8
Community				
Urban (23.0)	15	6	3	7
Suburban (50.3)	19	6	4	10
Rural (26.1)	33	5	9	19
Education				
Less than high school (10.5)	11	4	3	5
High school (29.5)	23	6	5	12
Some college (28.6)	26	6	5	15
College (31.4)	20	5	5	10
Annual income				
Less than 25,000 (16.9)	13	4	3	6
25,000–59,999 (29.2)	22	6	5	11
60,000–99,999 (27.6)	24	7	4	12
100,000 or more (26.3)	25	5	6	14
Military service				
Veteran (9.7)	44	10	9	25
Non-veteran (90.3)	19	5	4	10
Political views				
Liberal (20.2)	14	5	3	7
Moderate (46.3)	19	6	4	9
Conservative (31.5)	30	6	7	17

(continued)

Table 1. (continued)

Demographic (Percent Total Survey Population)	Any Firearm	Handgun Only	Long Gun Only	Both
Region				
Northeast (18.3)	15	3	4	7
Midwest (22.4)	23	4	6	12
South (36.9)	25	8	4	13
West (22.4)	20	5	4	11
Child under eighteen				
Yes (29.8)	19	5	7	9
No (70.2)	23	6	5	12
Grew up with a gun				
Yes (47.5)	35	7	8	20
No (48.0)	9	4	2	3
Don't know (3.2)	17	9	4	4

Source: Authors' compilation based on the National Firearms Survey.
Note: Reported values are percentage of respondents indicating ownership of the specified firearm.

Table 2. Given Reasons for Gun Ownership

	Protection From		Hunting	Other Sporting Use	Collection	Other
	People	Animals				
Gun type						
Handgun only, 1	0.78	0.10	0.03	0.00	0.16	0.03
Handgun only, >1	0.83	0.12	0.01	0.00	0.18	0.01
Long gun only, 1	0.36	0.14	0.46	0.17	0.11	0.46
Long gun only, >1	0.27	0.20	0.65	0.41	0.21	0.65
Handgun and long gun	0.72	0.27	0.55	0.47	0.36	0.55
Sex						
Male	0.60	0.20	0.49	0.32	0.37	0.44
Female	0.69	0.21	0.32	0.21	0.28	0.32
Age						
Eighteen to twenty-nine	0.60	0.21	0.38	0.26	0.39	0.38
Thirty to forty-four	0.67	0.18	0.41	0.30	0.38	0.41
Forty-five to fifty-nine	0.65	0.24	0.41	0.27	0.33	0.41
Sixty or older	0.58	0.18	0.41	0.29	0.32	0.41
Census region						
Northeast	0.53	0.18	0.40	0.29	0.37	0.40
Midwest	0.55	0.16	0.51	0.38	0.36	0.51
South	0.73	0.23	0.37	0.25	0.28	0.37
West	0.56	0.18	0.35	0.25	0.42	0.35

Source: Authors' tabulations based on the National Firearms Survey.

and more common among those from the South.

Gun Transfers

In addition to characterizing the stock of firearms in civilian hands, our survey provided information on the flow of guns in the United States over the past five years, including gun acquisitions, dispositions, and theft.

Firearms Acquisitions

We asked current gun owners a series of questions about the firearm they had acquired most recently. Approximately half said within the past five years (28 percent within the past two years, 21 percent between three and five years ago) and half (50 percent) more than five years ago (see tables 3, 4, and 5). Extrapolating to the U.S. population, we estimate that U.S. firearm owners acquired approximately seventy million guns in the past five years.[11]

The large majority of gun owners purchased their most recently acquired gun, with purchase more common for guns acquired in the past one to two years (86 percent) than for those acquired more distally (79 percent two to five years ago, 61 percent more than five years ago). Across all three periods, the most commonly acquired firearm was a handgun, with handguns constituting almost six of ten guns acquired in the past five years, and five of ten guns acquired more than five years ago. Stores (gun stores, sporting good stores, and so on) were the most common source of purchased guns, while gifts and inheritance were the most common form of nonpurchase transfer.

Firearms most recently acquired by gun owners tended to be new rather than used (see tables 6, 7, and 8). The proportion of new guns was higher among those acquired more recently; used guns account for four of ten firearms acquired more than five years ago, but only three of ten acquired in the past two years. The majority of new guns were purchased (89 percent in the past two years, 91 percent two to five years ago, 78 percent more than five years ago). Among used guns, nearly six of ten acquired more than five years ago were not purchased, versus only one-third of those acquired within the past two years. Inherited guns constitute 40 percent of used guns acquired more than five years ago, but only 16 percent of those acquired in the past two years, mirroring a decrease in the overall share of guns obtained by inheritance from 21 percent of those acquired more than five years ago to 4 percent of those acquired in the past two years.

The cost of the most recent firearm purchased (among respondents whose most recently acquired gun was purchased) was relatively evenly distributed around the mode of $250 to $500 (see table 9). Overall, used guns were less expensive than new guns and guns acquired longer ago were less expensive than

---

11. The NFS asked respondents who reported that they were current gun owners to describe when they acquired their most recently acquired firearm still in their possession and, separately, how many guns they had acquired in the past five years (regardless of whether those guns were still in their possession). Some respondents reported that they had acquired one or more guns during the past five years even though they had previously indicated that their most recent firearm acquisition (among the guns they currently owned) took place more than five years ago. Overall, when directly asked when they had most recently acquired a gun in their possession, 49 percent of people reported doing so within the past five years, whereas 62 percent said that they had acquired one or more firearms in the past five years when prompted to provide the number of firearms acquired (irrespective of whether those guns were still in their possession). In estimating that seventy million firearms were acquired over the past five years, we privileged the stem question to mitigate the well-established phenomenon of telescoping (that is, we excluded from our five-year estimate the 23 percent of respondents who reported acquiring at least one gun in the past five years yet also indicated their last acquisition was more than five years ago) (see table A1). Including respondents who initially reported that their most recent acquisition was more than five years ago increases our estimate of the total number of guns acquired over the past five years to eighty-five million. One possible explanation for this discrepancy is the tendency to telescope, which may have inflated the latter estimate. Alternatively, since only the second question explicitly asked respondents to consider guns that are no longer in their possession, these guns may have been excluded when respondents considered the first question.

Table 3. Distribution of Where Current Owners Acquired Most Recent Firearm, Less Than Two Years (28 Percent)

	All Guns (100%)	Handguns (59%)	Long Guns (40%)
Percent purchased at or from			
Any store	62	65	54
Family	2	3	1
Friend or acquaintance	6	6	7
Gun show	4	3	5
Pawn shop	5	4	6
Online	2	2	2
Other	3	3	4
All purchased firearms	84	86	79
Percent nonpurchased transfers			
Gift	8	8	9
Inheritance	4	3	8
Trade	0	0	0
Other	5	4	6
All nonpurchased firearms	17	15	23
All transfers	100		

Source: Authors' tabulations based on the National Firearms Survey.

Table 4. Distribution of Where Current Owners Acquired Most Recent Firearm, Two to Five Years Prior (21 Percent)

	All Guns (100%)	Handguns (60%)	Long Guns (39%)
Percent purchased at or from			
Any store	54	48	58
Family	3	2	4
Friend or acquaintance	9	11	8
Gun show	3	4	2
Pawn shop	6	7	3
Online	1	1	2
Other	3	3	4
All purchased firearms	79	76	81
Percent nonpurchased transfers			
Gift	11	16	8
Inheritance	8	6	9
Trade	1	0	0
Other	1	2	6
All nonpurchased firearms	21	24	19
All transfers	100		

Source: Authors' tabulations based on the National Firearms Survey.

Table 5. Distribution of Where Current Owners Acquired Most Recent Firearm, More Than Five Years Prior (50 Percent)

	All Guns (100%)	Handguns (51%)	Long Guns (48%)
Percent purchased at or from			
Any store	42	42	42
Family	3	2	3
Friend or acquaintance	7	9	5
Gun show	2	3	2
Pawn shop	3	4	2
Online	<1	1	0
Other	3	4	2
All purchased firearms	61	65	57
Percent nonpurchased transfers			
Gift	15	13	15
Inheritance	21	17	25
Trade	0	0	1
Other	3	4	2
All nonpurchased firearms	39	34	43
All transfers	100		

Source: Authors' tabulations based on the National Firearms Survey.

Table 6. Percentage of Where Current Owners' Most Recent Transfer Occurred, Less Than Two Years (28 Percent)

	Percent Transfers (100%)	New (71%)	Used (26%)
Percent purchased at or from			
Any store	62	78	16
Family	2	0	6
Friend or acquaintance	6	1	19
Gun show	4	3	6
Pawn shop	5	2	11
Online	2	1	5
Other	3	3	4
All purchased firearms	84	89	67
Percent nonpurchased transfers			
Gift	8	6	12
Inheritance	4	0	16
Trade	0	0	0
Other	5	5	5
All nonpurchased firearms	17	11	33
All transfers	100		

Source: Authors' tabulations based on the National Firearms Survey.

Table 7. Percentage of Where Current Owners' Most Recent Transfer Occurred, Two to Five Years Prior (21 Percent)

	Percent Transfers (100%)	New (61%)	Used (37%)
Percent purchased at or from			
Any store	54	79	10
Family	3	1	6
Friend or acquaintance	9	1	23
Gun show	3	3	3
Pawn shop	6	3	10
Online	1	1	2
Other	3	3	2
All purchased firearms	79	91	56
Percent nonpurchased transfers			
Gift	11	9	20
Inheritance	8	0	20
Trade	1	0	1
Other	1	1	0
All nonpurchased firearms	21	10	41
All transfers	100		

Source: Authors' tabulations based on the National Firearms Survey.

Table 8. Percentage of Where Current Owners' Most Recent Transfer Occurred, More Than Five Years Prior (50 Percent)

	Percent Transfers (100%)	New (71%)	Used (26%)
Percent purchased at or from			
Any store	42	69	9
Family	3	0	6
Friend or acquaintance	7	1	15
Gun show	2	3	2
Pawn shop	3	1	5
Online	1	1	0
Other	3	4	3
All purchased firearms	61	78	40
Percent nonpurchased transfers			
Gift	15	14	15
Inheritance	21	3	41
Trade	0	0	1
Other	3	3	2
All nonpurchased firearms	39	20	59
All transfers	100		

Source: Authors' tabulations based on the National Firearms Survey.

Table 9. Cost of Purchased Firearms, in U.S. Dollars

	$0–99	$100–249	$250–499	$500–999	$1,000 or more
All	4.2	18.0	48.1	25.1	4.6
Handguns	3.1	14.3	50.3	29.6	2.7
Long guns	5.1	22.8	45.4	19.3	7.5
New	2.5	14.3	49.9	28.0	5.3
Used	9.1	29.1	41.9	17.3	2.7
Five years or less	2.3	11.6	48.6	30.2	7.4
More than five years	6.9	26.1	46.7	18.6	1.7
Protection from strangers	3.6	15.3	51.0	27.1	3.1
Hunting	4.2	24.5	45.7	18.9	6.7
Sport shooting	6.7	15.3	48.9	25.2	5.0
Collection	2.6	17.7	42.4	28.2	9.0

Source: Authors' tabulations based on the National Firearms Survey.
Note: All figures in percentages.

those purchased more recently. The most commonly cited reason for buying a firearm was self-protection, a reason more common for those purchased within the last five years (43 percent) than more than five years ago (35 percent).

Firearm Dispositions
Approximately 5 percent of gun owners reported that they had sold or otherwise gotten rid of a gun in the past five years (the average number of guns disposed of was two). Of these, the large majority (71 percent) had sold the gun they disposed of most recently, 13 percent had given the gun as a gift, and 10 percent had traded it for something else. A few who had disposed of a gun (1 percent) reported having gotten rid of it in a buy-back program. When gun owners sold guns, they most often sold them to a friend directly (35 percent) or to a gun dealer (32 percent), 12 percent reporting that they had sold the gun via an online advertisement and another 14 percent having sold it to a family member (not shown).

Firearm Theft
Approximately 2.4 percent of gun owners (CI: 1.6–3.6) reported having had one or more stolen from them in the past five years, the mean number at 1.9 (a range of 1 to 6). Assuming that theft was evenly distributed across the years, we estimate that approximately 2.3 million guns were stolen over the past five years (five hundred thousand annually).

DISCUSSION
In 1994, when the National Survey of Private Ownership of Firearms (NSPOF) was conducted, Philip Cook and Jens Ludwig estimated an approximate 192 million guns in the hands of U.S. civilians (1997). In 2015, we estimate that that number has grown by more than seventy million to approximately 265 million. The guns acquired over the past twenty years are disproportionately handguns, the share of which in the total gun stock is now 42 percent, versus approximately 33 percent in 1994.

The shift we observe in the gun stock toward a greater proportion of handguns may reflect the decline in hunting and a change in motivations for firearm ownership and use (Smith 2001). Indeed, a perceived, and growing, need for self-protection appears to drive contemporary gun ownership in the United States (Pew Research Center 2013). Consistent with our finding that the majority of the guns that have been added to the gun stock are handguns and that gun owners in 2015 were more likely than gun owners in 1994 to report that they owned any handgun primarily for self-protection (76 percent versus 48 percent), we find that almost 70 percent of gun owners report that a primary reason for owning a gun is protection against people. Consistent with this trend, we find that respondents who owned only handguns were just as likely to live in an urban environment as a rural one, and to be demographically more diverse than owners of long guns (who, as a group, are more likely to be white, male, and rural).

Not only are there many more guns overall, there are also more gun owners (approximately 55 million from the NFS compared to approximately 44 million from the NSPOF), although the percentage of the adult population that owns guns has declined from 25 percent in the 1994 NSPOF (no confidence interval provided), to 22 (CI: 21–24) percent in 2015.[12] Indeed, gun owners today each own, on average, more guns (4.8 in the NFS versus approximately 4.3 in the NSPOF). Moreover, gun ownership appears to be somewhat more concentrated in 2015 than it was in 1994: the top 20 percent of gun owners owned 55 percent of the gun stock in 1994; they now own 60 percent.

In the absence of a gold standard against which to compare our estimates (of the sort that would render survey-based estimates largely unnecessary), two sources of administrative data—from the ATF and FBI—provide an opportunity to grossly validate results (ATF 2015; FBI 2016). Firearm manufacturing and import-export data available from the ATF suggest that, from 1899 through 2013 (the last year for which data are available), approximately 363 million firearms have been available for sale in the United States (see table A1).[13] Although guns are highly durable, it is reasonable to expect that every year some fraction is permanently removed from the marketplace through seizure, irrecoverable loss, or breakage. Following Cook, applying a 1 percent per year depreciation (permanent removal from use) rate to the available manufacturing data yields an estimated gun stock in 2013 of approximately 270 million (Cook 1993; Cook and Goss 2014). Assuming the number of guns was added to the market in 2014 (the last full year before our survey) was the same as the number added in 2015 (sixteen million, the largest number of guns manufactured or imported in U.S. history), the estimate of the U.S. gun stock (using the ATF data) increases to 285 million, close to the 265 million we estimate from our survey.[14]

Our estimate that approximately seventy million firearms changed hands within the past five years is also broadly consistent with estimates derived separately using—first—ATF data on firearm manufacturing, imports, and exports (which should track our estimates of new firearms acquired), and—second—National Instant Criminal Background Check System (NICS) background check data (which should correspond to the number of people who acquired firearms and underwent a background check). Given the percentage of people in the NFS who report that their most recently acquired gun was new (rather than used) and assuming that new guns correspond to the firearms that the ATF report enumerates, the total number of firearms acquired over the past five years should be approximately eighty-two mil-

12. A similar decline has been reported from the General Social Survey, in which personal gun ownership declined from 28 percent in 1994 to 22 percent in 2014 (Smith and Son 2015).

13. The data series presented in table A1 combines a summary (1899–1968), assembled from ATF reports on manufacturing plus imports (Newton and Zimring 1968), ATF data compiled by Gary Kleck (1969–1986, 1991), and the remainder from online ATF data (ATF 2015).

14. The NSPOF estimate of 192 million guns in 1994 is also remarkably consonant with ATF data up to 1994, applying the same 1 percent annual removal from market estimate. However, our estimate is 30 percent, not 15 percent lower than ATF figures. The estimate of approximately 270 million guns from our 2004 random digit dial telephone survey, appears to be an overestimate. Extrapolating from surveys to the U.S. population, especially for relatively rare events (such as owning an extremely large number of guns), has been shown to have the potential to lead to large overestimates. In the 2004 survey, two factors came into play: first, by 2004 RDD surveys were increasingly plagued, as our survey was, by low response rates, suggesting the possibility that even with the application of poststratification weights, results may not have been generalizable (and thus suitable for extrapolation) to the U.S. population. Second, because ownership of large numbers of guns is relatively uncommon, our estimates of the gun stock were sensitive to the inclusion (or exclusion) of respondents who reported that they owned large numbers of guns.

lion.[15] Our estimates based on ATF data may be an underestimate because they were calculated based on commerce data from a five-year period ending in 2013, the most recent year for which ATF data were available (and sales have been accelerating upward). Nonetheless, our estimates using NICS data are remarkably similar: eighty-three million (derived using our published finding that approximately 75 percent of gun owners who acquired their most recent firearm within the past five years underwent a background check for that acquisition, not shown).[16]

Our estimate of the number of guns stolen annually also squares well with external data sources, although our estimate that five hundred thousand guns are stolen annually is somewhat higher than the most recent gun theft estimate (233,000) reported from the NCVS. Overall, however, the number of guns stolen appears to have remained relatively stable over time. In the late 1980s, the NCVS estimated that approximately 340,000 firearms were stolen each year. Using data from the NSPOF, combined with data from a state-level survey that estimated the number of guns stolen per theft incident in that state, Cook and Ludwig estimate that slightly fewer than five hundred thousand guns per year were stolen in the United States in the mid-1990s.

The NFS used an existing probability-based online panel (KnowledgePanel) to examine U.S. gun ownership, whereas our 2004 survey and the NSPOF both relied on random digit dialing. It is possible that online panel surveys and random-digit dial (RDD) surveys elicit systematically different responses from survey participants, suggesting that comparisons over time (and across survey modes) should be undertaken with some caution. Even if it were possible (or desired) to conduct an RDD survey about gun ownership today, such a survey would be unlikely to be comparable to surveys from 1994 or 2004 due to increasingly poor response rates on telephone surveys (Link et al. 2008). Moreover, probability-based online samples have been found to reduce social desirability bias and yield more accurate results than telephone surveys (Chang and Krosnick 2009).

Although the NFS is thus likely to produce a good estimate of firearms in civilian hands, as well as to accurately characterize the flow of guns and other characteristics of gun ownership, some gun owners may nevertheless have chosen not to report their gun ownership on a survey, and some non–gun owners may have reported owning guns when in fact they do not. What evidence there is, however, suggests that gun owners appear to respond accurately with respect to their firearm ownership on surveys. Studies that have validated survey reports of gun ownership against administrative data have reported low levels of

---

15. Missing answers as to whether the most recently acquired gun was new (as opposed to used) were imputed, based on the assumption that the 3 percent of respondents with missing data with respect to whether their most recently acquired firearm was new or old, were missing at random. The estimate we arrive at using ATF data is higher (ninety-one million versus seventy million) if we do not restrict respondents to those who indicated in a stem question that they had acquired the last firearm currently in their possession within the past five years. The reason for this is that some of these respondents indicated that they had acquired a nonzero number of firearms in the past five years when asked directly how many firearms they had acquired regardless of whether they still had the firearm in their possession. Incorporating these respondents' answers into our estimate of the gun flow increased the estimate we arrived at using ATF data because the flow of all guns (both new and used) is derived by dividing the ATF enumeration of new guns by the percentage of new guns that our respondents reported were acquired in the past five years (and, ignoring the stem question restriction decreased the percentage of new guns from 68 percent to 62 percent).

16. If respondents were not required to indicate in the stem question that their most recently acquired firearm was acquired within the past five years, 69 percent of gun owners reported having undergone a background check with respect to their most recently acquired gun (and therefore the estimate of the number of firearms acquired over the past five years increases to ninety-one million). This number is likely to be an underestimate given that each NICS background check may result in the acquisition of more than one firearm (for additional details regarding background check data, see Miller, Hepburn, and Azrael 2017).

false negative reports (approximately 10 percent), and virtually no false positive reports (Kellermann et al. 1990; Rafferty et al. 1995). In the NFS, fewer than 1 percent of respondents refused to answer our stem question about household gun ownership, and none refused the subsequent question regarding whether they personally owned a gun. Nonetheless, it is likely that some groups of gun owners (such as those who possess firearms illegally, such as someone with a felony conviction), are not reflected in our estimates, and possible that nonresponse to some questions may affect the validity of our findings if those choosing not to answer a question differed systematically from those who did. Given that 2 percent or fewer of respondents refused to answer the vast majority of our questions about firearms, nonresponse bias among those in our survey is unlikely to have had a material influence on our findings.

CONCLUSION

As of 2015, we estimate approximately 265 million guns in the U.S. civilian gun stock, an increase of approximately seventy million guns since the mid-1990s. Over that time, the proportion of handguns in the gun stock—most often bought for self-protection—has grown (to more than 40 percent), as has the proportion of gun owners who own both handguns and long guns (to more than 75 percent). Although the proportion of U.S. adults who report owning guns has declined only modestly, from 25 percent in 1994 to 22 percent in 2015, fewer men own them (32 percent in 2015 versus 42 percent in 1994), slightly more women do (12 percent in 2015 versus 9 percent in 1994), and owners in general are more likely to have more guns (the mean number increased from four to five). Despite the increase in the average number of guns, the median owner owns only two (28 percent own one and 31 percent own two, accounting for 14 percent of the total U.S. stock); the 8 percent of all owners who own ten or more account for 39 percent of the gun stock (and 14 percent of owners own half the U.S. stock).

With respect to firearm transfers, we estimate that approximately seventy million firearms changed hands within the past five years, a number broadly consistent with manufacturing data from the ATF, the large majority of which were purchased, more so in the past two years (86 percent) than for those acquired more remotely (79 percent two to five years ago; 61 percent more than five years ago). Across all three periods, the most commonly acquired firearm was a handgun.

Guns not only move into but also out of the hands of owners. Five percent of gun owners in our sample reported having disposed of a gun within the past five years, most often (35 percent) through a sale to family or friends. Another 2.4 percent report having had a gun stolen within that time, accounting for an estimated five hundred thousand guns per year.

The National Firearms Survey provides the first nationally representative data about the stock and flow of guns in the United States since 2004 (and the second such since 1994). These data have the potential to ground public health, public safety and public policy discussions about guns and gun transfers in what we assume is largely the legal firearms market, which is where firearms, even those that end up in the gray or black market, all start out.

APPENDIX

Table A1. Estimation of Gun Stock Using Gun Manufacturing Data

Year	Total Guns (Millions)	Δ	Adjusted Estimate (.99)	Year	Total Guns (Millions)	Δ	Adjusted Estimate (.99)
1899–1945	47			1980	168	6	140
1946	48	1	48	1981	173	5	144
1947	51	3	50	1982	178	5	147
1948	53	2	52	1983	182	4	150
1949	55	2	53	1984	186	4	152
1950	58	3	56	1985	191	5	156
1951	60	2	57	1986	194	3	157
1952	62	2	58	1987	198	4	160
1953	64	2	60	1988	203	5	163
1954	66	2	61	1989	209	6	167
1955	67	1	62	1990	213	4	170
1956	69	2	63	1991	217	4	172
1957	71	2	64	1992	223	6	176
1958	73	2	66	1993	231	8	182
1959	75	2	67	1994	238	7	188
1960	78	3	69	1995	243	5	191
1961	80	2	71	1996	247	4	193
1962	81	1	71	1997	252	5	196
1963	84	3	73	1998	256	4	198
1964	86	2	75	1999	261	5	201
1965	89	3	77	2000	265	4	203
1966	93	4	80	2001	270	5	206
1967	97	4	83	2002	274	4	208
1968	102	5	87	2003	279	5	211
1969	107	5	92	2004	284	5	214
1970	112	5	96	2005	289	5	217
1971	117	5	100	2006	295	6	220
1972	122	5	104	2007	301	6	224
1973	128	6	109	2008	308	7	229
1974	135	7	115	2009	316	8	235
1975	140	5	118	2010	325	9	241
1976	146	6	123	2011	334	9	248
1977	151	5	127	2012	347	13	258
1978	156	5	131	2013	363	16	272
1979	162	6	135				

Source: Authors' compilation based on Newton and Zimring 1968, Kleck 1991, and ATF 2015.
Note: We apply a 1 percent depreciation (permanent removal from use) rate to each year's adjusted stock. Pre-1969 figures do not appear to include import (and net out export) data.

REFERENCES

Bureau of Alcohol, Tobacco, Firearms and Explosives (ATF). 2015. "Firearms Commerce in the United States: Annual Statistical Update 2015." Washington: U.S. Department of Justice.

Callegaro, Mario, and Charles DiSogra. 2008. "Computing Response Metrics for Online Panels." *Public Opinion Quarterly* 72(5): 1008–32.

Centers for Disease Control and Prevention (CDC). 2017. "Injury Prevention and Control." Web-based Injury Statistics Query and Reporting System (WISQARS). Atlanta, Ga.: Centers for Disease Control and Prevention, National Center for Injury Prevention and Control. Accessed July 3, 2017. https://www.cdc.gov/injury/wisqars/index.html.

Chang, Linchiat, and Jon A. Krosnick. 2009. "National Surveys via RDD Telephone Interviewing Versus the Internet: Comparing Sample Representativeness and Response Quality." *Public Opinion Quarterly* 73(4): 641–78.

Colby, Sandra L., and Jennifer M. Ortman. 2015. "Projections of the Size and Composition of the U.S. Population: 2014 to 2060." *Current Population Reports*, series P25, no. 1143. Washington: U.S. Census Bureau.

Cook, Philip J. 1993. "Notes on the Availability and Prevalence of Firearms."*American Journal of Preventive Medicine* 9(3): 33–38.

Cook, Philip J., and Kristin A. Goss. 2014. *The Gun Debate: What Everyone Needs to Know?* Oxford: Oxford University Press.

Cook, Philip J., and Jens Ludwig. 1996. *Guns in America: Results of a Comprehensive National Survey on Gun Ownership and Use*. Washington, D.C.: Police Foundation.

———. 1997. "Guns in America: National Survey on Private Ownership and Use of Firearms." *National Institute of Justice* Research in Brief. Washington: U.S. Department of Justice.

Federal Bureau of Investigation (FBI). 2016. "NICS Firearm Background Checks." Washington: U.S. Department of Justice. Accessed July 3, 2017. https://www.fbi.gov/file-repository/nics_firearm_checks_-_month_year.pdf/view.

Gallup. 2016. "In Depth Topics A to Z: Guns." Accessed July 3, 2017. http://www.gallup.com/poll/1645/guns.aspx.

Growth for Knowledge (GfK). 2013. "Knowledgepanel® Design Summary." Palo Alto, Calif.: GfK. Accessed August 18, 2017. http://www.knowledgenetworks.com/knpanel/docs/knowledgepanel(R)-design-summary-description.pdf.

Hepburn, Lisa, Matthew Miller, Deborah Azrael, and David Hemenway. 2007. "The U.S. Gun Stock: Results from the 2004 National Firearms Survey." *Injury Prevention* 13(1): 15–19. DOI: 10.1136/ip.2006.013607.

Kellermann, Arthur L., Frederick P. Rivara, Joyce Banton, Donald Reay, and Corine L. Fligner. 1990. "Validating Survey Responses to Questions About Gun Ownership Among Owners of Registered Handguns." *American Journal of Epidemiology* 13(6): 1080–84.

Kleck, Gary. 1991. *Point Blank: Guns and Violence in America*. New Brunswick, N.H.: Transaction Publishers.

Langton, Lynn. 2012. "Firearms Stolen During Household Burglaries and Other Property Crimes, 2005–2010." *BJS Crime Data Brief* no. NCJ-239436. Washington: U.S. Department of Justice. Accessed July 3, 2017. https://www.bjs.gov/content/pub/pdf/fshbopc0510.pdf.

Link, Michael W., Michael P. Battaglia, Martin R. Frankel, Larry Osborn, and Ali H. Mokdad. 2008. "A Comparison of Address-Based Sampling (ABS) Versus Random-Digit Dialing (RDD) for General Population Surveys." *Public Opinion Quarterly* 72(1): 6–27.

Miller, Matthew, Lisa Hepburn, and Deborah Azrael. 2017. "Firearm Acquisitions Without Background Checks: Results of a National Survey." *Annals of Internal Medicine* 166(4): 233–39.

Morin, Rich. 2014. "The Demographics and Politics of Gun-Owning Households." Washington, D.C.: Pew Research Center. Accessed July 3, 2017. http://www.pewresearch.org/fact-tank/2014/07/15/the-demographics-and-politics-of-gun-owning-households/.

Newton, George D., and Franklin E. Zimring. 1968. *Firearms and Violence in American Life*. A staff report submitted to the National Commission on the Causes and Prevention of Violence. Washington: U.S. Government Printing Office.

Pew Research Center. 2013. "Why Own a Gun? Protection Is Now Top Reason." Washington, D.C.: Pew Research Center. Accessed July 3, 2017. http://www.people-press.org/2013/03/12/why-own-a-gun-protection-is-now-top-reason/.

Rafferty, Ann P., John C. Thrush, Patricia K. Smith,

and Harry B. McGee. 1995. "Validity of a Household Gun Question in a Telephone Survey." *Public Health Reports* 110(3): 282–88.

Rand, Michael. 1994. "Guns and Crime: Handgun Victimization, Firearm Self-Defense, and Firearm Theft." *BJS* Crime Data Brief no. NCJ-147003. Washington: U.S. Department of Justice.

Smith, Tom W. 2001. "National Gun Policy Survey of the National Opinion Research Center: Research Findings." Chicago: National Opinion Research Center at the University of Chicago. Accessed July 3, 2017. http://www.norc.org/PDFs/publications/SmithT_Nat_Gun_Policy_2001.pdf.

Smith, Tom W., and Jaesok Son. 2015. "Trends in Gun Ownership, 1972–2014." Chicago: National Opinion Research Center at the University of Chicago. Accessed July 3, 2017. http://www.norc.org/PDFs/GSS%20Reports/GSS_Trends%20in%20Gun%20Ownership_US_1972-2014.pdf.

Wright, James D., Peter H. Rossi, and Kathleen Daly. 1983. *Under the Gun: Weapons, Crime, and Violence in America*. New York: Aldine de Gruyter.

Firearms Licensee Characteristics Associated with Sales of Crime-Involved Firearms and Denied Sales: Findings from the Firearms Licensee Survey

GAREN J. WINTEMUTE

Efforts to prevent firearm violence focus in part on federal licensees—gun dealers and pawnbrokers. Some licensees account for disproportionate sales of firearms later used in crime or denied because of failed background checks. These characteristics tend to co-occur and have been used to identify licensees who may be important point sources of firearms used in crime. Using data from a forty-three-state survey, this study finds licensee and community attributes associated with these characteristics, including sales of inexpensive handguns, exposure to illegal activity, and location in a major metropolitan area. Respondents with disproportionate sales and denied sales express increased concern about firearm violence and support for policies to prevent it, suggesting that some important sources of crime-involved firearms could be significant partners in prevention efforts.

Keywords: firearms, crime, violence, law enforcement

Firearm violence is a significant health and social problem in the United States. A total of 12,979 firearm homicides were recorded in 2015 and an estimated 284,910 "serious violent victimizations" involving firearms (CDC 2017; Bureau of Justice Statistics 2016).

Federally licensed retail sellers of firearms (gun dealers and pawnbrokers) play an important, complex, and mostly unintended role in the provision of firearms for criminal use. Although most criminal users acquire their firearms from unlicensed private parties (Vittes,

Garen J. Wintemute is Susan P. Baker–Stephen P. Teret Chair in Violence Prevention, director of the Violence Prevention Research Program, professor of emergency medicine at the University of California, Davis, an attending physician in the emergency department at UC Davis Medical Center, and director of the University of California Firearm Violence Research Center.

© 2017 Russell Sage Foundation. Wintemute, Garen J. 2017. "Firearms Licensee Characteristics Associated with Sales of Crime-Involved Firearms and Denied Sales: Findings from the Firearms Licensee Survey." *RSF: The Russell Sage Foundation Journal of the Social Sciences* 3(5): 58–74. DOI: 10.7758/RSF.2017.3.5.03. I am especially grateful to the retailers who participated in the survey, many of whom provided additional helpful comments. Barbara Claire, Vanessa McHenry, and Mona Wright provided expert technical assistance throughout the project. Dr. Tom Smith served as a consultant for the development of the survey questionnaire and gave extensive input. Jeri Bonavia, Kristen Rand, and Josh Sugarmann provided helpful reviews of a draft questionnaire. This research was supported in part by grants from the California Wellness Foundation and the Heising-Simons Foundation. Initial planning for the Firearms Licensee Survey was also supported in part by a grant from the Joyce Foundation. The study sponsors played no role in study design, collection, analysis, and interpretation of data, the writing of the report, or the decision to submit the paper for publication. The Institutional Review Board of the University of California, Davis approved this project. Direct correspondence to: Dr. Garen J. Wintemute at gjwintemute@ucdavis.edu, School of Medicine, University of California, Davis, 2315 Stockton Blvd., Sacramento, CA 95817.

Vernick, and Webster 2012), acquisition from licensees also occurs: directly through purchase (Scalia 2000; Harlow 2001) or theft (ATF 2000b; Braga and Kennedy 2001; Braga et al. 2012), or indirectly through surrogate—straw—purchases (ATF 2000b; Braga and Kennedy 2001; Braga et al. 2012; Wintemute 2007, 2009b; Mayors Against Illegal Guns 2008). Data from a national survey of licensees suggest more than thirty thousand attempted straw purchases annually (Wintemute 2013).

Anecdotal reports and criminal case evidence establish that some licensees knowingly participate in illegal firearm sales (ATF 2000b; Braga and Kennedy 2001; Wintemute 2009b; Sorenson and Vittes 2003; Wintemute 2010; City of New York 2009). Licensees themselves estimate that about 3 percent of their colleagues do so (Wintemute 2013). Other licensees refuse such transactions, act to prevent them, and report suspicious activity to law enforcement (ATF 2000b; Wintemute 2009b, 2010; City of New York 2009; NSSF 2000; Wintemute 2013).

The objective of this study is to further efforts to identify licensees who might be important *point sources* of firearms used in crime (Braga et al. 2002; Pierce et al. 2004). Such efforts have focused on two characteristics of licensees: disproportionate sales of firearms that are later recovered by law enforcement and subjected to ownership tracing by the Bureau of Alcohol, Tobacco, Firearms and Explosives (ATF), and frequent denials of sale by the Federal Bureau of Investigation (FBI) because the prospective purchaser has failed a background check (Pierce et al. 2004; Koper 2007; Wintemute, Cook, and Wright 2005; Wintemute 2009a; Wright, Wintemute, and Webster 2010; Koper 2013). These characteristics tend to occur together (Wintemute, Cook, and Wright 2005; Wintemute 2012). They may result from the licensee's business practices, clientele, or community characteristics that the licensee cannot control, willingness on the licensee's part to engage in illegal activity, or some combination of these. Prior studies in this area have been conducted on small samples, in limited geographic areas, or with limited data (Pierce et al. 2004; Koper 2007; Wintemute, Cook, and Wright 2005; Wintemute 2009a; Wright, Wintemute, and Webster 2010).

We conducted the Firearms Licensee Survey (FLS) in 2011 to gather detailed nationwide information on retail firearm commerce from licensees, along with their perspective and opinion on illegal commerce in firearms and selected firearm policy measures. The target population was the owners, managers, or other senior executives of licensees actively engaged in retail firearm sales. Previous reports from the survey address licensees' business and clientele characteristics (Wintemute 2012), frequency of and responses to attempted straw purchases and other illegal activities (Wintemute 2013), participation in illegal firearm sales by other licensees (Wintemute 2013), and beliefs regarding selected policy proposals (Wintemute 2014).

This final report from the FLS assesses which characteristics of licensees' businesses, clienteles, and communities are associated with the disproportionate sales of firearms that result in traces or with frequent denials of sale. The existence of such characteristics and their distribution among licensees could facilitate proactive identification of licensees who might be important point sources of crime-involved firearms. This in turn might provide a basis for interventions, ideally in collaboration with these licensees, to prevent firearm violence.

PRIOR RESEARCH

An early study of the uneven distribution of sales of firearms later used in crime finds that in 1998 more than 57 percent of all recovered firearms traced by ATF were first sold by just over 1 percent of federal firearms licensees (ATF 2000a). Firearm sales were also concentrated among relatively few licensees, however, leaving open the possibility that sales of large numbers of crime-involved firearms reflected nothing more than sales volume (FBI 2000).

This possibility was tested in a study of data for each handgun sold by the 421 licensees in California with sales of one hundred or more handguns annually between 1996 and 2000 (Wintemute, Cook, and Wright 2005). The study finds that it was not a likely explanation for the skewed distribution of sales of crime-involved firearms; some retailers sold crime-involved firearms not just frequently, but disproportionately—more frequently than expected based on sales volume alone. The strongest predictor of disproportionate sales of crime-involved firearms is the percentage of sales denied after a background check found the prospective purchaser to be a prohibited person.

This raises a seeming paradox: how are sales of crime-involved firearms increasing when a higher percentage of purchasers are being turned away? The study suggests as a potential resolution that "retailers who sell disproportionate numbers of crime guns also deal disproportionately with people who are at high risk of committing crimes with guns. Some of these people are prohibited from purchasing guns, usually because they have been convicted of serious crimes, and their detection by a background check increases denied sales for these retailers. But others at high risk would not be prohibited people" (Wintemute, Cook, and Wright 2005, 361). Individuals with nonprohibiting criminal records and straw purchasers are two examples of such high-risk, nonprohibited purchasers.

That study is limited by its reliance on data routinely collected by law enforcement agencies. A subsequent study adds information from observations in the field of sixty California licensees with disproportionate sales of crime-involved firearms and 240 controls, all drawn from the 573 California licensees with sales of fifty or more handguns annually (Wintemute 2009a). In multivariate analysis, denied sales are again an important predictor of case status; data collected on site add little. Based on a mediation analysis, this study raises the possibility that "some risk factors may be mediated by purchaser characteristics for which denied sales are a proxy measure." It suggests that some retailers might function as "bad guy magnets," following the lines of the argument in the previous paragraph, but did not address how bad guy magnetism might operate or the key question of whether and to what extent licensees might deliberately participate in activities that would create bad guy magnet status.

Other studies directly test licensees' willingness to participate in suspect or illegal sales. In these studies, research personnel propose to purchase a firearm under conditions that suggest a straw purchase. (A straw or surrogate purchase is one in which the ostensible purchaser is actually buying the firearm for someone else, who typically is a prohibited person or for some other reason wishes not to be recorded as the purchaser of the firearm. Straw purchases are felonies under federal law.) For example, Susan Sorenson and Katherine Vittes present handgun dealers with telephone callers who stated, "my girl/boyfriend needs me to buy her/him a handgun" and asked how to proceed (2003). Most dealers were willing to make the sale. A follow-up study uses only female callers and removes the ambiguity: "I need to buy a gun for my boyfriend. He knows what he wants, but asked me to buy it for him. Can I do that?" (Wintemute 2010). One in five respondents agreed to proceed. In this case, additional data were available; neither disproportionate sales of crime-involved firearms nor a high proportion of denied sales are associated with a yes response. Finally, an experimental study conducted at gun shows video-recorded licensees willingly participating in transactions that the licensees clearly believed to be straw purchases (City of New York 2009).

One of the goals of the Firearms Licensee Survey was to learn from retailers themselves how common they thought deliberate illegal behavior was among firearms licensees (Wintemute 2013). The relevant section of the questionnaire presents this introductory text: "*Shooting Sports Retailer* recently published an article about what they called 'bad apple' retailers, operating outside the law, who give a black eye to firearms retailers in general." Subjects were then asked, "In your opinion, what percentage of licensed retailers might be 'bad apples' who participate knowingly in illegal gun sales?" Estimates varied widely—yielding a median of 3 percent and interquartile range (IQR) of 1 to 10 percent. This result is consistent with law enforcement evidence that perhaps 5 to 10 percent of firearm trafficking operations involve deliberate participation by a firearms licensee (ATF 2000b; Braga and Kennedy 2001). By extrapolation to the 64,617 retail licensees as of June 2017, the FLS result yields an estimated 1,939 (range, 646 to 6,462) firearm dealers and pawnbrokers nationwide who knowingly sell firearms illegally (ATF 2017).

Subjects were then asked "When a straw purchase is taking place, about what percentage of the time, in your opinion, does the salesperson either strongly suspect or know for certain about it, but sell the gun anyway?" The result is similar to that for illegal sales—a median estimate of 4.5 percent and an IQR of 0 to 10 percent.

The FLS also sought to learn what motivations retailers themselves ascribed to licensees who broke the law (Wintemute 2013). Subjects were asked to rate the importance of five reasons for "a retailer's decision to participate knowingly in illegal gun sales." The options "he wants the extra income" and "he thinks that there is little risk of being caught and prosecuted" were seen as most important. Subjects were also asked to rate the importance of five reasons why "a retailer has more gun traces than would be expected from the number of guns he sells." The option most frequently rated as very important was "the retailer is known to 'go along' and not ask questions when selling a gun."

Respondents held a very negative view of retailers who participated in illegal activity. Asked to recommend sentencing for a retailer convicted of selling fifty firearms to a trafficking operation, their median term of imprisonment was ten years (IQR five to twenty years) and their median fine was $100,000 (IQR $25,000 to $250,000). These recommendations are very similar to those for an individual convicted of purchasing fifty firearms for a trafficking operation and exceeded those in federal sentencing guidelines.

METHODS

The design and execution of the survey are described in detail elsewhere and summarized here (Wintemute 2012, 2013; see also the appendix). The term *retailer* refers only to an individual person.

Identifying the Study Population

We used the February 2011 roster of federal firearms licensees to identify 55,020 retail licensees: dealers and gunsmiths (type 01 licenses), and pawnbrokers (type 02 licenses) (ATF 2012). Study eligibility was restricted to the 9,720 licensees who sold an estimated fifty or more firearms annually, based on data supplied by the FBI (see appendix). These data were not available for licensees in seven states: California, Connecticut, Hawaii, New Jersey, Nevada, Pennsylvania, and Virginia. A random sample of 1,601 licensees in the forty-three remaining states, stratified by license type, was drawn using PROC SURVEYSAMPLE in SAS software (SAS for Windows 2012). The sample size provides 95 percent confidence intervals of ±3 percent when equal proportions of respondents provided alternate responses to questions with two possible answers and the response rate was 60 percent (Dillman, Smyth, and Christian 2009).

Questionnaire Design

Recommendations by Don Dillman and colleagues guided the design of the questionnaire (Dillman, Smyth, and Christian 2009; Dillman, Gertseva, and Mahon-Haft 2005; see appendix). To provide a basis for estimating traced firearms as a proportion of firearms sold, subjects were asked three questions: "On average over the past five years, about how many times a year has ATF contacted your firearms business for help in tracing a gun?" "In 2010, about how many guns did your firearms business sell, including handguns, rifles, shotguns, and any other guns?" "About how many handguns did your firearms business sell in 2010?" To quantify denied sales, subjects were asked "On average over the past five years, about what percentage of gun buyers at your firearms business have been denied after a background check?"

Much of the questionnaire dealt with stigmatized behavior. To increase the validity of responses and minimize nonresponse bias, subjects were asked to estimate the frequency of and motivations for stigmatized behavior by others, not themselves.

Survey Implementation

The survey was conducted by mail, again following procedures developed by Dillman and his colleagues, beginning June 16, 2011 (Dillman, Smyth, and Christian 2009; see appendix). This time of slower business activity (FBI 2010a) was chosen to improve the response rate.

The questionnaire was not tested on a sample of licensed retailers out of concern for the possibility of adverse effects on the implementation of the survey should its existence be disclosed prematurely. In place of pretests, extensive, multisession cognitive interviews were conducted with two independent experts in the firearms industry and its practices. Three policy development experts reviewed a draft of the questionnaire.

The survey protocol required up to three questionnaire mailings; a $3 cash incentive was included in the first. During survey implementation, responses were monitored to detect unanticipated problems. Early on, the response rate for corporations with multiple licensees in the study population (chain stores) was lower than that for other subjects. Personalized letters were sent and follow-up phone calls made to the chief executive or regulatory officer of the twenty-five corporations with more than one licensee in our sample requesting that they authorize store managers to participate.

External Event Monitoring

To detect any external events that might affect the survey, we also established procedures to identify discussion of the survey on the Internet. The primary interest was in any attempt to discourage subjects from participating or to encourage collective or strategic responding. Searches were conducted daily on an array of relevant keywords and phrases, beginning one week before the first questionnaire mailing. Just two days after the first questionnaire was mailed, in fact, the National Shooting Sports Foundation (NSSF) issued a notice "strongly discouraging retailers from participating," which was widely circulated and, with minor modifications, issued a second time. The National Rifle Association posted a notice to retailers on its website shortly thereafter and distributed it as a personalized email, apparently to its entire membership (NRAILA 2011). A prior analysis suggests that the effect of these communications on results was small at most (Wintemute 2012).

Community Variables

Most sociodemographic data were aggregated at the county level. Population data were obtained from the 2010 Census (Census Bureau 2010). Poverty and unemployment data were obtained from the 2011 American Community Survey (Census Bureau 2011). Urban-rural status is expressed using the Department of Agriculture's 2013 Rural-Urban Continuum Code, a 9-point scale on which 1 represents counties in metropolitan areas of one million population or more and 9 represents those that are completely rural or have fewer than 2,500 urban residents and are not adjacent to a metropolitan area (U.S. Department of Agriculture 2013). Violent and property crime rates for 2010 were derived from counts provided by the Federal Bureau of Investigation (2010b). The state-level prevalence of firearm ownership was incorporated using a validated proxy measure, the proportion of all suicides committed with a firearm (Azrael, Cook, and Miller 2004). No nationwide county-level data or validated proxy measures are available for firearm ownership.

Data Management and Statistical Analysis

Response and refusal rates and questionnaire completeness were determined using established guidelines (AAPOR 2011). The response rate was the percentage of subjects in the sample who returned filled-out questionnaires. Complete questionnaires provided answers to more than 80 percent of questions, partial questionnaires to 50 percent to 80 percent, and break-off questionnaires to less than 50 percent.

Four respondents from Puerto Rico or the U.S. Virgin Islands were excluded. Respondents known not to be owners, managers, or other senior executives (n=21, of whom eighteen were salespeople) or of undetermined status (n=27) were excluded from analyses of respondents' opinions on policy proposals.

Based on results from prior research on these data (Wintemute 2012, 2013, 2014), the population of primary interest is defined as licensees who ranked in the top stratum (approximately a quartile) for traced firearms as a percentage of firearms sold (2 percent or higher), or for denied sales as a percentage of sales (5 percent or higher). For convenience, the term HTD is used to denote these high-trace or high-denial licensees. Three definitions of the population of primary interest were tested: respondents in the upper stratum for traced firearms, without regard to denied sales; those in the upper stratum for denied sales, without regard to traced firearms; and those in the upper stratum for both traced firearms and denied sales.

Continuous variables were stratified, generally into quartiles, to minimize effects due to outliers and clustering. Descriptive analyses used the Pearson or Mantel-Haenszel chi squared test to assess significance. Multivariable logistic regressions, expressing results as odds ratios with 95 percent confidence intervals model associations between the outcome and explanatory variables. Forward stepwise regression was used for multivariable models, with entry and retention criteria of $p \leq .30$ and $\leq .10$, respectively. The threshold for statistical significance was $p < .05$. Analyses were performed using SAS 9.4 for Windows (SAS for Windows 2012).

RESULTS

The survey's overall response rate is 36.9 percent. Of returned questionnaires, 96.3 percent are complete and 3.7 percent are partial. Individual question completion rates are 90 percent or higher; the 535 of 587 respondents eligible for this study (91.1 percent) provided information on sales, traces, and denials and could be classified as to HTD status.

Response rates for dealers and pawnbrokers are similar: 37.2 percent and 36.3 percent, respectively, $p=.75$. Further detail on response rates associated with licensee characteristics is reported elsewhere (Wintemute 2012). Response rates are below the overall rate among licensees in major metropolitan counties (Rural Urban Continuum code 1, 30.5 percent; code 2, 34.3 percent), and higher otherwise. Differences between respondents and nonrespondents on other community variables are small and not always statistically significant (data not shown).

Among respondents, 377 (64.2 percent) were dealers and 210 (35.8 percent) were pawnbrokers. The medians, interquartile ranges, and sample ranges (SR) for firearm traces and denials among all respondents, both expressed as percentages of firearm sales, are as follows: median 0.7, IQR 0–2, SR 0–29 for traces, and median 1, IQR 1–5, SR 0–70 for denials. After stratification, 235 licensees (43.9 percent) are classified as HTD.

Characteristics Associated with HTD Status

Pawnbrokers are overrepresented among HTD licensees (table 1). Sales of inexpensive handguns, exposure to attempted straw purchases, and theft of firearms are strongly associated with HTD status. Associations between HTD status and lower sales volume and more frequent sales to women are smaller but statistically significant. Among community characteristics (table 2), HTD status is particularly associated with the prevalence of firearm ownership. Associations are also smaller but statistically significant with the region in which the business was located (HTD licensees were most common in the South), with location in a major metropolitan county, and with increases in the violent crime rate, unemployment rate, and percentage of the population who were African American.

Findings for alternative definitions of the population of primary interest—respondents in the upper stratum for traced firearms, without regard to denied sales; those in the upper stratum for denied sales, without regard to traced firearms; and those in the upper stratum for both traced firearms and denied sales—are similar (data not shown).

In multivariate models (table 3), HTD status remains positively associated with sales of inexpensive handguns, exposure to illegal activity such as attempted straw purchases and theft, and location in the South or in a major metropolitan area. Large-volume licensees are least likely to have HTD status. The association with firearm ownership is inconsistent.

Opinions and Beliefs of HTD Respondents

Only respondents known to be owners, managers, or other senior executives were included in this analysis. HTD respondents were more likely than others to be concerned that their firearms might be stolen or used in a crime, and less likely to endorse the statement that "there are too many gun control regulations"

Table 1. Characteristics of Firearms Licensees

Characteristic	High-TD n (percentage)	Other n (percentage)	p
Licensee characteristics			
Type			.005
Dealer	136 (57.9)	209 (69.7)	
Pawnbroker	99 (42.1)	91 (30.3)	
Nature of licensee			.0002
Named individual	80 (34.0)	142 (47.3)	
Corporate, single location	119 (50.6)	140 (46.7)	
Corporate, multiple locations	36 (15.3)	18 (6.0)	
Sales			.04
≥500	46 (20.4)	95 (31.7)	
200–499	73 (32.3)	80 (26.7)	
100–199	56 (24.8)	67 (22.3)	
<100	51 (22.6)	58 (19.3)	
Handgun sales as percentage of sales			.52
≥75	29 (13.1)	38 (13.0)	
50–74	91 (41.0)	103 (35.3)	
25–49	45 (20.3)	76 (26.0)	
0–24	57 (25.7)	75 (25.7)	
Inexpensive handgun sales as percentage of handgun sales			<.0001
≥50	97 (42.9)	75 (25.4)	
25–49	46 (20.4)	49 (16.6)	
10–24	43 (19.0)	78 (26.4)	
0–9	40 (17.7)	93 (31.5)	
"Tactical or modern sporting" rifle sales as percentage of rifle sales			.75
≥20	47 (20.4)	77 (26.3)	
6–19	58 (25.1)	53 (18.1)	
2–5	67 (29.0)	83 (28.3)	
0–1	59 (25.5)	80 (27.3)	
Multiple sales as percentage of sales			.21
≥5	74 (31.5)	69 (23.0)	
2–4	50 (21.3)	78 (26.0)	
1–1.9	56 (23.8)	83 (27.7)	
<1	55 (23.4)	70 (23.3)	
Gun show sales as percentage of sales			.21
>0	28 (11.1)	47 (15.7)	
0	207 (88.1)	252 (84.3)	
Internet sales as percentage of sales			.98
≥10	33 (14.0)	34 (11.3)	
>0, <10	30 (12.8)	55 (18.3)	
0	172 (73.2)	211 (70.3)	
Clientele characteristics			
Sales to law enforcement as percentage of sales			.16
≥10	78 (33.5)	78 (26.1)	
5–9	51 (21.9)	69 (23.1)	

Table 1. (continued)

Characteristic	High-TD n (percentage)	Other n (percentage)	p
1–4	59 (25.3)	95 (31.8)	
<1	45 (19.3)	57 (19.1)	
Sales to women as percentage of sales			.02
≥25	64 (27.4)	65 (21.8)	
11–24	61 (26.1)	72 (24.1)	
6–10	54 (23.1)	62 (20.8)	
0–5	55 (23.5)	99 (33.2)	
Exposure to illegal activity			
Attempted straw purchase, past year			<.0001
≥Monthly	27 (11.5)	23 (7.7)	
>1 or 2	44 (18.7)	33 (11.1)	
1 or 2	110 (46.8)	126 (42.3)	
0	54 (23.0)	116 (38.9)	
Attempted undocumented purchase, past year			.16
≥Monthly	29 (12.3)	30 (10.1)	
>1 or 2	19 (6.8)	21 (7.1)	
1 or 2	69 (29.4)	70 (23.5)	
0	121 (51.5)	177 (59.4)	
Theft of firearms, past five years			.0002
Yes	77 (33.2)	57 (19.1)	
No	155 (66.8)	242 (80.9)	

Source: Author's tabulation.

Table 2. Characteristics of Firearms Licensees' Communities

Characteristic	High-TD n (percentage)	Other n (percentage)	p
Region			.004
Midwest	47 (20.0)	100 (33.3)	
Northeast	5 (2.1)	10 (3.3)	
West	43 (18.3)	42 (14.0)	
South	140 (59.6)	148 (49.3)	
Urban-rural status (RUCC code)			.03
1	60 (25.5)	51 (17.0)	
2	58 (24.7)	66 (22.0)	
3–5	55 (23.4)	99 (33.0)	
6–9	62 (26.4)	84 (28.0)	
Total population			.44
≥290,000	68 (28.9)	62 (20.7)	
≥100,000, <290,000	52 (22.1)	82 (27.3)	
≥35,000, <100,000	49 (20.9)	83 (27.7)	
<35,000	66 (28.1)	73 (24.3)	

(continued)

Table 2. (*continued*)

Characteristic	High-TD n (percentage)	Other n (percentage)	p
Firearm suicide, percentage of all suicide			.03
≥62	76 (32.3)	63 (21.0)	
≥57.13, <62	48 (20.4)	90 (30.0)	
≥52.10, <57.13	71 (30.2)	73 (24.3)	
<52.10	40 (17.0)	74 (24.7)	
Violent crime rate			.03
≥497	58 (26.9)	65 (22.7)	
≥310, <497	62 (28.7)	66 (23.1)	
≥178, <310	53 (24.5)	77 (26.9)	
≥0, <178	43 (19.9)	78 (27.3)	
Property crime rate			.23
≥3,804	53 (24.5)	69 (24.1)	
≥2,880, <3,804	61 (28.2)	62 (21.7)	
≥2165, <2,880	52 (24.1)	75 (26.2)	
≥0, <2,165	50 (23.2)	80 (28.0)	
Unemployment, percentage			.009
>10.4	70 (29.8)	55 (18.3)	
≥8.7, ≤10.4	59 (25.1)	81 (27.0)	
>7, <8.7	52 (22.1)	82 (27.3)	
≤7	54 (23.0)	82 (27.3)	
Poverty, percentage			.63
≥19	61 (26.0)	69 (23.0)	
≥16, <19	58 (24.7)	77 (25.7)	
≥12, <16	59 (25.1)	82 (27.3)	
<12	57 (24.3)	72 (24.0)	
African American, percentage			.02
≥18.9	74 (31.5)	63 (21.0)	
≥6, <18.9	54 (23.0)	71 (23.7)	
>1.1, <6	49 (20.9)	83 (27.7)	
≤1.1	58 (24.7)	83 (27.7)	
Hispanic, percent			.13
>10	65 (27.7)	76 (25.3)	
≥5.6, ≤10	61 (26.0)	65 (21.7)	
≥2.5, <5.6	57 (24.3)	74 (24.7)	
<2.5	52 (22.1)	85 (28.3)	
Male age fifteen to twenty-nine, percentage			.20
>11.1	60 (25.5)	72 (24.0)	
≥9.9, ≤11.1	65 (27.7)	66 (22.0)	
≥8.98, <9.9	57 (24.3)	83 (27.7)	
<8.98	53 (22.6)	79 (26.3)	

Source: Author's tabulation.

Table 3. Multivariate Regression Results

Characteristic	Odds Ratio	95 Percent Confidence Interval	
Sales			
500+	0.4	0.2	0.7
200–499	0.8	0.4	1.5
100–199	0.9	0.5	1.8
<100	Referent		
Inexpensive handgun sales, percentage of handgun sales			
≥50	3.4	1.9	5.9
25–49	2.1	1.1	4.0
10–24	1.3	0.7	2.3
0–9	Referent		
Attempted straw purchase, past year			
≥Monthly	3.1	1.3	7.2
>1 or 2	3.5	1.7	7.0
1 or 2	1.5	0.9	2.5
Never	Referent		
Theft of firearms, past five years			
Yes	2.7	1.7	4.5
No	Referent		
Region			
Midwest	0.4	0.2	0.8
Northeast	0.3	0.1	1.4
West	1.0	0.5	2.0
South	Referent		
Urban-rural status (RUCC code)			
1	2.5	1.3	4.7
2	1.7	0.9	3.1
3–5	0.9	0.5	1.5
6–9	Referent		
Firearm suicide, percentage of all suicide			
≥62	0.9	0.4	2.2
≥57.13, <62	0.4	0.2	0.9
≥52.10, <57.13	1.8	0.9	3.4
<52.10	Referent		

Source: Author's tabulation.

(table 4). Their estimate of the percentage of retailers who "participate knowingly in illegal gun sales" was higher than that for other respondents (median 5 [2–10] and 2 [1–5], respectively, $p<.0001$). They were more likely to support a background check requirement for all firearm sales and most expansions of current criteria for denial of firearm purchase. Differences in support for expanded denial criteria are not always statistically significant, in part

Table 4. Respondent Characteristics and Beliefs

Characteristic	Hi-TD n (percentage)	Other n (percentage)	p
"Private ownership of guns is essential for a free society"			.46
Agree	219 (94.0)	287 (96.3)	
Neutral	10 (4.3)	5 (1.7)	
Disagree	4 (1.7)	6 (2.0)	
"It is too easy for criminals to get guns in this country"			.08
Agree	142 (61.5)	152 (51.5)	
Neutral	44 (19.1)	78 (26.4)	
Disagree	45 (19.5)	65 (22.0)	
"My guns might be stolen"			.02
Very concerned	69 (30.0)	59 (19.7)	
Somewhat concerned	72 (31.3)	107 (35.7)	
Not at all concerned	89 (38.7)	134 (44.7)	
"I might sell a gun that gets used in a crime"			.0006
Very concerned	70 (30.6)	72 (24.0)	
Somewhat concerned	103 (45.0)	104 (34.7)	
Not at all concerned	56 (24.5)	124 (41.3)	
"There are too many gun control regulations"			.05
Very concerned	87 (37.7)	128 (42.7)	
Somewhat concerned	83 (35.9)	117 (39.0)	
Not at all concerned	61 (26.4)	55 (18.3)	
Estimated percentage of retailers who make illegal sales			<.0001
≥10	89 (39.4)	60 (21.4)	
4–9	50 (22.1)	57 (20.4)	
1–3	64 (28.3)	123 (43.9)	
<1	23 (10.2)	40 (14.3)	
Estimated percentage of straw purchases with retailer aware and participating			.51
≥10	95 (41.9)	98 (34.6)	
4–9	23 (10.1)	47 (16.6)	
1–3	39 (17.2)	52 (18.4)	
<1	70 (30.8)	86 (30.4)	
Policy proposals			
Require "that gun sales by private individuals include background checks"			.002
Favor	151 (64.3)	152 (50.7)	
Neutral	34 (14.5)	55 (18.3)	
Oppose	50 (21.3)	93 (31.0)	
Expand denial criteria: "persons convicted of this crime... should not be able to purchase handguns"			

Table 4. (*continued*)

Characteristic	Hi-TD n (percentage)	Other n (percentage)	p
Possession of equipment for illegal drug use	189 (82.9)	229 (79.0)	.26
Assault and battery, not involving a lethal weapon or serious injury	166 (72.2)	189 (64.1)	.049
Resisting arrest	133 (57.8)	145 (49.7)	.06
Publicly displaying a firearm in a threatening manner	205 (88.7)	243 (82.9)	.06
Expand denial criteria: "persons with this condition . . . should not be able to purchase handguns"			
Alcohol abuse, with repeated cases of alcohol-related violence	210 (90.9)	264 (89.5)	.59
Alcohol abuse, with repeated cases of DUI (driving under the influence) or similar offenses	166 (72.5)	197 (67.7)	.24
Serious mental illness, history of violence	232 (99.2)	294 (98.7)	.60
Serious mental illness, history of alcohol or drug abuse	229 (97.9)	278 (95.9)	.20
Serious mental illness, no violence, alcohol, or drug abuse	213 (91.4)	263 (89.8)	.52

Source: Author's tabulation.

because large majorities of respondents from both HTD and other licensees supported all proposed expansions—except those convicted of resisting arrest.

DISCUSSION

In this forty-three-state sample of active federal firearms licensees, variation was considerable in the self-reported frequency of sales of firearms that were later traced and in the proportion of sales that were denied. Particularly noteworthy are associations between status as a licensee for which these events occur most commonly and sales of inexpensive handguns, exposure to other forms of illegal activity (attempted straw purchases and theft), and location in a major metropolitan area or in the South. These findings are consistent with those of prior research (Pierce et al. 2004; Koper 2007; Wintemute, Cook, and Wright 2005; Wintemute 2009a; Wright, Wintemute, and Webster 2010; Koper 2013).

As discussed earlier, these findings suggest that some licensees are the focus of an array of efforts to acquire firearms for criminal purchases. Attempted straw purchases and denied sales represent failed efforts; they are, almost certainly, attempted purchases by persons with criminal intent or by prohibited persons. Thefts and, arguably, a substantial portion of sales of firearms that are later used in crime represent successes. These "bad guy magnet" licensees could be identified as part of routine law enforcement operations because trace records are available to law enforcement agencies from ATF and denial counts for individual licensees can be obtained from the FBI through the Freedom of Information Act.

No implication is intended that the HTD licensees among respondents are deliberately involved in any of the illegal activities associated with status as a bad guy magnet. On the contrary, it is clear from the findings presented here and explored further elsewhere that, at least among these respondents, levels of concern about criminal use of firearms and support for efforts to intervene rise with exposure to illegal activity (Wintemute 2013, 2014). Response bias might be particularly important, of course; it is quite plausible that licensees who deliberately participate in illegal commerce are unlikely to participate in a survey such as this. Certainly, respondents in this survey frequently attributed criminal motives to other licensees who have high frequencies of trace requests and denied sales (Wintemute 2013, 2014). Further research on the causes and mediators of disproportionate sales of firearms that were later traced, and on disproportionate denied sales, is sorely needed.

The opinions and beliefs of the HTD licensees in this study suggest that among licensees who serve as important point sources for firearms used in crime is likely a subset interested in collaborative efforts to prevent firearm violence. The existing Don't Lie for the Other Guy campaign is an example of such an effort, but it has never been fully implemented (NSSF 2000). An earlier report from this survey finds that respondents who refused to participate in illegal purchases did not always alert law enforcement and other licensees when such attempts occurred (Wintemute 2013). Licensees could be encouraged to make such notifications routinely and advertise in advance their intent to do so. Perhaps the existing Don't Lie campaign's message could be twofold: Don't Lie for the Other Guy and If You Try, We Will Turn You In.

Financial incentives could play an important role. Rewards could be offered to licensees who provided information leading to the prosecution of persons attempting straw purchases, for example. More important, perhaps, substantial rewards could be offered for assistance in identifying the small proportion of licensees who deliberately participate in illegal commerce. Respondents to this survey clearly believed that such licensees exist. For that matter, such deliberate participation has been directly observed and documented under appropriate conditions (Wintemute 2007, 2009b). Tips from licensees identify trafficking operations (ATF 2000b; Braga and Kennedy 2001), and some speak publicly about the illegal activities of others (Shapiro 2008; Wintemute 2009b).

A follow-up survey might usefully explore licensees' willingness to participate in a collaborative effort of this type to prevent firearm violence, contingent on such factors as the size of the rewards being offered, offers of public recognition for performing a public service (or perhaps the opposite—assurances of anonymity), and the like. An encouraging precedent has been set by collaborative efforts between health professionals and firearm retailers to prevent suicide, which are under way in several locations (Vriniotis et al. 2015; Brink 2014).

Limitations

Overall study limitations are reviewed in detail elsewhere (Wintemute 2012); no additional limitations apply just to this portion of the study. The study population was restricted to licensees with estimated sales above a specific threshold; licensees from seven states were excluded because the necessary data were not available. The response rate is comparable to that of others using similar methods for establishment surveys, including the developer of those methods (Paxson, Dillman, and Tarnai 1995; Kriauciunas, Parmigiani, and Rivera-Santos 2011). An effort was made to interfere with the execution of the survey, but it appeared to have little if any effect (Wintemute 2012). We rely on self-report throughout, which is particularly important for data on firearm traces and denied sales. Given that much of the Firearms Licensee Survey concerned stigmatized behavior, nonresponse bias remains a concern. No alternative data on traces are available, given statutory restrictions on release of those data under the so-called Tiahrt amendments. External validation does exist for the median denial percentage that respondents reported, which is similar to the nationwide percentage that the Bureau of Justice Statistics reports (Frandsen et al. 2013).

CONCLUSION

Disproportionate sales of crime-involved firearms and high proportions of denied sales identify a subset of federal firearms licensees that may be of particular interest for prevention efforts. Status as a pawnbroker, sales of inexpensive handguns, and exposure to illegal activities such as straw purchases and firearm theft are associated with those characteristics. At least among survey respondents, those characteristics are associated with increased levels of support for policies to prevent firearm violence that might affect retail commerce in firearms. Possibilities for collaborative efforts should be explored. Respondents with and without these characteristics estimated that a small but significant minority of licensees were deliberately involved in illegal activities, suggesting that traditional law enforcement approaches will remain of primary importance.

APPENDIX: METHODS

These materials are modified from the supplement to a previous report from the Firearms Licensee Survey.

Identifying the Study Population

In response to our request under the Freedom of Information Act, the FBI provided a tabulation of background checks on prospective firearm purchasers performed by its National Instant Criminal Background Check System (NICS checks), specific to the individual licensees requesting the checks. Data were for the eighty-eight days from November 13, 2010, through February 9, 2011. These dates were not chosen deliberately; the data were compiled as soon as possible after our request was approved. Because records are retained for only eighty-eight days, data for a longer period are not available.

The number of NICS checks a licensee requests does not equal the number of firearms that the licensee sells, for several reasons. Nonetheless, NICS checks are a reasonable proxy measure for retail firearm transactions. The 9,720 licensees having ten checks or more in the FBI data (representing roughly fifty firearm sales or redemptions per year) account for 17.7 percent of all retail licensees on ATF's roster (Wintemute 2012).

No licensees from California, Connecticut, Hawaii, New Jersey, Nevada, Pennsylvania, and Virginia were included in the FBI's tabulation. Licensees in these states contact a state agency, not the FBI, to request NICS checks (Adams and Frandsen 2005). These states need not identify requesting licensees when transmitting NICS check requests and are excluded because their data are incomplete (Andrew F. Clay, personal communication, December 9, 2011). These states accounted for 12.6 percent of all retail licensees on ATF's roster.

A random sample of 1,601 licensees in the forty-three remaining states, stratified by license type, was drawn using PROC SURVEY SAMPLE in SAS software (SAS 2012). The sample included 16.5 percent of licensees in the sampling frame.

Questionnaire Design

The questionnaire comprised thirty-eight questions on twelve pages. Pretests on retailers were not conducted because implementation could be affected were the study's existence disclosed. This concern proved well founded (Wintemute 2012). We conducted multisession cognitive interviews with two independent experts who had extensive knowledge of firearms industry practices, and three policy experts reviewed a draft questionnaire.

Survey Implementation

The survey design required up to three questionnaire mailings, with a reminder postcard between the first and second. We included a $3 cash incentive in the first. A cover letter explained that the survey was intended "to understand better the unique perspective of firearms licensees on important social issues and the firearms business itself" and to collect "the first nationwide information on the day-to-day business experience of firearms licensees."

During implementation, monitoring determined that licensees affiliated with chain stores had a lower response rate. We sent personalized letters to the chief executive or regulatory officer of the twenty-five corporations with more than one licensee in our sample, requesting that they authorize individual store managers to participate. Multiple attempts were made to contact each corporate officer by telephone.

We established procedures to detect discussion of the survey on the Internet, our primary interest being in attempts to discourage subjects from participating or to encourage collective or strategic responding.

Data Management and Statistical Analysis

We entered data as questionnaires were received, using dual-entry procedures and automated and manual comparisons. The average annual percentage of sales that were denied and number of trace requests, each over five years, were converted to percentages of firearm sales in 2010.

REFERENCES

Adams, Devon B., and Ronald J. Frandsen. 2005. "Survey of State Procedures Related to Firearm Sales, Midyear 2005." Report no. NCJ 214645. St. Louis, Mo.: U.S. Department of Justice, Bureau of Justice Statistics.

American Association for Public Opinion Research (AAPOR). 2011. *Standard Definitions: Final Dispositions of Case Codes and Outcome Rates for Surveys*, 7th ed. Oakbrook Terrace, Ill.: AAPOR.

Azrael, Deborah, Philip J. Cook, and Matthew Miller. 2004. "State and Local Prevalence of Firearms Ownership Measurement, Structure, and Trends." *Journal of Quantitative Criminology* 20(1): 43–62.

Braga, Anthony A., Philip J. Cook, David M. Kennedy, and Mark H. Moore. 2002. "The Illegal Supply of Firearms." In *Crime and Justice: A Review of Research*, edited by Michael Tonry. Chicago: University of Chicago Press.

Braga, Anthony A., and David M. Kennedy. 2001. "The Illicit Acquisition of Firearms by Youth and Juveniles." *Journal of Criminal Justice* 29(2): 379–88.

Braga, Anthony A., Garen J. Wintemute, Glenn L. Pierce, Philip J. Cook, and Greg Ridgeway. 2012. "Interpreting the Empirical Evidence on Illegal Gun Market Dynamics." *Journal of Urban Health* 89(5): 779–93.

Brink, Susan. 2014. "Gun Shops, Public Health Officials Find Common Ground: A String of Suicides Prompted Gun Store Owners in New Hampshire to Adopt a Voluntary Self-Regulation Program." *U.S. News & World Report*, December 4. Accessed July 30, 2016. http://www.usnews.com/news/articles/2014/12/04/gun-shops-public-health-officials-work-together-to-prevent-suicide.

Bureau of Alcohol, Tobacco and Firearms (ATF). 2000a. "Commerce in Firearms in the United States." Washington: U.S. Department of Justice.

———. 2000b. "Following the Gun: Enforcing Federal Laws Against Firearms Traffickers." Washington: U.S. Department of Justice.

Bureau of Alcohol, Tobacco, Firearms and Explosives (ATF). 2012. "Downloadable Lists of Federal Firearms Licensees (FFLs)." Accessed October 26, 2012. http://www.atf.gov/about/foia/ffl-list.html.

———. 2017. "Report of Active Firearms Licenses—License Type by State Statistics." Accessed June 27, 2017. https://www.atf.gov/firearms/docs/undefined/report-active-firearms-licenses-license-type-state-statistics-june-2017/download.

Bureau of Justice Statistics. 2016. "NCVS Victimization Analysis Tool (NVAT)." Washington: U.S. Department of Justice, Bureau of Justice Statistics. July 29, 2016. http://www.bjs.gov/index.cfm?ty=nvat.

Centers for Disease Control and Prevention (CDC). 2017. "Welcome to WISQARS." National Center for Injury Prevention and Control. Accessed July 15, 2017. http://www.cdc.gov/injury/wisqars/index.html.

City of New York. 2009. "Gun Show Undercover: Report on Illegal Sales at Gun Shows." New York: The City of New York.

Dillman, Don A., Arina Gertseva, and Taj Mahon-Haft. 2005. "Achieving Usability in Establishment Surveys through the Application of Visual Design Principles." *Journal of Official Statistics* 21(2): 183–214.

Dillman, Don A., Jolene D. Smyth, and Leah Melani Christian. 2009. *Internet, Mail, and Mixed-Mode Surveys: The Tailored Design Method*, 3rd ed. Hoboken, N.J.: John Wiley & Sons.

Federal Bureau of Investigation (FBI). 2000. "National Instant Criminal Background Check System (NICS): Operations Report (November 30, 1998–December 31, 1999)." Washington: U.S. Department of Justice.

———. 2010a. "Total NICS Background Checks." Washington: U.S. Department of Justice. Accessed November 2010. https://www.fbi.gov/file-repository/nics_firearm_checks_-_month_year.pdf/view.

———. 2010b. "Crime by County 2010" [dataset]. Washington: U.S. Department of Justice.

Frandsen, Ronald J., Dave Naglich, Gene A. Lauver, and Allina D. Lee. 2013. "Background Checks for Firearm Transfers, 2010—Statistical Tables." Report NCJ 238226. Washington: U.S. Department of Justice, Bureau of Justice Statistics.

Harlow, Caroline Wolf. 2001. "Firearm Use by Offenders." Report NCJ 189369. Washington, DC: U.S. Department of Justice, Bureau of Justice Statistics.

Koper, Christopher S. 2007. "Crime Gun Risk Factors: Buyer, Seller, Firearm, and Transaction Characteristics Associated with Gun Trafficking and Criminal Gun Use." Philadelphia: Jerry Lee Center of Criminology.

———. 2013. "Crime Gun Risk Factors: Buyer, Seller, Firearm, and Transaction Characteristics Associated with Gun Trafficking and Criminal Gun Use." *Journal of Quantitative Criminology* 30(2): 285–315.

Kriauciunas, Aldas, Anne Parmigiani, and Miguel Rivera-Santos. 2011. "Leaving Our Comfort Zone: Integrating Established Practices with Unique Adaptations to Conduct Survey-Based Strategy Research in Nontraditional Contexts." *Strategic Management Journal* 32(9): 994–1010.

Mayors Against Illegal Guns. 2008. "Inside Straw Purchasing: How Criminals Get Guns Illegally." New York: Mayors Against Illegal Guns.

National Rifle Association Institute for Legislative Action (NRAILA). 2011. "Warning — Anti-Gun Survey of Firearms Dealers Under Way!" [email communication to Garen J. Wintemute].

National Shooting Sports Foundation (NSSF). 2000. "Don't Lie for the Other Guy." Accessed January 25, 2013. http://www.dontlie.org.

Paxson, M. Chris, Don A. Dillman, and John Tarnai. 1995. "Improving Response to Business Mail Surveys." In *Business Survey Methods,* edited by Brenda G. Cox, David A. Binder, B. Nanjamma Chinnappa, Anders Christianson, Michael J. Colledge, and Phillip S. Kott. New York: John Wiley & Sons.

Pierce, Glenn L., Anthony A. Braga, Raymond R. Hyatt Jr., and Christopher S. Koper. 2004. "Characteristics and Dynamics of Illegal Firearms Markets: Implications for a Supply-Side Enforcement Strategy." *Justice Quarterly* 21(2): 391–422.

SAS for Windows. 2012. "SAS for Windows." Cary, N.C.: SAS Institute.

Scalia, John. 2000. "Federal Firearm Offenders, 1992–98." Report NCJ 180795. Washington: U.S. Department of Justice, Bureau of Justice Statistics.

Shapiro, Oliver. 2008. "Rogue Retailers: Innocent until Proven Guilty? Or Guilty by Profession?" *Shooting Sports Retailer* 26(1): 50–52, 54, 56, 113.

Sorenson, Susan B., and Katherine A. Vittes. 2003. "Buying a Handgun for Someone Else: Firearm Dealer Willingness to Sell." *Injury Prevention* 9(2): 147–50.

U.S. Census Bureau. 2010. "United States Census 2010." Washington: U.S. Department of Commerce. Accessed February 24, 1014. https://www.census.gov/2010census/.

———. 2011. "American Community Survey, 2011." Washington: U.S. Department of Commerce. Accessed July 15, 2017. https://www.census.gov/programs-surveys/acs/.

U.S. Department of Agriculture. 2013. "Rural-Urban Continuum Codes." Accessed March 26, 2014. http://www.ers.usda.gov/data-products/rural-urban-continuum-codes/documentation.aspx4.

Vittes, Katherine A., Jon S. Vernick, and Daniel W. Webster. 2012. "Legal Status and Source of Offenders' Firearms in States with the Least Stringent Criteria for Gun Ownership." *Injury Prevention* 19(1): 26–31.

Vriniotis, Mary, Catherine Barber, Elaine Frank, Ralph Demicco, and the New Hampshire Firearm Safety Coalition. 2015. "A Suicide Prevention Campaign for Firearm Dealers in New Hampshire." *Suicide and Life-Threatening Behavior* 45(2): 157–63.

Wintemute, Garen J. 2007. "Gun Shows Across a Multistate American Gun Market: Observational Evidence of the Effects of Regulatory Policies." *Injury Prevention* 13(3): 150–56.

———. 2009a. "Disproportionate Sales of Crime Guns among Licensed Handgun Retailers in the United States: A Case-Control Study." *Injury Prevention* 15(5): 291–99.

———. 2009b. *Inside Gun Shows: What Goes on When Everybody Thinks Nobody's Watching*. Sacramento, Calif.: Violence Prevention Research Program.

———. 2010. "Firearm Retailers' Willingness to Participate in an Illegal Gun Purchase." *Journal of Urban Health* 87(5): 865–78.

———. 2012. "Characteristics of Federally Licensed Firearms Retailers and Retail Establishments in the United States: Initial Findings from the Firearms Licensee Survey." *Journal of Urban Health* 90(1): 1–26.

———. 2013. "Frequency of and Responses to Illegal Activity Related to Commerce in Firearms: Findings from the Firearms Licensee Survey." *Injury Prevention* 19(6): 412–20.

———. 2014. "Support for a Comprehensive Background Check Requirement and Expanded Denial Criteria for Firearm Transfers: Findings from the Firearms Licensee Survey." *Journal of Urban Health* 91(2): 303–319.

Wintemute, Garen J., Philip J. Cook, and Mona A. Wright. 2005. "Risk Factors Among Handgun Retailers for Frequent and Disproportionate Sales of Guns Used in Violent and Firearm Related Crimes." *Injury Prevention* 11(6): 357–63.

Wright, Mona A., Garen J. Wintemute, and Daniel W. Webster. 2010. "Factors Affecting a Recently-Purchased Handgun's Risk for Use in Crime Under Circumstances That Suggest Gun Trafficking." *Journal of Urban Health* 87(3): 352–64. Long-Term

PART III

Response to Gun Regulation and Enforcement

Long-Term Trends in the Sources of Boston Crime Guns

ANTHONY A. BRAGA

Analyses of firearm trace data, most collected over relatively brief periods, suggest that a noteworthy share of guns used in crime were recently diverted from legal commerce. This article analyzes a longitudinal database on firearm recoveries by the Boston Police Department between 1981 and 2015 and successfully traced handguns between 1991 and 2015. The percentage of high-capacity semiautomatic pistols among recovered handguns increased dramatically in the 1980s and 1990s. A persistent share of traced handguns were imported from licensed dealers in southern states and an increasing share first purchased at licensed dealers in New Hampshire and Maine. These analyses suggest that market disruption strategies may reduce illegal diversions of new handguns from licensed dealers and the passage of one-handgun-a-month laws may influence where criminals get their guns.

Keywords: firearms, gun trafficking, gun control, gun laws, firearm tracing

The question of whether the illegal supply of guns to criminals and juveniles can be disrupted has been vigorously debated in policy circles and in the literature on firearms and violence (see, for example, Cook, Braga, and Moore 2011; Kleck and Wang 2009). Estimates suggest that only about one of every six firearms used in crime was legally obtained (Reiss and Roth 1993). To the extent that criminals and juveniles in particular jurisdictions are supplied with guns through systematic gun trafficking, focused regulatory and investigative resources may be useful in disrupting the illegal supply of firearms to criminals (Braga et al. 2002). Unlike other contraband, the illegal supply of guns does not begin with illegal smuggling or in clandestine factories. Virtually every crime gun in the United States starts out in the legal market. This suggests a problem with illegal gun acquisition from regulated and

Anthony A. Braga is Distinguished Professor of Criminology and Criminal Justice and director of the School of Criminology and Criminal Justice at Northeastern University, a fellow of the American Society of Criminology, a fellow and past president of the Academy of Experimental Criminology, and the 2014 recipient of its Joan McCord Award.

© 2017 Russell Sage Foundation. Braga, Anthony A. 2017. "Long-Term Trends in the Sources of Boston Crime Guns." *RSF: The Russell Sage Foundation Journal of the Social Sciences* 3(5): 76–95. DOI: 10.7758/RSF.2017.3.5.04. This research was supported by funds provided by the Rappaport Institute for Greater Boston, Everytown for Gun Safety, and the Fund for a Safer Future. I would like to thank Boston mayor Martin Walsh, Boston police commissioner William Evans, superintendent Paul Fitzgerald, sergeant detective Catherine Doherty, Desiree Dusseault, Richard Laird, Ted Alcorn, and James Sullivan for their valuable assistance in the completion of this research. Points of view in this document are those of the author and do not necessarily represent the official position of the City of Boston or the Boston Police Department. Direct correspondence to: Dr. Anthony A. Braga at a.braga@northeastern.edu, School of Criminology and Criminal Justice, Northeastern University, 360 Huntington Ave., Boston, MA 02115.

unregulated legal sources and a corresponding need to intervene in these markets to make obtaining firearms for criminal use more expensive, inconvenient, or legally risky.

Effective supply-side efforts could help increase the price of guns sold to prohibited persons and increase the effective price of acquiring guns—the time and hassle required to make a connection to buy guns (see Moore 1973, 1976). The benefit of this approach would be an increased incentive for criminals and juveniles to economize on gun possession and use. As guns become more scarce and valuable, they will be slower to buy and quicker to sell. Thus, prohibited persons would have guns for shorter periods over the course of their criminal careers (Kennedy 1994). Unfortunately, direct evidence is scant that successful regulatory and enforcement actions against supply lines of guns to criminals and juveniles will actually reduce availability and hence gun use in crime (Wellford, Pepper, and Petrie 2005). Further research on the structure of illegal gun markets and experimentation with market disruption tactics is sorely needed.

The Bureau of Alcohol, Tobacco, Firearms and Explosives (ATF) is charged with regulating firearms commerce and enforcing federal firearms law. Historically, with the support of local, state, and federal law enforcement partners, ATF has pursued cases against armed career criminals and firearms traffickers (2000, 2002). The strategic analysis of firearms trace data to identify gun traffickers is a key component of ATF's efforts to address the illegal supply of guns. ATF encourages state and local agencies to engage comprehensive firearms tracing under which all firearms recovered by the police are submitted for tracing to determine where they were first sold and by whom they were first purchased. The resulting database of trace results is the raw material for improved intelligence on the channels through which criminals acquire guns (Cook and Braga 2001).

The use of firearms trace data to describe the sources of crime guns and to evaluate the impact of policy interventions on criminal access to and use of guns remains controversial. For instance, critics suggest that these data may be limited by police decisions on which recovered guns to submit for tracing (Bea and Burton 1992; Kleck and Wang 2009). However, comprehensive tracing of all firearm recoveries reduces some of the bias in trace data introduced by police decision making. Jurisdictions that submit all confiscated guns for tracing can be confident that the resulting database of trace requests is representative of a well-defined "population" of guns recovered by police during a particular period and a reasonable "sample" of guns used in crime (Cook and Braga 2001). Trace data have been used to describe the structure of illegal gun markets serving criminals (Kennedy, Piehl, and Braga 1996a; Braga et al. 2012) and in a number of policy evaluations (such as Weil and Knox 1996; Koper and Roth 2001; Braga and Pierce 2005).

This article presents a descriptive analysis of a unique longitudinal database on firearm recoveries by the Boston Police Department (BPD) between 1981 and 2015 and successfully traced recovered handguns between 1991 and 2015. These data are used to describe long-term trends in the types of firearms recovered, examine changes in the characteristics of first retail sales of traced handguns, and assess the influence of several policy interventions on the age and sources states of traced handguns over time in Boston. The following section briefly reviews the empirical evidence on the illegal supply of guns to criminals.

EMPIRICAL EVIDENCE ON ILLEGAL GUN MARKETS

Much of the empirical evidence on the illegal supply of guns comes from analyses of ATF firearm trace data and firearms trafficking investigations that indicate some percentage of the guns used in crime were recently diverted from legal firearms commerce (ATF 2000, 2002; Braga et al. 2012; Cook and Braga 2001; Pierce et al. 2004). Several findings are of particular note. First is that new guns are recovered disproportionately in crime (Cook and Braga 2001; Pierce et al. 2004; Zimring 1976). Another is that some licensed firearm retailers are disproportionately frequent sources of crime guns and are linked to more guns traced by ATF than would be expected from their overall volume of gun sales (on reasons for these patterns, see Wintemute, Cook, and Wright 2005). Separately, under test conditions, significant proportions of licensed retailers and private party gun sellers will knowingly participate in illegal gun sales (Sorenson and Vittes 2003; Wintemute 2010). In addition, on average, about one-third of guns used in crime in any community are acquired in that community, another third from elsewhere in the same state, and a third from other states (ATF 2002; Cook and Braga 2001). Last are the long-standing interstate trafficking routes for crime guns, typically from states with weaker gun regulations to those with stronger ones. The best known of these is the so-called Iron Pipeline—from the Southeast to the Middle Atlantic and New England (Cook and Braga 2001; Pierce et al. 2004).

Analyses of ATF firearm trafficking investigation data reveal that illegal gun traffickers exploit an incredibly leaky legal firearms commerce system. For instance, a 2000 report examining 1,530 gun trafficking investigations made by ATF between July 1, 1996, and December 31, 1998, found that more than eighty-four thousand firearms were diverted legal to illegal commerce (ATF 2000). The report identified the primary gun trafficking pathways as scofflaw and negligent firearms dealers, straw-man legal purchasers who provide guns to criminals, and illegal diversions through secondary market sources such as gun shows, flea markets, and want ads. The analysis also revealed the organized theft of firearms from licensed dealers, common carriers, and residences as illegal diversion pathways. Moreover, ATF found that 61 percent of the cases involved the diversion of twenty or fewer firearms, and concluded that most but not all gun trafficking investigations involve a relatively small number of firearms (2000). The two largest cases involved the illegal diversion of some eleven thousand and ten thousand firearms, respectively.

Recent analyses of data drawn from the 2004 Survey of Inmates in State Correctional Facilities, the 2004 Survey of Inmates in Federal Correctional Facilities, and the 2002 Survey of Inmates in Local Jails suggest that very few illegal gun users directly acquire their guns through theft. Philip Cook, Susan Parker, and Harold Pollock find that only 4 percent of male respondents age eighteen to forty in the first two years of their prison term who admitted in the survey interview that they had a gun at the time of crime reported directly stealing their most recent crime gun. These authors further document that 10 percent of recently incarcerated state prison inmates who carried a gun indicated that they purchased that gun from a licensed dealer, such as a gun store or pawnbroker (2015). Most of the transactions—roughly 70 percent—were with social connections (friends and family) or with street sources (fences, drug dealers, illicit gun brokers, and gangs). These sources may well include traffickers who are buying from retail outlets and selling to prohibited persons.

Despite multiple illegal sources of firearms for criminals, ethnographic research suggests that illegal gun markets may not work very well in particular urban environments. Some evidence indicates considerable frictions in the underground market for guns in Chicago (Cook et al. 2007). These frictions were due primarily to the underground gun market being both illegal and thin—that is, the number of buyers, sellers, and total transactions was small, and relevant information on reliable sources of guns were scarce. The same research further reveals that Chicago street gangs helped overcome these market frictions, but economic interests caused gang leaders to limit supply primarily to gang members, and even then transactions were usually loans or rentals with strings attached. Thin underground gun markets may be particularly vulnerable to focused gun market disruption strategies.

A growing body of evaluation evidence suggests that enforcement and regulatory interventions focused on retail sales practices can generate subsequent reductions in new guns recovered in crime. In Detroit and Chicago, the number of guns recovered within a year of first retail sale from someone other than the original purchaser was sharply reduced after undercover police stings and lawsuits targeted scofflaw retail dealers (Webster et al. 2006). In Milwaukee, the number of guns recovered within a year of first retail sale from someone other than the original purchaser significantly decreased after voluntary changes in the sales practices of a gun dealer that received negative publicity for leading the United States in selling the most guns recovered by police in crime (Webster, Vernick, and Bulzacchelli 2006). In Chicago, an analysis of recovered crime handguns found that the 1994 implementation of the Brady Handgun Violence Prevention Act was associated with a marked decrease in crime handguns imported from states required to institute the provisions of the act (Cook and Braga 2001). The Brady Act mandated licensed dealers to conduct a criminal background check on all handgun buyers and required a one-week waiting period before transferring the gun to a criminal. The Cook and Braga (2001) analysis suggests that the Brady Act made interstate gunrunning from lax-control states less profitable by making it more difficult for traffickers to buy handguns from licensed dealers in those states.

The case for a supply-side approach to gun violence is generally supported by the empirical evidence on illegal gun market dynamics. However, rigorous research is sorely needed to determine whether supply-side interventions can actually affect the availability of guns to criminals. As the National Research Council's Committee to Improve Research Information and Data on Firearms concludes, "it is simply not known whether it is actually possible to shut down illegal pipelines of guns to criminals nor the costs of doing so" (Wellford, Pepper, and Petrie 2005, 8). Experimental evidence also needs to be developed to determine whether interventions designed to limit illegal transfers of firearms can indeed reduce gun violence.

GUNS AND SERIOUS GUN VIOLENCE IN BOSTON

Massachusetts is well known for having some of the strongest gun laws in the United States. In 2013, the Brady Campaign to Prevent Gun Violence ranked Massachusetts gun laws as the sixth strongest in the fifty states.[1] Importantly, Massachusetts regulates all secondhand gun transactions by requiring records of ownership transfers, thefts, and losses to be reported to the state (Braga and Hureau 2015). Massachusetts has also been noted as having very low prevalence of gun ownership relative to other U.S. states (Azrael, Cook, and Miller 2004). Survey research suggests that only 12.8 percent of Massachusetts households reported owning a gun (Okoro et al. 2005), versus 31 percent nationwide (Smith and Son 2015). A 2010 Harvard School of Public Health representative survey of Boston residents estimates that only 3.7 percent of respondents report that someone in their household owns a handgun (see Braga and Cook 2016).

Like many cities in the United States, Boston suffered a dramatic increase in gun violence in the late 1980s and early 1990s (Kennedy, Piehl, and Braga 1996a). Preceded by the arrival of crack cocaine in 1986, this epidemic, measured as a gun homicide problem, started in 1988 and was contained mostly within Boston's young black male population residing in a few disadvantaged neighborhoods (Braga 2003). Gangs and criminally active youth were at the core of the situation (Kennedy, Braga, and Piehl 1997). Boston experienced a sudden downturn in related violence in the mid- to late 1990s; however, the change was associated with the implementation of a strategic gang violence reduction initiative (Braga et al. 2001).

Gun violence surged again in Boston during the mid-2000s. Research conducted during this period once more revealed that it could be characterized as being driven by gang conflicts and highly concentrated among a small number of high-risk places and high-risk people. Roughly 5 percent of Boston's street block faces and intersections generated about 74 percent of fatal and nonfatal shooting incidents between 1980 and 2008 (Braga, Papachristos, and Hureau 2010). These hot spots were located in and proximate to gang turf and drug market areas and occupied small geographies within disadvantaged neighborhoods. In 2006, only 1 percent of Boston's population between the ages of fourteen and twenty-four were mem-

---

1. See "2013 State Scorecard," http://www.bradycampaign.org/2013-state-scorecard (accessed July 5, 2017). The Brady Campaign ranked all fifty states based on thirty policy approaches to regulating guns and ammunition, such as: background checks on gun sales; reporting lost or stolen firearms; and prohibiting dangerous people from purchasing weapons.

bers of street gangs involved in gun violence; at the same time, gang-related disputes generated more than two-thirds of gun homicides, and gang members were involved as offenders, victims, or both in nearly 70 percent of nonfatal shootings (Braga, Hureau, and Winship 2008). In a recent study of one disadvantaged Boston community, roughly 85 percent of all gunshot victims were in a single co-offending network representing less than 5 percent of the community's population (Papachristos, Braga, and Hureau 2012). Once again, a deterrence-based gang violence reduction strategy was credited with reducing serious gun violence in Boston during the late 2000s (Braga, Apel, and Welsh 2013; Braga, Hureau, and Papachristos 2014).

Most people arrested for illegal gun possession in Boston are not otherwise law-abiding individuals. In 2014, the BPD arrested 485 people for illegal gun possession and 228 for violent gun offenses. Eighty percent of the adult arrestees were found to have criminal records, and judging by criminal-history data, illegal gun possessors were as involved in crime as those who were arrested for gun violence—murder, robbery, and assault (Braga and Cook 2016). These data suggest that Boston has an ongoing problem with criminal access to firearms.

SOURCES OF CRIME GUNS

The Boston Gun Project was a problem-oriented policing initiative expressly aimed at reducing homicide victimization among youths in Boston in the mid-1990s (Kennedy, Braga, and Piehl 1996a). It represented an innovative partnership between researchers and practitioners to assess the city's youth homicide problem and implement an intervention designed to have a substantial near-term impact on the problem. Project research shows that the problem of youth homicide was concentrated among a few chronically offending gang-involved youth (Kennedy, Braga, and Piehl 1996a). The same research also shows that firearms associated with youth, especially with gang youth, tended to be semiautomatic pistols, often quite new and apparently only recently diverted from retail. Many of these guns were first sold at retail in Massachusetts or smuggled into Boston from out of state. The project began in early 1995 and implemented what is now known as the Operation Ceasefire intervention beginning on May 15, 1996. The intervention had two main elements: the "pulling levers" focused deterrence strategy to prevent gang violence and a direct law enforcement attack on illicit firearms traffickers supplying youth with guns.[2]

Boston Gun Project research initially focused on understanding and addressing the local illicit firearms market serving youth age twenty-one and younger. Youth gun acquisition was largely driven by fear, self-protection, and status concerns arising from a high-risk street environment dominated by violent gangs, drugs, and guns (Kennedy, Piehl, and Braga 1996a). Interviews with youth probationers in Boston reveal that guns were fairly easy to acquire either by buying them illegally or by borrowing them from friends and associates (Kennedy, Piehl, and Braga 1996a). For style reasons and to avoid being caught with an older gun that may have already been used in a violent crime, youth probationers expressed a strong preference for "new in the box" semiautomatic pistols.

To unravel the nature of the illegal gun market, the Boston Gun Project research team analyzed ATF firearms trace data for 1,550 firearms recovered from youth age twenty-one and younger in Boston between January 1991 and May 1995 (Kennedy, Piehl, and Braga 1996a). Some 82 percent of the recovered firearms were handguns and more than half were semiautomatic pistols. Recovered semiautomatic pistols were concentrated among a few calibers, such

---

2. Focused deterrence strategies honor core deterrence ideas, such as increasing risks faced by offenders, while finding new and creative ways of deploying traditional and nontraditional law enforcement tools. According to a 2001 National Institute of Justice evaluation, the intervention was associated with a 63 percent reduction in Boston youth homicide and similar large reductions in nonfatal serious gun violence (Braga et al. 2001). A more recent systematic review and meta-analysis of focused deterrence programs indicates that these initiatives generate statistically significant reductions in crime (Braga and Weisburd 2012).

as 9mm, .380, and .25. Roughly 52 percent of the firearms were successfully traced to their first retail sale. Almost 20 percent were not traced because the serial numbers had been obliterated. An analysis of the source states of traceable guns revealed that Boston had problems with diversions from both local and out-of-state federal firearms licensees (FFLs). Despite strict state controls on firearms commerce, 34 percent of traceable guns were first sold at retail in Massachusetts. Nearly 32 percent were first sold at retail in loose-control southern states, most notably along the I-95 Iron Pipeline—Florida, Georgia, Virginia, North Carolina, and South Carolina.

The time between a firearm's first sale at retail and subsequent recovery in crime is popularly known as time-to-crime (Pierce et al. 2004). Law enforcement investigators consider that a fast time-to-crime, defined by ATF as three years or less, suggests that a firearm may have been recently illegally diverted from retail outlets (ATF 2002): 35 percent of traceable Boston youth guns were fast time-to-crime guns. For all traceable new firearms, the first retail purchaser was a different person than the youth from whom the gun was recovered, suggesting a recent illegal diversion from legitimate firearms commerce.

Based on this analysis, the Operation Ceasefire gun market disruption strategy was appropriately focused on the illegal diversion of new handguns from retail outlets in Massachusetts, southern states along Interstate 95, and elsewhere (Braga and Pierce 2005). The key elements of the strategy were sevenfold:

> Expanded focus of local, state, and federal authorities to include *intrastate* firearms trafficking in Massachusetts in addition to interstate trafficking.
>
> Focused enforcement attention on traffickers of the makes and calibers of handguns most used by gang members.
>
> Focused enforcement attention on traffickers of handguns that had short time-to-crime intervals and, thus, were most likely to have been trafficked. The ATF Boston Field Division implemented an in-house tracking system that flagged handguns whose traces revealed a short time-to-crime interval.
>
> Focused enforcement attention on traffickers of handguns used by the city's most violent gangs.
>
> Attempts to restore obliterated serial numbers of confiscated handguns and subsequently investigate trafficking based on these restorations.
>
> Support for these enforcement priorities through strategic analyses of data generated by the Boston Police Department and ATF's comprehensive tracing of crime guns and by developing leads from the systematic debriefing of gang-affiliated arrestees and those involved in violent crime.
>
> Deliberate communication of successful investigations and prosecutions of gun traffickers to deter others from diverting firearms from retail sources to criminals and youth in Boston.

Half of the ATF gun trafficking investigations launched as part of this strategy focused on firearms illegally diverted from FFLs by straw purchasers. An impact evaluation in 2005 found that the gun market disruption strategy significantly reduced the illegal supply of new handguns to Boston criminals (Braga and Pierce 2005). However, the evaluation also suggests that gun traffickers may have substituted older handguns purchased through secondary market transactions to avoid enforcement attention.

As mentioned, the Boston gun market disruption strategy was implemented in conjunction with a powerful deterrence-based strategy to reduce gang violence. The National Institute of Justice–sponsored evaluators credited the Operation Ceasefire deterrence strategy with the sudden, large impact on youth homicide and gun violence (Braga et al. 2001). Their assessment that the principal impact was a demand-side, deterrence-based effect rather than a supply-side effect was based on two observations. First, it seemed implausible that supply-side efforts were responsible for the abrupt reductions in gun-related violence over the summer of 1996. Boston trafficking cases followed that reduction, rather than anticipated it. Second, antitrafficking efforts in Boston did nothing to reduce the existing stockpile of illegally acquired and possessed firearms in Boston. Those guns held by gang members in Boston in May of 1996 were, for the most part, still held by them several months later when the violence reached its new, lower equilibrium. The immediate change was not in the extent of gun ownership but in gun use. Although it was unlikely that market disruption strategy had a meaningful short-term impact on serious gun violence, the available evidence suggests that the intervention had a meaningful longer-term impact on the illegal supply to Boston of newer handguns (Braga and Pierce 2005).

Boston has been the site of an ongoing series of research inquiries into the illegal supply of guns to criminals. Like others, Boston-based studies have generally analyzed the sources of illegal guns during specific periods, such as the early 1990s or late 2000s, rather than long-term trends. This article presents a descriptive analysis of a unique longitudinal data set on gun recoveries in Boston to uncover developmental trends in illegal gun market characteristics and dynamics that would be missed in existing cross-sectional data analyses. These data are also used to assess the impacts of two well-known policy interventions, one-gun-a-month laws and gun buy-back programs, on the characteristics of Boston crime guns.

DATA

This article uses detailed BPD firearm recovery data to examine long-term gun trends in Boston. The Ballistics Unit keeps records on the basic characteristics of all firearms recovered by BPD officers (type, manufacturer, model, and caliber-gauge). Prior to 1991, these data were maintained in carefully organized paper record files. Paper records on N=8,753 firearms recovered between 1981 and 1990 were entered into a computerized database for a previously completed research study (see Braga 2003). The data were acquired and supplemented with gun recovery data maintained by the BPD in their comprehensive firearms trace database.

The Gun Control Act of 1968 (GCA) established a set of requirements that allows any given firearm to be traced from its manufacture or import to its first sale by a retail dealer (Zimring 1975; Cook and Braga 2001). The GCA mandates that each new firearm, whether manufactured in the United States or abroad, be marked with a serial number. In addition, the GCA requires all FFLs, including manufacturers, importers, distributors, and retail dealers, to maintain records of all firearms transactions. Firearms traces can be unsuccessful for a variety of reasons. ATF trace data can provide policy-relevant insights on illegal gun market dynamics when conclusions are based on careful analyses that are coupled with clear acknowledgments of data limitations (Cook and Braga 2001; Wellford, Pepper, and Petrie 2005).

The BPD has been comprehensively submitting all recovered firearms to ATF for tracing since 1991 (Kennedy, Piehl, and Braga 1996a; Braga and Pierce 2005). Between 1991 and 2015, the BPD recovered 15,888 firearms in illegal gun possession offenses (62.3 percent), public places (28.8 percent), violent crimes (6.3 percent), and drug offenses or other crimes (2.6 percent) that were subsequently submitted to ATF for tracing. This research analyzes trace data for the N=12,909 handguns recovered by the BPD during this period (81.3 percent of 15,888). Long guns, such as rifles and shotguns, were not included in the analyses. Handguns are the majority of crime guns recovered by the BPD. Some 58.3 percent (7,521 of 12,909) recovered between 1991 and 2015 were successfully traced to the first retail purchaser. Traces were not successful for pre-1968 manufacture (16.3 percent), obliterated serial numbers (13.7 percent), and data entry issues on the trace form (8.2 percent) or in dealer records (3.5 percent).

TRENDS IN FIREARM RECOVERIES, 1981–2015

Figure 1 presents yearly trends in the total number of firearms and the total number of handguns the BPD recovered between 1981 and 2015. Nearly 78 percent of the total (24,641) were handguns (19,157). The number of recovered guns peaked in 1990 with 1,153 recoveries, and dropped to a low of 319 in 1999. The yearly number of handguns recovered closely followed the total number of firearms recovered. Figure 1 also shows that the share of recovered firearms that were handguns narrowed after 1996. Be-

Figure 1. Guns Recovered by Boston Police Department

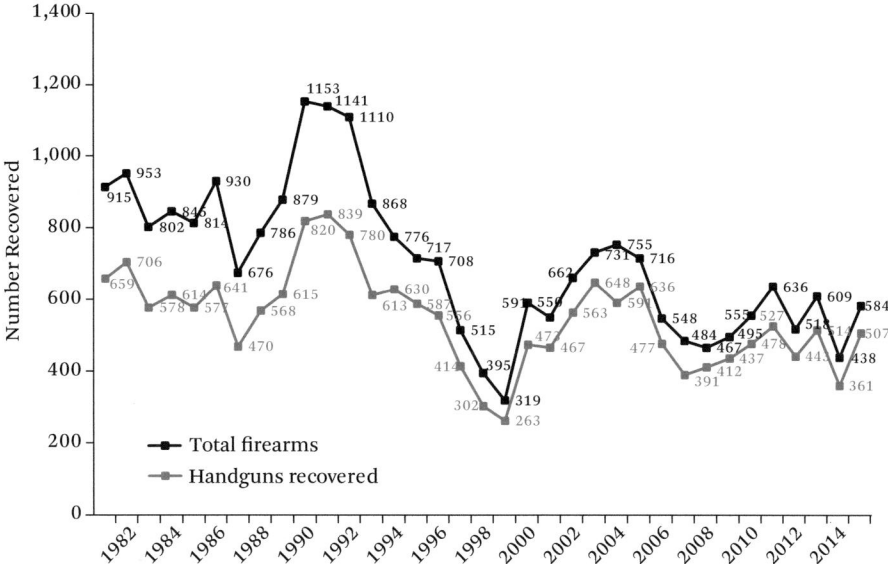

Source: Author's calculations.

Figure 2. Handgun Recoveries and Homicides in Boston

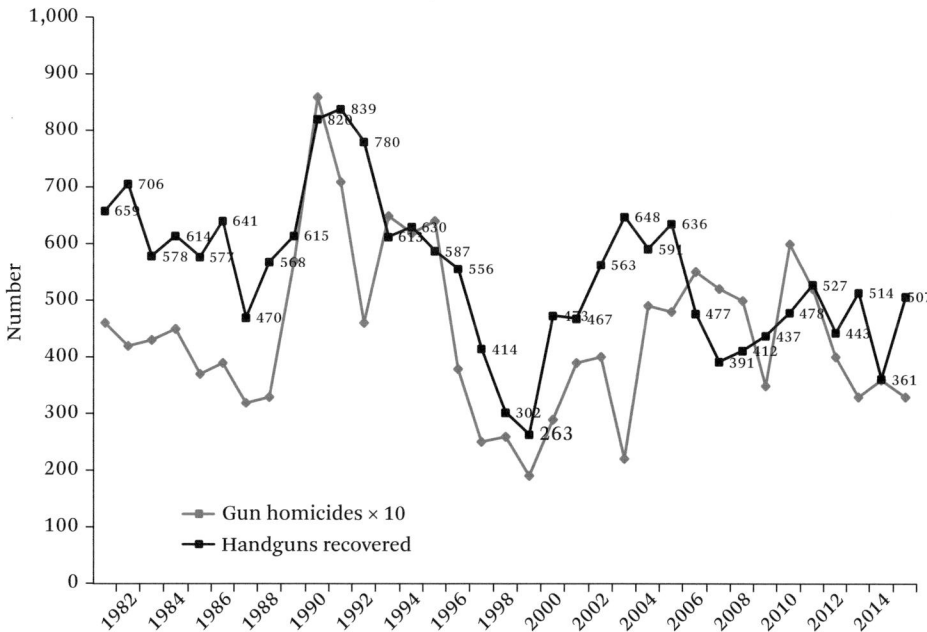

Source: Author's calculations.

tween 1981 and 1996, almost 73 percent were handguns. Between 1997 and 2015, slightly more than 84 percent were.

Figure 2 presents the yearly numbers of handgun recoveries and of gun homicides in Boston between 1981 and 2015. Because the numbers of handgun recoveries were much greater, those of gun homicides were multi-

Table 1. Types and Calibers of Recovered Handguns in Boston

		Percentages				
Period	N	Semi-automatic	.22, .25, .32	.38, .357	.380, 9mm	.40, .44, .45
1981–1985	3134	34.6	44.9	38.6	7.5	4.3
1986–1990	3114	41.6	44.2	33.2	14.0	5.1
1991–1995	3449	60.9	38.3	23.3	30.2	4.8
1996–2000	2008	74.2	38.9	23.9	27.5	6.8
2001–2005	2905	75.7	29.2	20.9	29.7	12.9
2006–2010	2195	65.7	26.4	20.6	33.4	18.0
2011–2015	2,352	66.6	26.7	20.7	31.7	19.9

Source: Author's calculations.

plied by ten so that both trends could be represented on the same graph. Although yearly trends diverge in particular years, such as 1992 and 2003, gun homicides and handgun recoveries both show sudden increases between the late 1980s and early 1990s, steep declines between the middle and late 1990s, and more modest increases in the early to middle 2000s. The two trends have a Pearson's cross-temporal correlation coefficient $r=0.574$ ($p<.01$), suggesting a strong positive association between yearly number of handgun recoveries and yearly number of gun homicides.

Changes over time in the types and calibers of recovered handguns are summarized in table 1. Between 1981 and 1985, higher-capacity semiautomatic pistols represented "only" 34.6 percent of all handguns recovered. During this period, the vast majority of recovered handguns were revolvers (63.5 percent) and only a small share were derringers (1.6 percent). The proportion of semiautomatic pistols among recovered handguns increased dramatically over the course of the late 1980s, 1990s, and 2000s, reaching a peak of 75.7 percent between 2001 and 2005. The share of semiautomatic pistols then decreased moderately to roughly 65 percent between 2006 and 2015.

Consistent with the shift toward greater shares of semiautomatic pistols, the calibers of recovered handguns also changed over time. Between 1981 and 1985, medium-powered .380 and 9mm handguns represented only 7.5 percent of all handguns recovered. The share quadrupled to 30.2 percent between 1991 and 1995 and remained steadily more than 25 percent through 2015. In contrast, the share of .38 and .357 handguns declined from 38.6 percent between 1981 and 1985 to 20.7 percent between 2011 and 2015. Recoveries also shifted from lower-powered to high-powered handguns over the study period. Between 1981 and 1985, lower-powered .22, .25, and .32 handguns accounted for almost 45 percent of all recoveries; higher-powered .40, .44, and .45 handguns represented only 4.3 percent. By 2011 through 2015, .22, .25, and .32 handguns represented only 26.7 percent of recoveries; nearly 20 percent were .40, .44, and .45 handguns.

TRENDS IN KEY TRAFFICKING INDICATORS FOR TRACED HANDGUNS, 1991–2015

Obliterated Serial Numbers

The recovery of a firearm with an obliterated serial number is viewed as a strong indicator that a trafficker was involved in the illegal diversion of the firearm from legal commerce (ATF 2000, 2002; Cook and Braga 2001; Kennedy, Piehl, and Braga 1996a). Because defacing the serial number on a firearm is itself a crime (see 18 U.S.C. § 922(k)), obliterated numbers establish that a criminal possessed the gun at some time and is strong evidence that some past possessor wanted to obstruct tracing and prevent the firearm from being linked to a past transfer. Gun traffickers are likely to want to impede tracing so that they cannot be linked with their criminal associates, such as straw purchasers or a corrupt licensed dealer. Obliterated serial numbers were found on a modest

Figure 3. Handguns and Obliterated Serial Number Handguns

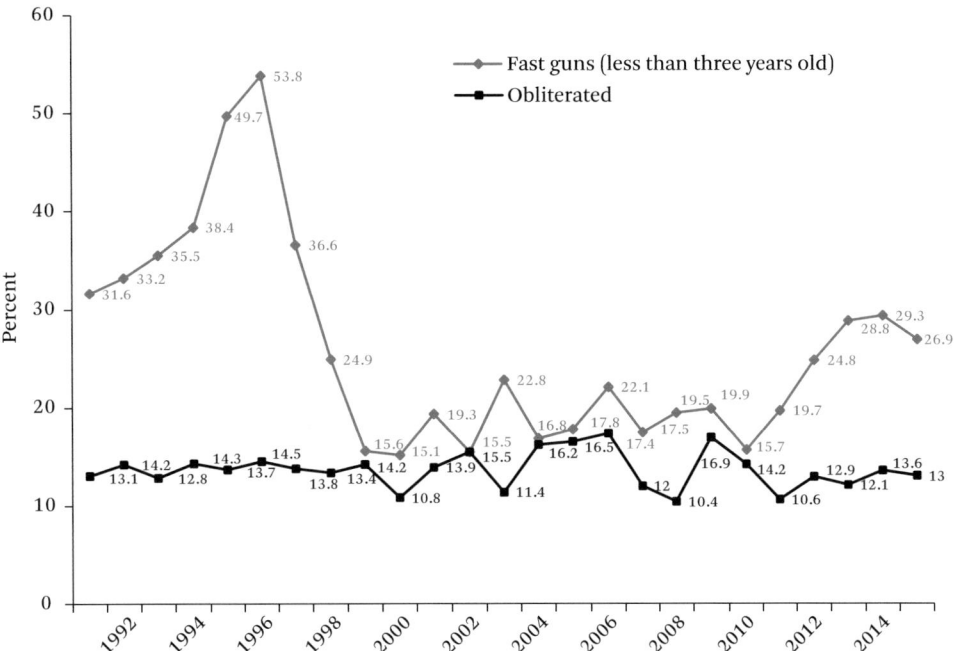

Source: Author's calculations.

share of handguns recovered by the BPD over time. Between 1991 and 2015, the trend in the yearly share of handguns recovered with obliterated serial numbers was stable, between roughly 10 percent and 17 percent per year (see figure 3). For the entire 1991 to 2015 period, 13.7 percent (1,763 of 12,909) had obliterated serial numbers.

BPD Crime Lab specialists, however, can sometimes restore obliterated serial numbers, and traces of guns can then proceed. Between 1995 and 2003, the BPD and ATF Boston Field Division made a concerted effort to restore and trace 910 firearms recovered with obliterated serial numbers as part of a special initiative to focus their enforcement efforts on the guns that seemed most likely to be trafficked (Braga and Pierce 2005). During this period, roughly 45 percent had their serial numbers successfully restored and subsequently traced to a first retail purchaser. These guns were a blend of new and secondhand firearms predominately purchased from out-of-state licensed dealers. Because as many as one in six recovered handguns have obliterated serial numbers in any given year, restoring defaced numbers seems to be high-value activity to generate investigative leads on gun traffickers diverting firearms from both primary and secondary market sources.

Age of Traced Handguns

As described, a traced firearm with a short time-to-crime is generally regarded as an indicator that the weapon may have been recently diverted from an FFL. Figure 3 presents the annual percentage of traced Boston handguns with a time-to-crime of three years or less between first retail sale and BPD recovery. Between 1991 and 1996, the share increased from 31.6 percent to 53.8 percent. The Operation Ceasefire gun trafficking strategy was associated with a large post-1997 reduction in the percentage of handguns recovered with fast time-to-crime (Braga and Pierce 2005). As figure 3 suggests, the annual percentage of fast time-to-crime handguns dropped sharply in 1997 and 1998. Between 1999 and 2011, the trend was relatively stable and only 18.4 percent of all traced handguns (638 of 3,475) had a fast time-to-crime. The rate remained above 25 percent between 2012 and 2015.

The Anthony Braga and Glenn Pierce evaluation used multivariate regression analyses to estimate the effects of the Operation Ceasefire intervention on new handguns recovered in crime between January 1991 and December 2003 (2005). To distinguish intervention effects from measurable rival causal factors, the final model controlled for existing linear and nonlinear trends, seasonal variation, Boston violent crime trends, handgun recovery numbers, trace result variations, and the February 1994 implementation of the Brady Handgun Violence Prevention Act. The analysis was supplemented by a postintervention-only comparison of Boston trends in new handgun recoveries to new handgun recovery trends in fourteen Youth Crime Gun Interdiction Initiative (YCGII) cities. YCGII cities participated in an ATF program that required local police departments to trace all recovered crime guns. The trends in the comparison group suggested that the Boston trend was unique.

In their review of the Boston evaluation, Gary Kleck and Sung-Yung Wang speculate that the reported decline in the share of new recovered crime handguns was not due to the effects of the intervention but instead driven by a decline in Boston's burglary rate during the same period (2009). To support this assertion, the authors report a strong positive correlation between the percentage of crime guns with a time-to-crime of three years or less and Boston's burglary rate as reported in the Uniform Crime Reports between 1996 and 2003 ($r=0.89$). The Braga and Pierce analysis did not control for trends in Boston's burglary rate (2005).

To investigate whether burglary explained the decrease in new handguns recovered by the BPD over time, a covariate was added to the original Braga and Pierce model to account for Boston's monthly burglary rate for the full evaluation time period of January 1991 through December 2003. Following the Braga and Pierce model development strategy, the effects of Operation Ceasefire on the recovery of new handguns in Boston was estimated using ordinary least squares linear regression models. The impact on the percentage of recovered handguns that were new in Boston was measured at a one-year lag (dummy variable capturing the effect post–June 1, 1997). The dependent variable is, once again, the monthly percentage of traced recovered handguns that were recovered within three or fewer years of the first retail sale.

Table 2 presents the original results and those of the revised model that included the Boston burglary rate. A quick comparison of the regression coefficients between the two models reveals no substantive changes when the Boston burglary rate covariate is included. Controlling for other covariates, the burglary rate is not significantly associated with the percentage of new recovered handguns, which suggests that the causal relationship between burglary and new recovered handguns is spurious when other factors are considered. Table 2 also reveals that the lagged effects of the intervention on the percentage of recovered handguns that were new remained robust to the addition of the burglary rate covariate to the model. Holding the other predictor variables constant, the intervention was associated with a statistically significant 22.3 percent reduction in the mean monthly percentage of all recovered handguns that were new. This revised analysis suggests that the Operation Ceasefire strategy did affect the prevalence of new handguns recovered in Boston crime.

Source States of Traced Handguns

Figure 4 presents yearly trends in share of traced recovered handguns from selected source states between 1991 and 2015. Consistent with prior research, FFLs in Massachusetts consistently generated the largest share of Boston's recovered handguns relative to those from other states (see Kennedy, Piehl, and Braga 1996a; Braga and Hureau 2015). Between 1991 and 2007, the yearly proportion of traced handguns first purchased at Massachusetts FFLs generally varied between about 30 percent and almost 42 percent. In 2008, the share originating from Massachusetts FFLs dropped to 20.4 percent, followed by a steady increase over the next several years. In 2013, 46 percent of the traced handguns were first purchased at the Massachusetts FFLs. This one-year spike was mostly driven by a small number of seizures of multiple firearms from individuals who were once legal purchasers but became illegal pos-

Table 2. OLS Regressions, Effects of Operation Ceasefire

	Percentage of New Handguns					
	New Handguns			Controlling for Boston Burglary Rate		
Variable	B	(SE)	t	B	(SE)	t
Ceasefire (one-year lag)	−.227	(.040)	−5.65***	−.223	(.045)	−4.954***
Burglary rate	—		—	.00003	(.000)	.218
Trend	.001	(.002)	.285	.001	(.003)	.355
Trend²	−.000006	(.000)	−.281	−.000008	(.000)	−.627
N violent gun crimes	.000	(.000)	1.00	.000	(.001)	.859
N handguns received	−.002	(.001)	−2.29*	−.002	(.001)	−2.29*
Percent handguns with no age	.182	(.094)	1.93	.184	(.095)	1.93
Brady Law enacted	.106	(.048)	2.27*	.108	(.049)	2.23*
Intercept	.253	(.135)	1.88	.254	(.133)	1.91
N		156			156	
R²		.599			.599	
F-test		11.346***			10.676***	
Durbin-Watson test		1.74			1.77	

Source: Author's compilation based on Braga and Pierce 2005.
Note: Month dummy variables included in both regression models but not shown here.
*p < .05; **p < .01; ***p < .001

Figure 4. Source States of Traced Handguns in Boston

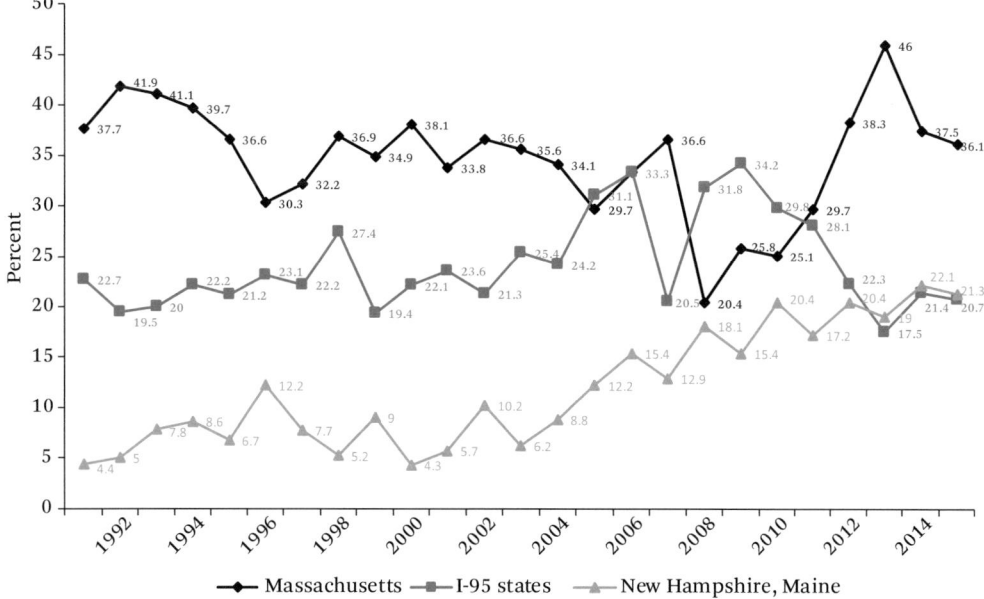

Source: Author's calculations.

sessors after a felony conviction or domestic assault incident.

A recent study examined whether Massachusetts state-level private gun transfer data could be used to understand how in-state secondary market transactions may influence the supply of handguns to Boston criminals (Braga and Hureau 2015). Using trace data on Boston recoveries between 2007 and 2013, traced Boston crime handguns first sold at Massachusetts license dealers were matched to state secondhand gun transfer data. Many crime handguns with records of secondary market transactions in Massachusetts moved rapidly from private transfer to police recovery, suggesting an in-state problem with illegal transfers to high-risk and prohibited persons. Unfortunately, important transaction data on the in-state sources of nearly 63 percent of recovered handguns were not readily available to law enforcement agencies. Braga and David Hureau conclude that a highly problematic gap between having strong gun laws in place and actually enforcing their provisions exists in Massachusetts (2015). This lack of enforcement seems to contribute to the relatively large number of crime guns directly or indirectly originating from Massachusetts FFLs over time.[3]

Traced handguns recovered in Boston tended to be imported from FFLs in two distinct geographic regions of states with less restrictive gun control laws: either nearby New Hampshire and Maine, or the Iron Pipeline states of Virginia, North Carolina, South Carolina, Georgia, and Florida. Between 1991 and 2004, about 23 percent of traced handguns were imported from FFLs in those five southern states and only 7.5 percent from the two northern ones. Between 2005 and 2015, the share of traced handguns imported from FFLs in the southern states increased slightly to 26.3 percent. However, during this same period, the share of traced handguns imported from FFLs in New Hampshire and Maine more than doubled, to 17.7 percent. ATF and BPD investigators suggest that drug trafficking supply lines from Boston into southern New Hampshire and Maine have intensified as high property values in the Boston area have caused a population shift to less expensive, out-of-state properties within commuting distance of the city; Boston gang members and other criminals increasingly export illegal drugs into New Hampshire and Maine, and import illegal guns from these loose gun control states (see, for example, Bever 2014).

To some observers, a crime gun with an out-of-state origin is not necessarily an indicator that a gun runner illegally moved the gun across state lines. Other explanations for this movement are possible, such as an owner legally moving to another state and having the firearm stolen from their new residence (Kleck and Wang 2009). Massachusetts state law requires all gun owners, including those who move into the state with their firearms, to report firearm losses and thefts to local and state police department. When recovered Boston crime guns are submitted to the BPD Ballistics Unit for processing, firearm examiners run the manufacturers and serial numbers through the National Crime Information Center (NCIC) stolen gun database and record whether the recovered crime gun was reported stolen.

To further examine out-of-state origin as an indicator of illegal gun diversions, NCIC data collected by the BPD Ballistics Unit on N=1,479 handguns recovered by the BPD between 2007 and 2014 and subsequently traced to FFLs located outside Massachusetts were analyzed. Despite a state law requiring such reporting, not a single recovered handgun traced to FFLs outside Massachusetts was reported to NCIC as stolen. It is possible that law-abiding gun owners might be reluctant to report stolen guns to authorities or lacked enough information on stolen guns to file an accurate report. These problems, however, would affect recently transplanted residents and long-term residents alike. For comparative purposes, stolen gun re-

---

3. In comparison, only 12 percent of traceable firearms recovered by the New York City Police Department (NYPD) between 2010 and 2015 were first purchased at an FFL in New York State (trace data provided as part of an ongoing research partnership with NYPD to examine the sources of New York City crime guns). New York State has strong gun laws that are similar to Massachusetts gun laws. See the 2013 Brady Campaign scorecard (http://www.bradycampaign.org/2013-state-scorecard, accessed July 3, 2017).

cords were analyzed for 2007 to 2014 handguns traced to a Massachusetts FFL and not found to be recovered in the hands of the first retail purchaser. BPD Ballistic Unit records indicated that 10.8 percent (62 of 572) had been reported stolen to NCIC before recovery by BPD officers. If theft of guns from recently transplanted residents was a persistent problem, a similar stolen gun reporting rate would be expected. The "guns stolen from new residents" explanation for the interstate movement of crime guns therefore does not seem to apply to traced Boston crime guns imported from other states. Philip Cook and his colleagues come to a similar conclusion in their analysis of the sources of Chicago crime guns (2015).

USING LONGITUDINAL TRACE DATA IN POLICY EVALUATION

Effects of Limiting Handgun Purchases on Interstate Gun Trafficking

During the early 1990s, the Commonwealth of Virginia earned a reputation as a key source state for firearms illegally trafficked to cities in the northeastern United States (Larson 1994). In July 1993, Virginia enacted a law limiting individual handgun purchases to one per thirty-day period. The intention of the law was to limit the ability of illegal gun traffickers to make multiple purchases of handguns in a single transaction, thereby undermining the economic incentive generated by diverting multiple handguns from Virginia FFLs. Douglas Weil and Rebecca Knox used ATF trace data to examine the locations of crime gun purchases before (September 1989 through June 1993) and after (July 1993 through March 1995) the enactment of Virginia's one-handgun-per-month law (1996). Their analyses reveal noteworthy reductions, after passage of the bill, in the share of guns traced to Virginia FFLs for firearms traced from anywhere in the United States and for firearms traced from northeast corridor states.

The findings of the Weil and Knox evaluation are limited by the uncertain quality of the available ATF firearms trace information (1996). As the authors openly report, that used in their study was not collected in a comprehensive manner. It represented only the recovered crime guns that law enforcement agencies in study locations decided to submit to ATF for tracing. The trends and patterns documented by their analyses were therefore biased to an unknown degree. As described earlier, the BPD has been comprehensively tracing all recovered firearms since January 1, 1991. These comprehensive data allow a clearer assessment of the impact of the July 1993 law limiting handgun purchases to one per month on the movement of handguns from retail purchases at Virginia FFLs to recovery by the BPD.

In this partial replication of the Weil and Knox analysis, the sources of traced handguns recovered in Boston were compared for eighteen-month periods before (January 1991 through June 1993) and after (July 1993 through December 1995) implementation of the law. Between January 1991 and December 1995, 55.1 percent of handguns (1,893 of 3,438) recovered by the BPD were successfully traced by ATF to the first retail purchaser. Purchase dates were examined to determine whether Boston-recovered handguns were purchased at Virginia and other FFLs in I-95 southern states before or after the law was implemented. Virginia's one-handgun-per-month law was repealed in March 2012. To determine whether the repeal of the law affected interstate transfers of Boston crime guns, the sources of traced handguns recovered in Boston were compared for twenty-six months before (January 2010 through February 2012) and forty-six months after (March 2012 through December 2015). Between January 2010 and December 2015, 62.3 percent of handguns (1,764 of 2,830) recovered by the BPD were successfully traced by ATF to the first retail purchaser.

Table 3 presents the estimated odds ratios that a Boston-recovered handgun was purchased from a Virginia FFL relative to an FFL in another I-95 southern state for the implementation and repeal of Virginia's one-handgun-a-month law. Before the law was implemented, 20.1 percent of recovered handguns originating from an I-95 southern state were first purchased at a Virginia FFL; after the implementation, only 7.8 percent were. The likelihood that a Boston handgun would be traced to a Virginia FFL relative to licensed dealers elsewhere in I-95 southern states decreased by

Table 3. Estimated Odds Ratios, Recovered Handgun Purchases

Traced to I-95	Before Law		After Law		Odds Ratio (95% CI)
	N	Percentage	N	Percentage	
After July 1993 law implementation comparison, January 1, 1991–December 31, 1995					
Southern state FFL	403	100.0	128	100.0	0.337
Virginia FFL	81	20.1	10	7.8	(0.169–0.671)
Other FFL	322	79.9	118	92.2	$Chi^2 = 10.33$
					$p = .0013$
After March 2012 law repeal comparison, January 1, 2010–December 31, 2015					
Southern state FFL	251	100.0	65	100.0	1.878
Virginia FFL	27	10.8	12	18.5	(0.893–3.943)
Other FFL	224	89.2	53	81.5	$Chi^2 = 2.83$
					$p = .0925$

Source: Author's calculations.

66.3 percent after the one-gun-a-month law took effect (OR=0.337, $p<.01$). Fifteen years later, before the law was repealed, 10.8 percent of recovered handguns originating from an I-95 southern state were first purchased at a Virginia FFL; after repeal, the figure was 18.5 percent. Although not statistically significant at the $p<.05$ level, the likelihood that a Boston handgun would be traced to a Virginia FFL relative to licenses dealers elsewhere in I-95 southern states increased by 87.8 percent after the law was repealed (OR=1.878, $p<.10$). These results are congruent with the findings of Weil and Knox's 1996 study and suggest that restricting handgun purchases to one per month may change where criminals get their guns.

Influence of Buy-Back Programs on Characteristics of Recovered Guns

Gun buy-backs involve a government or private group paying individuals to turn in guns they possess. Participants turning in guns are paid via cash disbursements, gift cards, or other compensation. To encourage participation by criminals, these programs do not require participants to identify themselves and do not maintain any records of the individuals who turned firearms in. The recovered guns are then destroyed. Despite empirical evidence that suggests gun buy-backs do not reduce violence, municipalities continue to implement these programs (Wellford, Pepper, and Petrie 2005; but see Leigh and Neill 2010). At least three problems are associated with the violence reduction theory underlying gun buy-backs: the guns turned in are the least likely to be used in criminal activities; because replacement guns are easy to acquire, the decline of guns on the street may be smaller than the number of guns that are turned in; and the likelihood that any particular turned-in gun will be used in crime is very low (Wellford, Pepper, and Petrie 2005).

Gun buy-back program implementers have responded to the empirical evidence by developing strategies to increase the likelihood that high-risk guns are turned in by high-risk individuals (Braga and Wintemute 2013). These strategies have included targeted advertising to young people in urban neighborhoods affected by high levels of gun violence and graded incentives to encourage the recovery of handguns and assault weapons. In response to community concerns over periodic outbreaks of serious gun violence, the City of Boston implemented gun buy-back programs three times: in 1993–1994, 2006, and 2014–2015. The characteristics of guns recovered during each period are presented in table 4.

In 1993 and 1994, a nonprofit crime preven-

Table 4. Characteristics of Firearms Recovered from Buybacks

	1993–1994	2006	2014–2015
N firearms	1,556	1,019	430
Percent handgun	56.1	85.7	89.1
Percent semiautomatic pistol	17.1	34.7	40.5
Percent .380, 9mm, .40, .45	1.9	26.1	11.4
Percent obliterated	4.3	4.1	3.9
Percent traced to first retail purchaser	11.1	33.9	44.2
Percent three years or less from first retail sale	4.1	9.2	5.3
Percent first sold at retail in I-95 states	15.7	18.8	13.7

Source: Author's calculations.

tion agency conducted buy-backs with the BPD and the Suffolk County district attorney, offering $50 per gun and recovering 2,158 guns (see Kennedy, Piehl, and Braga 1996b). BPD and ATF attempted to trace the chain of ownership from manufacturer to first retail purchaser of 1,566 (72.6 percent) of these: all 1,288 from 1993 but only the first 278 (31.9 percent) of 870 from 1994. BPD and ATF stopped comprehensive tracing efforts after finding that many were not traceable. Only 11 percent (173) were successfully traced to the first retail purchaser. BPD noted that licensed gun dealers from the suburbs used the event to clear their inventories of secondhand firearms that were worth less than the $50 incentive.

In 2006, then Boston mayor Thomas M. Menino, BPD, and numerous faith-based and community organizations launched the Aim for Peace gun buy-back program (see Braga and Wintemute 2013). It included four new programmatic elements designed to increase the number of handguns brought in from neighborhoods suffering from high levels of violence:

> Target gift cards for $200 were given for each handgun. Rifles and shotguns were accepted, but no incentives were provided.
>
> Individuals who turned in firearms had to prove that they were Boston residents before receiving a gift card. The names of participants were not associated with any recovered guns or recorded in any way.
>
> As in 1993–1994, BPD district stations served as gun drop-off locations. However, recognizing that some residents may not be comfortable walking into a police station with a gun, BPD also set up drop-off operations at eight community locations, such as churches and nonprofit organization offices, in neighborhoods with high rates of gun violence.
>
> A sophisticated communications campaign sought to engage Boston's youth via a podcast, more than thirty billboards in strategic locations frequented by city youth, and saturation advertising on city buses, subway cars, train stations, and bus stops.

The program operated from June 12 through July 14 and recovered 1,019 firearms; BPD attempted to trace all of them.

Beginning in March 2014 and continuing throughout 2015, mayor Martin J. Walsh and the BPD implemented the Your Piece for Peace program, which included some of the design features of the 2006 buy-back. Once again, the BPD provided a $200 Visa gift card for each turned-in handgun and, though long guns were accepted, no incentives were provided. Individuals were also required to prove they were Boston residents before they received a gift card. Although the launch of the program was publicized in the local media, it did not have the strategic advertising initiatives of its 2006 predecessor. The 2014–2015 buy-back did not have community-based drop-off locations and walk-in gun exchanges were limited to BPD district stations. Community members could, however, call the BPD and make arrangements for an officer to pick up firearms from their residences. Although the program operated for an extended twenty-two months (and continued through 2016), the program yielded only 430 firearms. The BPD submitted all the buy-back guns to ATF for tracing.

Relative to the 1993–1994 program, the 2006 buy-back yielded more handguns, especially higher-powered semiautomatic pistols (table 4).[4] The 1993–1994 buy-back recovered more older long guns than newer handguns associated with the youth gun violence epidemic of the period (Kennedy, Piehl, and Braga 1996b). Although similar numbers of guns from the 1993–1994 and 2006 buy-backs had obliterated serial numbers, a much higher number from the 2006 program were successfully traced by ATF (Braga and Wintemute 2013). Relative to 1993–1994, the 2006 firearms were more likely to have been purchased within three years of their first retail sale and more likely to have originated from dealers along the Iron Pipeline. The 2014–2015 buy-back yielded fewer guns but did secure more handguns and semiautomatic pistols than its predecessors. ATF was also able to successfully trace 44.2 percent of the 2014–2015 guns, notably more than the earlier programs.

The features of the 2014–2015 program may have unintentionally diminished the overall number of recovered handguns and reduced the share of higher-powered semiautomatic pistols taken off Boston streets relative to the 2006 program. Traceable firearms were also less likely to have included newer guns that were first sold at retail outlets in the I-95 southern states. As described elsewhere in this article, increasing the number of recovered guns with these indicators provides law enforcement agencies with additional opportunities to identify and apprehend gun traffickers. Unfortunately, the 2014–2015 buy-back recovered fewer high-risk handguns than its immediate predecessor. Gun criminals in disadvantaged neighborhoods may have not been aware of the opportunity to turn in their guns given the lack of strategic advertising in the later program. Among those who were aware, some may have been dissuaded by the prospects of walking into a police station with a gun or calling the police to schedule a gun pick-up.

These analyses suggest that program design may matter when attempting to encourage high-risk individuals to turn in their guns. However, the first two programs did not reduce levels of gun violence in Boston after implementation (Kennedy, Piehl, and Braga 1996b; Braga and Wintemute 2013). Over the course of the 2014–2015 program, the number of fatal and nonfatal shooting victims increased by 14 percent from 214 in 2014 to 244 in 2015. These findings suggest that, even with program design modification that improved the kinds of guns turned in, buy-back programs are not an effective market intervention to reduce gun violence.

CONCLUSION

The longitudinal analyses of Boston firearm recovery and trace data shed some policy-relevant insight on evolving illegal gun market dynamics serving criminals in one jurisdiction. First, they suggest that handguns recovered by the BPD became increasingly deadly over time. Beginning in the 1990s, higher-capacity semiautomatic pistols capable of shooting larger numbers of bullets replaced revolvers as the most frequently recovered type of handgun in Boston. Equally concerning, the share of smaller caliber handguns among BPD recoveries diminished over the 2000s as the prominence of larger caliber handguns increased. This transition from revolvers to semiautomatic pistols recovered by law enforcement agencies mirrors national trends in handgun production in the United States between the 1980s and 1990s (Wintemute 2006). Given the increased killing power of handguns in the civilian firearms stock, it is imperative to block

---

4. As Braga and Wintemute note, the available data suggest that improvements in the guns recovered were driven by changes in buy-back design features rather than secular changes in the underlying distribution of crime guns during the intervening years (2013). In 1993 and 1994, the BPD submitted 1,637 recovered crime guns to ATF for tracing: 75.8 percent were handguns and 48.4 percent were traceable. In 2006, the BPD submitted 554 recovered crime guns to ATF for tracing: 89.5 percent were handguns and 53.9 percent were traceable. The 2006 guns more closely resembled the stock of crime guns.

access by criminals, juveniles, and other high-risk individuals.

Like many other U.S. cities, the bulk of Boston's serious gun violence problem is generated by a relatively small number of criminally active gang members (Braga 2003; Braga, Hureau, and Winship 2008; see also, for example, Papachristos and Wildeman 2014; Papachristos et al. 2015). Boston gun criminals seem to be supplied by illegal diversions of handguns from both out-of-state and in-state FFLs. The age of recovered handguns, as measured as the time between the first retail sale and confiscation by the BPD, has also increased, suggesting a problem with the illegal diversion of older firearms from secondary market sources.

Massachusetts gun laws should provide state and local law enforcement agencies with the necessary tools to regulate secondary transfers of firearms within the state. Unfortunately, as Braga and Hureau suggest, little enforcement and regulatory attention seems to be paid to the problem of suspicious transfer patterns in Massachusetts (2015). Long-term trends document a noteworthy share of traced handguns originating from FFLs in I-95 southern states and an increasing share from those in nearby New Hampshire and Maine. The lack of paperwork on secondary market transfers in these lax gun control states, however, makes launching investigations into interstate gun trafficking operations of older firearms very difficult.

Strategic enforcement programs focused on the illegal diversion of new firearms from primary markets may reduce the availability of new guns to criminals (Webster et al. 2006; Webster, Vernick, and Bulzacchelli 2006). The analyses presented here strengthened the case that the anti–gun trafficking component of Boston's Operation Ceasefire strategy did indeed reduce the prevalence of new handguns recovered by the BPD. What is more, this study suggests that the presence of state one-gun-per-month laws do influence where criminals acquire guns. Unfortunately, whether these market-based interventions reduced the overall availability of guns to criminals and whether supply-side interventions have a measureable impact on gun violence remain unclear. Modifying the programmatic features of buy-back programs in Boston seemed to increase the share of recovered semiautomatic pistols that could be traced to their retail origins. However, the implementation of gun buy-back programs in Boston was not associated with any gun violence reductions.

Rational debate on gun policy requires detailed information on crime guns. ATF currently produces modest summaries of the characteristics of crime gun traces for the fifty states, the District of Columbia, U.S. territories, Canada, Mexico, and the Caribbean (www.atf.gov/statistics/index.html). Unlike the national and city-level trace reports generated by the now-defunct Youth Crime Gun Interdiction Initiative (ATF 2002), ATF's current state-level crime gun summaries do not involve external academics and do not provide more rigorous and detailed analyses of crime gun sources, trends, and patterns. ATF should return to publishing these more detailed annual crime gun trace reports overseen by external academics. The Boston illegal gun market research summarized and extended here highlights the policy-relevant findings that can be generated through ongoing academic analyses of ATF trace data and local police data.

REFERENCES

Azrael, Deborah, Philip J. Cook, and Matthew Miller. 2004. "State and Local Prevalence of Firearms Ownership: Measurement, Structure, and Trends." *Journal of Quantitative Criminology* 20(1): 43–62.

Bea, Keith, and Michael J. Burton. 1992. "'Assault Weapons': Military-Style Semi-Automatic Firearms Facts and Issues." *CRS Report no. 92-434*. Washington, D.C.: Government Printing Office.

Bever, Fred. 2014. "When Mass. Criminals Want a Gun, They Often Head North," WBUR News, February 24. Accessed July 3, 2017. http://www.wbur.org/2014/02/24/gun-trafficking-into-massachusetts.

Braga, Anthony A. 2003. "Serious Youth Gun Offenders and the Epidemic of Youth Violence in Boston." *Journal of Quantitative Criminology* 19(1): 33–54.

Braga, Anthony A., Robert Apel, and Brandon C. Welsh. 2013. "The Spillover Effects of Focused Deterrence on Gang Violence." *Evaluation Review* 37(3–4): 314–42.

Braga, Anthony A., and Philip J. Cook. 2016. "The Criminal Records of Gun Offenders." *Georgetown Journal of Law and Public Policy* 15(1): 1–16.

Braga, Anthony A., Philip J. Cook, David M. Kennedy, and Mark H. Moore. 2002. "The Illegal Supply of Firearms." In *Crime and Justice: A Review of Research*, vol. 29, edited by Michael Tonry. Chicago: University of Chicago Press.

Braga, Anthony A., and David M. Hureau. 2015. "Strong Gun Laws Are Not Enough: The Need for Improved Enforcement of Secondhand Gun Transfer Laws in Massachusetts." *Preventive Medicine* 79 (October): 37–42.

Braga, Anthony A., David M. Hureau, and Andrew V. Papachristos. 2014. "Deterring Gang-Involved Gun Violence: Measuring the Impact of Boston's Operation Ceasefire on Street Gang Behavior." *Journal of Quantitative Criminology* 30(1): 113–39.

Braga, Anthony A., David M. Hureau, and Christopher Winship. 2008. "Losing Faith? Police, Black Churches, and the Resurgence of Youth Violence in Boston." *Ohio State Journal of Criminal Law* 6(1): 141–72.

Braga, Anthony A., David Kennedy, E. Waring, and Anne M. Piehl. 2001. "Problem-Oriented Policing, Deterrence, and Youth Violence: An Evaluation of Boston's Operation Ceasefire." *Journal of Research in Crime and Delinquency* 38(3): 195–225.

Braga, Anthony A., Andrew V. Papachristos, and David M. Hureau. 2010. "The Concentration and Stability of Gun Violence at Micro Places in Boston, 1980–2008." *Journal of Quantitative Criminology* 26(1): 33–53.

Braga, Anthony A., and Glenn L. Pierce. 2005. "Disrupting Illegal Firearms Markets in Boston: The Effects of Operation Ceasefire on the Supply of New Handguns to Criminals." *Criminology and Public Policy* 4(4): 717–48.

Braga, Anthony A., and David L. Weisburd. 2012. "The Effects of Focused Deterrence Strategies on Crime: A Systematic Review and Meta-Analysis of the Empirical Evidence." *Journal of Research in Crime and Delinquency* 49(3): 323–58.

Braga, Anthony A., and Garen J. Wintemute. 2013. "Improving the Potential Effectiveness of Gun Buyback Programs." *American Journal of Preventive Medicine* 45(5): 668–71.

Braga, Anthony A., Garen J. Wintemute, Glenn L. Pierce, Philip J. Cook, and Greg Ridgeway. 2012. "Interpreting the Empirical Evidence on Illegal Gun Market Dynamics." *Journal of Urban Health* 89(5): 779–93.

Bureau of Alcohol, Tobacco and Firearms (ATF). 2000. *Following the Gun: Enforcing Federal Laws Against Firearms Traffickers*. Washington, D.C.: Bureau of Alcohol, Tobacco and Firearms.

———. 2002. *Crime Gun Trace Analysis (2000): National Report*. Washington, D.C.: Bureau of Alcohol, Tobacco and Firearms.

Cook, Philip J., and Anthony A. Braga. 2001. "Comprehensive Firearms Tracing: Strategic and Investigative Uses of New Data on Firearms Markets." *Arizona Law Review* 43: 277–309.

Cook, Philip J., Anthony A. Braga, and Mark H. Moore. 2011. "Gun Control." In *Crime and Public Policy*, rev. ed., edited by James Q. Wilson and Joan Petersilia. New York: Oxford University Press.

Cook, Philip J., Richard J. Harris, Jens Ludwig, and Harold A. Pollock. 2015. "Some Sources of Crime Guns in Chicago: Dirty Dealers, Straw Purchasers, and Traffickers." *Journal of Criminal Law and Criminology* 104(4): 717–59.

Cook, Philip J., Jens Ludwig, Sudhir Venkatesh, and Anthony A. Braga. 2007. "Underground Gun Markets." *Economic Journal* 117(524): 558–88.

Cook, Philip J., Susan T. Parker, and Harold A. Pollack. 2015. "Sources of Guns to Dangerous People: What We Learn by Asking Them." *Preventive Medicine* 79(1): 28–36.

Kennedy, David M. 1994. "Can We Keep Guns Away from Kids?" *American Prospect* 18(1): 74–80.

Kennedy, David M., Anthony A. Braga, and Anne M. Piehl. 1997. "The (Un)Known Universe: Mapping Gangs and Gang Violence in Boston." In *Crime Mapping and Crime Prevention*, Crime Prevention Studies, vol. 8, edited by David Weisburd and J. McEwen. Monsey, N.Y.: Criminal Justice Press.

Kennedy, David M., Anne M. Piehl, and Andrew A. Braga. 1996a. "Youth Violence in Boston: Gun Markets, Serious Youth Offenders, and a Use-Reduction Strategy." *Law and Contemporary Problems* 59(1): 147–96.

———. 1996b. "Gun Buy-Backs: Where Do We Stand and Where Do We Go?" In *Under Fire: Gun Buy-Backs, Exchanges, and Amnesty Programs*, edited by Martha R. Plotkin. Washington, D.C.: Police Executive Research Forum.

Kleck, Gary, and Shun-Yung Kevin Wang. 2009. "The Myth of Big-Time Gun Trafficking and the

Overinterpretation of Gun Trace Data." *UCLA Law Review* 56: 1233–94.

Koper, Christopher S., and Jeffrey A. Roth. 2001. "The Impact of the 1994 Federal Assault Weapons Ban on Gun Markets: An Assessment of Multiple Outcome Measures and Some Lessons for Policy Evaluation." *Journal of Quantitative Criminology* 17(1): 239–66.

Larson, Erik. 1994. *Lethal Passage: The Story of a Gun*. New York: Crown Publishers.

Leigh, Andrew, and Christine Neill. 2010. "Do Gun Buybacks Save Lives? Evidence from Panel Data." *American Law and Economics Review* 12(2): 462–508.

Moore, Mark H. 1973. "Achieving Discrimination in the Effective Price of Heroin." *American Economic Review* 63(2): 193–206.

———. 1976. *Buy and Bust: The Effective Regulation of an Illicit Market in Heroin*. Lexington, Mass.: Heath.

Okoro, Catherine A., David E. Nelson, James A. Mercy, Lina S. Balluz, Alex E. Crosby, and Ali H. Mokdad. 2005. "Prevalence of Household Firearms and Firearms Storage Practices in 50 States and the District of Columbia." *Pediatrics* 116(3): e370–76.

Papachristos, Andrew V., Anthony A. Braga, and David M. Hureau. 2012. "Social Networks and the Risk of Gunshot Injury." *Journal of Urban Health* 89: 992–1003.

Papachristos, Andrew V., Anthony A. Braga, Eric Piza, and Leigh S. Grossman. 2015. "The Company You Keep? The Spillover Effects of Gang Membership on Individual Gunshot Victimization in a Co-Offending Network." *Criminology* 53(4): 624–49.

Papachristos, Andrew V., and Christopher Wildeman. 2014. "Network Exposure and Homicide Victimization in an African American Community." *American Journal of Public Health* 104(1): 143–50.

Pierce, Glenn L., Anthony A. Braga, Raymond R. Hyatt, and Christopher S. Koper. 2004. "The Characteristics and Dynamics of Illegal Firearms Markets: Implications for a Supply-Side Enforcement Strategy." *Justice Quarterly* 21(2): 391–422.

Reiss, Albert J., and Jeffrey A. Roth, eds. 1993. *Understanding and Preventing Violence*, vol. 1. Washington, D.C.: National Academies Press.

Smith, Tom W., and Jackson Son. 2015. "General Social Survey Final Report: Trends in Gun Ownership in the United States, 1972–2014." Chicago: National Opinion Research Center at University of Chicago.

Sorenson, Susan B., and Katherine A. Vittes. 2003. "Buying a Handgun for Someone Else: Firearm Retailer Willingness to Sell." *Injury Prevention* 9(2): 147–50.

Webster, Daniel W., Jon S. Vernick, and Maria T. Bulzacchelli. 2006. "Effects of a Gun Dealer's Change in Sales Practices on the Supply of Guns to Criminals." *Journal of Urban Health* 83(5): 778–87.

Webster, Daniel W., April M. Zeoli, Maria T. Bulzacchelli, and Jon S. Vernick. 2006. "Effects of Police Stings of Gun Dealers on the Supply of New Guns to Criminals." *Injury Prevention* 12(4): 225–30.

Weil, Douglas S., and Rebecca C. Knox. 1996. "Effects of Limiting Handgun Purchases on Interstate Transfer of Firearms." *Journal of the American Medical Association* 275(22): 1759–61.

Wellford, Charles F., John V. Pepper, and Carol V. Petrie, eds. 2005. *Firearms and Violence: A Critical Review*. Committee to Improve Research and Information on Firearms. Washington, D.C.: National Academies Press.

Wintemute, Garen J. 2010. "Guns and Gun Violence." In *The Crime Drop in America*, rev. ed., edited by Alfred Blumstein and Joel Wallman. New York: Cambridge University Press.

Wintemute, Garen J., Philip J. Cook, and Mona A. Wright. 2005. "Risk Factors Among Handgun Retailers for Frequent and Disproportionate Sales of Guns Used in Violent and Firearm Related Crimes." *Injury Prevention* 11(6): 357–63.

Zimring, Franklin E. 1975. "Firearms and Federal Law: The Gun Control Act of 1968." *Journal of Legal Studies* 4(1): 133–98.

———. 1976. "Street Crime and New Guns: Some Implications for Firearms Control." *Journal of Criminal Justice* 4(1): 95–107.

A Comparative Analysis of Crime Guns

MEGAN E. COLLINS, SUSAN T. PARKER, THOMAS L. SCOTT, AND CHARLES F. WELLFORD

Information is limited on how firearms move from legal possession to illegal possession and use in criminal activities, largely because of data collection capacity and a lack of recent, exhaustive recovery data across jurisdictions. This article includes both an analysis of firearms trace data and prisoner interviews across multiple jurisdictions: New Orleans, Louisiana, Prince George's County, Maryland, and Chicago, Illinois. Findings indicate that recoveries and trace successes vary across jurisdictions and by type of crime. Jurisdiction regulations were associated with the proportion of guns purchased in state and time to recovery but not with purchaser characteristics. Interviews from imprisoned offenders in two jurisdictions revealed the most common method of obtaining a crime gun was to steal it or buy it off the street.

Keywords: firearms and violent crime, transfer of firearms, criminal acquisition of firearms

Acknowledging that the Second Amendment to the U.S. Constitution guarantees the right of individuals to possess firearms, and that the overwhelming majority of those who own firearms use them in lawful ways, the public, policymakers, and law enforcement leaders nonetheless agree that criminals should not have access to guns, and certainly not for criminal purposes (see U.S. Supreme Court opinion in *District of Columbia v. Heller*, 554 U.S. 570 [2008]; for an analysis of this decision, see Gast 2005). Although violent crime has generally been declining since the mid-1990s,[1] firearms continue to produce a substantial threat to public safety,

---

Megan E. Collins is an associate with the Crime & Justice Institute at Community Resources for Justice. **Susan T. Parker** is senior data scientist at CivicScape. **Thomas L. Scott** is a PhD student in the Department of Criminology and Criminal Justice at the University of Maryland. **Charles F. Wellford** is professor emeritus in the Department of Criminology and Criminal Justice at the University of Maryland.

© 2017 Russell Sage Foundation. Collins, Megan E., Susan T. Parker, Thomas L. Scott, and Charles F. Wellford. 2017. "A Comparative Analysis of Crime Guns." *RSF: The Russell Sage Foundation Journal of the Social Sciences* 3(5): 96–127. DOI: 10.7758/RSF.2017.3.5.05. Authors are listed alphabetically to reflect their equal contributions to this article. The work of Collins, Scott, and Wellford was supported by a subcontract from the International Association of Chiefs of Police (IACP) as part of an award from the National Institute of Justice (The Epidemiology of Gun Crime). Susan Parker's work was supported by awards from the Joyce Foundation (Grant ID 13-34817) and the National Institute of Justice (2014-MU-CX-0013) to the University of Chicago's Crime Lab. Neither the Joyce Foundation, the IACP, nor the National Institute of Justice is responsible for the content of this article. Three anonymous reviewers provided very helpful comments, especially Reviewer A, whose observations resulted in very important modifications to the article. Direct correspondence to: Charles F. Wellford at wellford@umd.edu, 2220 LeFrak Hall, University of Maryland, College Park, MD 20742.

1. Acknowledging the 3.1 percent increase in the violent crime rate between 2014 and 2015, we refer here to the greater trend that saw the national violent crime rate decrease from approximately 636.6 per hundred thousand inhabitants in 1996, to 372.6 per hundred thousand in 2015 (FBI 2016).

and are utilized in a majority of homicides in the United States (for a detailed review of gun violence in the United States, see Cook and Pollack 2017). Overall, the lethality and seriousness of crime in the United States is greater than in any other industrialized democracy, largely because of the extent of gun possession and use by criminals (Cook and Pollack 2017; Wellford, Pepper, and Petrie 2005).

However, information on how guns are acquired for use in crimes is dated, incomplete, and inconclusive (Wellford, Pepper, and Petrie 2005); the collection of information regarding gun acquisition is made more difficult by limitations placed on the Bureau of Alcohol, Tobacco, Firearms and Explosives (ATF) by Congress and other federal agencies.[2] As a result, useful information on how guns move from legal possession to illegal possession and use in criminal activities is extremely limited. In part, it was this condition that prompted the National Institute of Justice (NIJ) to form a topical working group on firearms and violence. The working group concluded that

> New efforts be undertaken to use improved methodologies to study and better understand the ways in which all criminals who use guns in the commission of their crimes acquire those guns. The first step in this effort would be the development of methodologies that would provide better estimates of gun acquisition than those used in the 1990 studies. . . . this research area should include studies of the "life cycle" of crime guns (tracing guns from the gun crime to the manufacturer, identifying all intermediate owners and possessors and their means of acquisition). This research would assist in identifying possible new ways to disrupt acquisition of guns for use in crimes. (NIJ 2011, 2–3)

These conclusions mirror those of a 2005 National Academy of Sciences report, which stated that "arguments for and against a market-based approach (to restricting access to guns) are now largely based on speculation, not on evidence from research" (Wellford, Pepper, and Petrie 2005, 8). This lack of actionable information about the sources of crime guns has made it more difficult for law enforcement leaders to develop effective, empirically based responses to violence in their jurisdictions.[3]

This article documents our efforts to better understand how guns that are used in acts of violence move from first legal sale to use in a crime in three jurisdictions: New Orleans, Louisiana, Prince George's County, Maryland, and Chicago, Illinois. To be clear, many guns used in crimes are obtained legally and may be used by the original purchaser; this article seeks to better understand both licit and illicit methods of acquiring crime guns. We do so using two sources of data: the trace results of guns recovered by law enforcement, focusing on those used in violent crimes, and surveys and interviews with individuals arrested for and convicted of gun crimes. Although these sources have been used in prior studies, this article is unique in that it assesses these data across three qualitatively different jurisdictions, which differ in their crime profile, composition, location, and the degree to which gun sales are regulated.

LITERATURE REVIEW
Despite the relative prevalence of gun crime in the United States, knowledge about the life cy-

---

2. Even though in recent years the Congress has reduced the limitations it imposed on the ATF that made it nearly impossible for the agency to provide trace data to law enforcement agencies and researchers, our research has faced numerous additional obstacles created by the agency that greatly lengthened the time it took to receive the information that the current law allows (for a summary of the history of these limitations, see http://smartgunlaws.org, accessed July 12, 2017).

3. For example, during a 2009 Police Executive Research Forum symposium on guns and crime, Paul Helmke of the Brady Center to Prevent Gun Violence remarked, "One of the crucial things is that it's hard to figure out where the guns come from. Guns start out in a legal market, but they fairly quickly get into an illegal market. One of the things we encourage every police department to look at it is where the guns come from. If we had a better idea of where the guns are coming from and how they get to the gangbangers, then we could figure out some strategies to stop them" (Kanter and Fischer 2010, 14).

cles of crime guns is lacking. A particularly large gap in research relates to how firearms become diverted from the legal, primary market, composed of manufacturers, wholesalers, and distributors, to the police recovering them in the hands of criminals. As policymakers continue to debate the merits of supply-side firearms legislation, understanding the breadth and nature of the licit and illicit marketplaces that control the flow of guns in the United States is critical.

Some of the guns used during the commission of violent crimes may be obtained through legal channels.[4] Research indicates, however, that few criminals purchase their firearms directly from licensed dealers (Braga et al. 2012; Vittes, Vernick, and Webster 2012; Wright and Rossi 1994). This is critical in the context of estimating the size of crime gun markets, given that only the size of the legal primary market may be reliably quantified at the national level.[5] Conversely, the field relies on estimates to approximate the sizes of the legal secondary market and the illegal market, the latter of which consists of guns obtained through straw purchase, unlicensed street dealers, theft, and other unlawful channels (Cook and Pollack 2017; Koper and Reuter 1996; Wright and Rossi 1994).[6]

It therefore follows that when firearms purchased exclusively through the primary market are recovered by law enforcement, the full history of the gun may be mapped out with a relatively high rate of success. Conversely, because of low levels of documentation, once firearms enter the secondary or illegal markets, tracing crime guns from first purchase to use in a crime becomes exceedingly difficult (Wellford, Pepper, and Petrie 2005). The firearms literature therefore is lacking in crime gun sources and details regarding the secondary and illicit firearms markets. Two methods previously used in attempts to identify sources of recovered crime guns also used in this study are firearms traces and interviews or surveys with known gun offenders. To date, many studies have been limited to certain geographies (as national reporting of most official gun data is prohibited), with nongeneralizable samples. This article seeks to improve on these by concurrently employing both trace and interview-survey methods across three distinct sites.

Trace Studies

Efforts to understand the scope and nature of the illicit gun market have relied largely on gun traces using ATF databases such as eTrace.[7] Because of restrictions on data collection and record sharing, these are almost exclusively conducted at the local level and require the local agencies' cooperation and willingness to share

---

4. Legally purchased guns may be acquired through either a primary market, which involves the retail sale of a firearm by a federal firearms licensee (FFL), or a secondary market, in which a firearm is transferred between two unlicensed parties (Cook and Ludwig 1996; Wachtel 1998; Cook and Pollack 2017). The primary market can include the wholesale transfer of guns as well as the retail sale of a single gun to a private individual; these sales typically occur in gun stores, sporting good outlets, pawn shops, and licensed in-home businesses. Conversely, the legal secondary market is more informal, occurring through newspaper or internet classified ads, word of mouth, gun shows, and purchases or gifting between family and friends (Cook and Pollack 2017).

5. Guns legally acquired through the primary market should be traceable to the initial sale, as FFLs must record the source and identifying properties of every firearm obtained and sold; additionally, the individual purchasing from the FFL must provide identification to ensure they are not prohibited from doing so (Cook and Pollack 2017).

6. Firearms obtained through the secondary market are often entirely lawful, but are not as easily traced or documented. Instead these transfers typically occur quickly and without formal recordkeeping or payment of fees; as such, the overall size of the secondary market is unknown (Cook and Ludwig 1996; Cook and Ludwig 1996).

7. eTrace is a web-based firearms trace request system available to accredited domestic and international law enforcement agencies to assist in tracing firearms purchased in the United States. Through this interface, law enforcement can electronically submit firearms trace requests, monitor trace progress, get completed results, and query trace data. More than 5,600 law enforcement agencies are registered with eTrace (ATF 2015; Lisko and Arends 2015).

information. These studies have produced somewhat fragmented and at times inconsistent results on the sources of crime guns and the nature of the illicit gun market.

In one such study, Julius Wachtel assessed records for 5,002 firearms recovered by law enforcement agencies in the Los Angeles area between 1988 and 1995; 82 percent of the guns were recovered by the Los Angeles Police Department, and the remainder by law enforcement from Los Angeles County or nearby communities (1998). Of the recovered firearms, 6 percent had been reported stolen. The initial purchaser and the possessor at the time of recovery were fully identified for 1,599 of the 5,002 guns; in 14 percent of these instances, the gun was seized from the initial retail purchaser. Traces of the firearms recovered in the Los Angeles area were successful approximately half of the time: state records had data for 47 percent of handguns shipped to a California dealer, and the ATF National Tracing Center successfully identified the first retail dealer for the remaining 46 percent.[8] Similarly, a trace study conducted by Philip Cook and his colleagues reveals a 65.5 percent trace success rate for five years (2009 through 2013) of requests submitted to the ATF National Trace Center by the Chicago Police Department (CPD) (2015).[9] Interestingly, traces for nongang guns were slightly more successful than traces for gang-related guns.

Two of the trace studies focused on illicit gun trafficking markets (Moore 1981; Wachtel 1998). One examined the closed case files of thirteen street gun dealing (that is, dealing without a license) investigations between 1974 and 1976 and found the predominant source of street firearms dealers to be through purchases from licensed dealers and residential thefts (Moore 1981). The other reviewed case studies of domestic gun trafficking investigations conducted by the ATF in Los Angeles between 1992 and 1995 (Wachtel 1998).[10] Three-quarters of the trafficked guns (n=14,328) were initially purchased at wholesale, either by licensed dealers (90 percent) or by unlicensed street vendors using a forged license (10 percent). Fourteen percent of the trafficked guns were initially purchased from retail dealers, nearly half (42 percent) by straw purchasers. Unlike Mark Moore, Wachtel finds no instances of residential theft (Moore 1981; Wachtel 1998).

In addition to yielding inconsistent findings at times, trace studies also have inherent bias. These studies rely on police submitting guns to be traced, which occurs only in a particular set of cases—presumably those believed to be important, and those that they may not be able to solve using other means (Cook and Braga 2001). Results from guns submitted to be traced may therefore be biased to reflect more serious, complicated cases, rather than a more representative cross-section of violent gun crime.

Trace studies are also criticized by some for failing to be geographically representative (Braga et al. 2002). However, few efforts have been made to capture these trends at a national level. For example, in 2010 Mayors Against Illegal Guns assessed national trace statistics for 2009. Overall, 238,107 guns recovered at crime scenes in the United States were submitted for tracing to the ATF National Tracing Center, of which 145,321 (61 percent) were successfully traced to a source state. The firearm was recovered in the same state in which it was initially purchased 70 percent of the time (n=102,067; Mayors Against Illegal Guns 2010). Another national study reports the most prolific traffickers to be corrupt federal firearms licensees (FFLs), which made up 9 percent of ATF investigations but nearly half of the guns accounted for (ATF 2000a). Conversely, although straw purchases made up nearly half of ATF investigations, they yielded few trafficked guns per investigation. Firearms stolen from manufacturers, licensed retailers, resi-

---

8. A noteworthy obstacle to these traces was that dealers failed to supply sales or disposition information for 40 percent (n=765) of guns traced to their location.

9. The guns submitted for traces were recovered between January 1, 2009, and September 17, 2013, from individuals younger than forty at the time of the recovery (Cook et al. 2015).

10. These investigations either led to a conviction or were still proceeding through the courts at the time of the study.

dences, and shipping carriers accounted for more than one-quarter of investigations (ATF 2000a). Given the moderate success rate of trace requests and the restrictions to generalizability, supplemental methods have been used for gun market research, most notably surveys or interviews with offenders.

Gun Offender Survey and Interview Studies

Studies using trace data can provide information on some elements of gun markets, but are unlikely to offer much insight into the largely undocumented secondary and illegal markets. Instead, interviews or surveys with arrested or convicted gun offenders can provide additional information about how crime guns are typically acquired. These studies range in generalizability, some focusing on specific jurisdictions or offender groups (for example, gang affiliated or juveniles), and others, such as the Survey of Inmates in Local Jails (SILJ) and Survey of Inmates in State Correctional Facilities (SISCF), nationally representative of persons held in state prisons and local jails (Cook et al. 2015). However, gaining offender cooperation in discussing illegal transactions may have prevented full participation or candor in some of these studies. A description of findings elicited from offender surveys and interviews with regard to crime gun sources is presented in table 1, though it is not an exhaustive review:

As with the trace studies, findings regarding illicit gun markets and acquisition of crime guns are also mixed when offenders are interviewed or surveyed. However, the most common source of firearms across most of the surveys was family and friends (Beck et al. 1993; Cook et al. 2007; Sheley and Wright 1993).

In general, adding interview research has provided a much richer picture of offender gun acquisition processes than trace-based studies alone. For example, a 1992 study of one hundred imprisoned "armed career criminals" found five primary sources for the offenders' guns, most of which were in secondary or illegal markets. These sources included private parties (off-the-street sales), involvement with criminal acts or associates, retail firearms, flea markets or gun shows, and relatives (ATF 1992). More recently, Cook and colleagues (2007) interviewed gang members, gun dealers, professional thieves, prostitutes, police, public school security guards, and teenagers in Chicago, and supplemented their findings with data from government surveys of recent arrestees in twenty-two cities, and administrative data. Using a mixed-method approach, they conclude that the underground gun market in Chicago is relatively thin, potentially because of gang monopolies in certain markets or activities, the police, or neighborhood-specific factors. Additionally, they reveal trends in acquisition and time to crime relevant to neighborhood crime rates. Contrary to research focused on more organized trafficking, Philip Cook and his colleagues (2007) and Daniel Webster and his colleagues (2002) find straw purchasing to be rare among juveniles in Chicago and Maryland, respectively, juveniles rarely leaving their communities to get guns.

Implications

Despite numerous legislative and administrative barriers to conducting a thorough assessment of crime gun markets, room for improvement on current methods remains. For example, the majority of the trace studies are limited to individual municipalities, which are more often than not in high regulation states such as California, New York, and Massachusetts (Moore 1981; Wachtel 1998). Similar studies are lacking for areas with weaker gun regulations, such as some states in the southern and midwestern United States. Additionally, inmate surveys are typically conducted independently of trace studies, rather than in the same jurisdiction. By applying both methodologies to the same jurisdiction, we can gain a deeper understanding of the supply chain of crime guns, from the initial purchase, identified through a trace, to the offenders' point of acquisition, as uncovered through the prisoner interviews. This study joins these two methods and addresses some of the gaps in the research discussed.

DESCRIPTION OF TRACE DATA

This study takes a multimethod approach to explore the supply chain of guns used in crimes from first legal sale to recovery by law enforcement following use in a crime. Two forms of data are used, as mentioned: trace results of

Table 1. Summary of Prior Crime Gun Source Research

Authors	Year	Method	Firearm Source
Wright et al.	1983	Interviewed imprisoned felons	50 percent borrowed or bought from friends 32 percent theft 16 percent bought from store
Wright and Rossi	1986	Survey of criminals about last handgun	43 percent purchased (FFL or pawnshop) 32 percent stole 9 percent borrowed 7 percent traded 8 percent received as a gift
Beck et al.	1993	Interviewed imprisoned felons	31 percent from family/friends 28 percent black market, drug dealer, fence[a] 27 percent purchased from store 9 percent theft
Sheley and Wright	1993	Interviewed delinquents and inner city youths (incarcerated and in high school)	30 percent from friends 22 percent on the street 21 percent drug dealer or addict 12 percent theft 7 percent bought at store 6 percent family members
Decker and Pennell	1995	Interviewed arrestees	45 percent illegal firearms market 13 percent theft
Survey of Inmates in Local Jails (SILJ)	2002	Surveyed individuals who used or possessed a gun when the offense occurred	45 percent friends and family 24 percent fence, street, drug dealer 19 percent gun store or pawn shop 7 percent other
Survey of Inmates in State Correctional Facilities (SISCF)	2004	Surveyed males eighteen to forty in first two years of prison term and admit they had a gun at time of crime	37 percent friends and family 31 percent fence, street, drug dealer 10 percent gun store/pawn shop 8 percent other
Cook et al.	2007	Interviews with nongang affiliated youths	40 percent relative 33 percent someone affiliated with a gang 17 percent licensed security guard 6 percent broker 2 percent other
Cook and Goss	2014	National survey of prisoners serving less than two years	41 percent friends and family 32 percent illegal or street 12 percent retail 14 percent other

Source: Authors' tabulation based on Wachtel (1998, 222) and Cook et al. (2015, app. A).
[a] "Fence" refers to businessmen who deal in large quantities of goods, often stolen from trucks or warehouses.

Table 2. Jurisdictional Characteristics

	Prince George's County	New Orleans	Chicago
Firearm suicides/suicides, 2011[a]	0.6	0.6	0.3
Population, 2010[b]	863,420.0	343,829.0	2,695,598.0
Number of sworn police officers, 2010[c]	1,562.0	1,452.0	12,515.0
Population/number of sworn police officers, 2010	552.8	236.8	215.4
Estimated police budget, number sworn officers, 2010[d]	159,169.3	90,448.1	97,642.5
Number of part 1 index crimes, 2010[c]	33,162.0	15,000.0	56,591.0
Number of index crimes, number sworn officers, 2010	21.2	10.3	4.5
Proportion of violent index crimes involving a gun[e]	0.5	0.4	0.4
Percentage of white population, 2010[b]	19.2	33.0	45.0
Percentage of black population, 2010[b]	64.5	60.2	32.9
Percentage of Hispanic population, 2010[b]	14.9	5.2	28.9
Percentage of foreign population, 2010[b]	20.7	6.0	20.9

Source: Authors' calculations.
[a] CDC 2016.
[b] U.S. Census Bureau 2010.
[c] FBI 2011.
[d] Estimated by taking the average of the 2007 and 2013 values from Law Enforcement Management and Administrative Statistics (LEMAS), U.S. Department of Justice.
[e] Police departments and UCR.

guns used in violent crimes and submitted by local police agencies for tracing; and observations and opinions of incarcerated individuals on the nature of gun markets in the jurisdiction of their offense. These sources provide insight into when and where crime guns were first purchased, how they were acquired by violent offenders, and when they were recovered by law enforcement.[11] These data were collected from three diverse jurisdictions, selected to reflect differences in population characteristics, crime, gun enforcement, and the regulation of gun sales and transfers.

Jurisdictions

The three jurisdictions sampled are New Orleans, Louisiana, Chicago, Illinois, and Prince George's County, Maryland. In selecting these sites, we sought jurisdictions in states that were markedly different in the degree to which their laws and regulations monitor and control gun sales and possession. Although this study does not test the impact of these differences, the results from the analysis presented here may be helpful in identifying additional research necessary to better understand the relationship between regulations and crime gun acquisition. Reviews by independent oversight and advocacy organizations highlight the legislative and regulatory differences between the three jurisdictions. For example, the Law Center to Prevent Gun Violence issues an annual scorecard, which in 2014 gave the state of Maryland a grade of A- (the highest grade given), Illinois a B+, and Louisiana an F (2014).

In addition to regulatory disparities, these

---

11. In the firearms literature the time between first legal sale and tracing is referred to as *time to crime*. This time is typically found to be between five and seven years. This article references it as *time to recovery* because the weapon could have been used in crimes before the one in which it was recovered. Even with trace data and inmate interviews it remains unclear how and when the weapon moved from the initial legal owner to the person who uses it in a crime (when that offender is not also the original purchaser). In New Orleans and Prince George's County, we are seeking to better understand this period by interviewing first legal purchasers; these results will be reported in later work.

jurisdictions differ in other ways that may affect gun markets (table 2). For example, in 2010, the 1,452 sworn police officers of the New Orleans Police Department (NOPD) served the entire city of New Orleans, which has a population of roughly 344,000 (FBI 2011; U.S. Census 2010). During this period, the officers responded to approximately fifteen thousand Part I index crimes. In 2011 and 2012, 40 percent of violent index crimes involved a gun, including 70 percent of homicides, 50 percent of robberies, and 30 percent of aggravated assaults.[12] Unfortunately, no reliable data are available on variation in gun prevalence across U.S. regions. A common proxy that correlates highly with survey-based estimates of gun prevalence is the proportion of suicides committed with a firearm (Azrael, Cook, and Miller 2004). Using this measure obtained from the Centers for Disease Control and Prevention (CDC) Underlying Cause of Death Database, we find that more than 60 percent of completed suicides in New Orleans were committed with a firearm.

The New Orleans gun crime landscape is measurably different from Prince George's County, Maryland, which claims a population of 863,420 and is policed by approximately 1,562 sworn officers who responded to just over thirty-three thousand Part I index crimes in 2010 (FBI 2011; U.S. Census 2010). The Prince George's Police Department (PGPD) quantifies crime data using a different metric than the standard FBI Uniform Crime Report (UCR) measures; specifically, publicly available PGPD crime data quantify gun crime differently than NOPD and do not include a count of robbery incidents. To aid in cross-jurisdictional comparisons, this study uses UCR crime numbers for Prince George's County. To best estimate the number of gun crimes that occurred, the proportion of crimes that involved a gun (based on numbers provided by PGPD) was multiplied by UCR crime incidents.

Additionally, because estimates of the number or proportion of robberies committed with a firearm between 2012 and 2013 were unavailable, the proportion of robberies in which a firearm was used in Maryland in 2012 was exploited to estimate this number (FBI 2013, table 21). The proportion of violent crimes involving a firearm in Prince George's County is somewhat consistent with New Orleans, in that approximately 51 percent of violent index crimes involved a firearm, including 74 percent of homicides, 43 percent of robberies, and 55 percent of aggravated assaults. In Prince George's County in 2011, 58 percent of completed suicides were committed with a firearm.

Last, Chicago greatly differs from the other two locations, boasting a population of nearly 2.7 million residents and the nation's second largest police force, of more than 12,500 sworn officers as of 2010 (FBI 2011; U.S. Census 2010). From 2011 to 2013, this department responded to well over fifty-six thousand violent Part I index crimes, of which 39 percent involved a firearm, including 85 percent of homicides, 64 percent of robberies, and 20 percent of aggravated assaults. Chicago has an estimated lower level of gun prevalence because only around 30 percent of suicides are committed with a firearm, which is about half the proportion in New Orleans and Prince George's County.

The demographics of the three locations also differed in 2010: Chicago had a larger white population (45 percent) than New Orleans (33 percent) and Prince George's County (19 percent), a smaller African American population (33 percent) than New Orleans (60 percent) and Prince George's County (65 percent), and a larger Hispanic population (29 percent) than both New Orleans (5 percent) and Prince George's County (15 percent). New Orleans had a much smaller foreign-born population (6 percent) than Chicago and Prince George's County (20.9 percent and 20.7 percent, respectively) (U.S. Census 2010). The jurisdictions were similar in terms of other demographics, such as sex and age composition. We did not control for those differences because this descriptive analysis seeks to explore and document—rather than explain—differences.

Based on these conditions, we hypothesized the following from differences in police presence, density of gun ownership, demo-

---

12. These gun crime statistics were obtained through personal communication with the New Orleans Police Department.

graphics and other factors. We cannot test these factors within the purview of this research, but their consideration may inform future research. Consistent with research, we expected that in low regulation states guns were more likely to be purchased in-state. Additionally, the increased density of firearm ownership in New Orleans and Prince George's County over Chicago may make acquisition from social connections or theft a more certain avenue for obtaining a gun simply because more individuals are likely to possess one. On the other hand, more lax gun regulations may make gun store purchases more attractive to individuals in New Orleans. In Chicago, we might expect fewer individuals to purchase guns from a gun store given the availability of guns either trafficked from or purchased in Indiana, a low regulation state bordering the city. In Prince George's County, it is possible, given relatively stringent gun regulations and a proximate source state in Virginia, that individuals may behave similarly with regard to reliance on connections or the illegal market as sources of firearms. With currently available data, we cannot, of course, test any of these hypotheses but they are useful context for future research.

Trace Data

We received the trace results for all guns submitted by the NOPD, PGPD, and CPD to the ATF for tracing over a two-to-three-year period.[13] The guns submitted for tracing include those used during the commission of crimes as well as those recovered by police but not directly used in a crime (for example, taken from a person, found in public places, confiscated during investigation for other crimes, and the like). Not all guns submitted by these jurisdictions were successfully traced, which could be due to missing records, obliterated serial numbers, or the age of the gun. In short, although the trace data are the only source against which to identify the original purchaser of each gun recovered, they do not cover all crime guns and are not available for all recovered guns. As part of our results, we analyze a random sample of gun crime police reports from one jurisdiction where a firearm was either recovered or not recovered to better understand the selection process leading to the recovery of a firearm following a gun crime. To our knowledge, this is the first attempt to empirically understand the differences in distribution of guns between instances when one is recovered from a possessor and one is not.

Firearms were recovered in about one-quarter of the violent gun crimes that occurred in New Orleans between 2011 and 2012. The crime codes used in Chicago appear to reflect the police practice of targeting firearms for recovery; this difference may account for that between Chicago and the other two jurisdictions.[14] It appears that those tasked with completing eTrace requests may use broader categories to populate this field rather than specifying the exact crime type the recovered firearm was associated with. Thus these values are underestimated to an unknown extent. Again, it is difficult to know exactly how many guns were recovered in Prince George's County, given the way PGPD calculates gun crimes. Using the UCR estimate described earlier, however, only 11 percent of violent gun crimes resulted in a recovered firearm. Despite the limitations of disaggregating the proportion of recovered guns by crime type in Chicago and Prince George's County, each jurisdiction shows that guns were most likely to be recovered in homicides, followed by aggravated assaults, whereas they were unlikely to be recovered in armed robberies.

The trace data used in this report concern

---

13. Although the data come from the same source, variation is entirely possible in how fields are entered, coded, and maintained across the jurisdictions. This demands caution when attempting to draw comparisons across jurisdictions.

14. The crime codes Firearm under Investigation (n=8,281, 44.9 percent) and Possession of Weapon (n=4,043, 21.3 percent) make up a disproportionate number of records relative to their corresponding arrest incidents in other jurisdictions but tie with Chicago for weapons offenses. We note the volume of police stops during our study time period as a possible factor in the large volume of weapon charges. For more information, see "Stop and Frisk in Chicago," http://www.aclu-il.org/sites/default/files/wp-content/uploads/2015/03/ACLU_Stopand Frisk_6.pdf (accessed October 1, 2017).

only recovered firearms that were submitted to the ATF. It is possible, and in fact likely, that crimes in which a gun is recovered differ from those in which one is not. To estimate the potential differences between these conditions, we used a random selection of NOPD police reports from 2011 and 2012 to compare crimes in which a gun was recovered and crimes in which a gun was used but never recovered (table 3).[15] The incidents in which a firearm was recovered were more likely to result in an arrest and more likely to kill or injure the victim than when a gun was not recovered. Differences in victim and offender characteristics were also discernable.

As mentioned, not all recovered guns submitted to the ATF were successfully traced.[16] The proportion of successful traces varied across jurisdictions, New Orleans showing greater success (74.0 percent) than either Chicago (60.9 percent) or Prince George's County (63.2 percent) (tables 4 and A6). Traces were unsuccessful for several reasons, the most common of which bieng quite similar across jurisdictions: age of the gun; a missing, invalid, or obliterated serial number; the dealer or manufacturer being out of business or deceased; and an FFL not having the necessary paperwork available. We cannot adjust our results for these differences, but they should be kept in mind while interpreting any analyses of trace data. Too often these data are interpreted as if they were more complete measures of original sources of crime guns.[17]

RESULTS OF TRACE ANALYSES

Using trace data from New Orleans, Prince George's County, and Chicago, we explored patterns related to source states (where the gun was acquired by the first purchaser), crime type, time to recovery, FFL concentrations, and purchaser and possessor demographics.[18] Because trace data do not represent a random or systematic sample of firearms from a jurisdiction, but instead reflect police practices, recordkeeping, and other factors, we analyzed select subsets of recovered crime guns, purchasers, or possessors. For example, we assessed four crime types associated with the recovered crime guns (violent, property, weapon, and drug), expecting recovered firearms associated with violent arrestees to be associated

---

15. Although we initially conducted a multivariate logistic regression, interpreting the results was ineffectual due to small cell sizes for some variables and differences in the distribution of available information between recovered and unrecovered gun crimes (for example, no aggravated assaults were reported for gun crimes when a firearm was not recovered). For these reasons, we rely on the descriptive table to display how these gun crimes differ.

16. Based on conversations with ATF personnel at the National Tracing Center, we define a successful trace as one that produces the full name and date of birth of the first legal purchaser.

17. In addition, the ATF does not attempt to ensure the accuracy and completeness of information submitted by agencies seeking trace requests. Although this may not matter for the operational use of trace results for specific cases, it does matter for the use of trace results for strategic and research purposes.

18. ATF trace data are generated to inform law enforcement investigations, not academic research. It thus appears that information is not always entered uniformly in eTrace (such as whether to populate optional fields), resulting in varying amounts of missing data across jurisdictions. To accommodate this factor, and to be as inclusive as possible without sacrificing accuracy, we provide the number of cases resulting from varying restrictions to our denominator in table A1. Throughout this manuscript we make comparisons using all successful traces as our denominator, but it is important to remember that the jurisdictions vary in the amount of missing cases due both to an unsuccessful trace and local data maintenance practices. Researchers must be careful when using a data source that is so incomplete, where the correlates of incompleteness are not well understood, and when the source does not conduct appropriate error checks. The fact that our review of trace results across jurisdictions found similar results in terms of levels of tracing and reasons for unsuccessful traces should not be taken as a demonstration of the accuracy or representativeness of the trace data. Rather, our comparison of trace results for recovered and unrecovered guns, combined with the small percentage of guns that are recovered in each jurisdiction supports the call for stronger, more comprehensive data sources for crime gun research (see, for example, Wellford, Pepper, and Petrie 2005). We expand on this issue in our conclusion.

Table 3. Gun Recovery in New Orleans, 2011–2012

	Gun Recovered (N=202) n, percentage	No Gun Recovered (N=250) n, percentage
Crime type		
Aggravated battery	53, 26.2	72, 28.8
Armed robbery**	27, 13.4	141, 56.4
Homicide**	60, 29.7	36, 14.4
Aggravated assault**	55, 27.2	0
Negligent injury**	6, 3.0	0
Illegal carry weapon	1, 0.5	0
Fraudulent report	0	1, 0.4
Status		
Open**	75, 37.1	182, 72.8
Cleared by arrest**	121, 59.9	65, 26.0
Time of crime		
12:01–4:00 am*	29, 14.4	51, 20.4
4:01–8:00 am	11, 5.5	20, 8.0
8:01–12:00 pm	21, 10.4	18, 7.2
12:01–4:00 pm	31, 15.4	31, 12.4
4:01–8:00 pm	51, 25.3	47, 18.8
8:01–12:00 am*	59, 29.2	83, 33.2
Offender race		
Black**	138, 89.0	198, 98.5
White**	12, 7.7	2, 1.0
Hispanic**	4, 2.6	0
Other	1, 0.7	1, 0.0
Offender sex		
Male**	137, 87.8	198, 98.5
Female**	19, 12.2	3, 1.5
Offender under twenty-four		
Yes**	50, 38.8	40, 61.5
No**	79, 61.2	25, 38.5
Number of offenders		
One offender*	110, 67.5	127, 57.7
Multiple offenders*	53, 32.5	93, 42.3
Victim race		
Black**	164, 82.4	178, 72.0
White**	24, 12.1	47, 19.0
Hispanic	10, 5.0	17, 6.9
Other	1, 0.5	5, 2.0
Victim sex		
Male	152, 76.4	198, 79.8
Female	47, 23.6	50, 20.2

Table 3. (continued)

	Gun Recovered (N=202) n, percentage	No Gun Recovered (N=250) n, percentage
Victim under twenty-four		
Yes	48, 27.7	62, 26.2
No	125, 72.3	175, 73.8
Victim injury		
No injury**	72, 36.0	122, 49.0
Minimum injury	8, 4.0	12, 4.8
Treat and discharge	4, 2.0	10, 4.0
Hospitalized	58, 29.0	72, 28.9
Death**	58, 29.0	33, 13.3

Source: Authors' calculations.
*$p < .1$, two-tailed proportional z-test
**$p < .05$, two-tailed proportional z-test

Table 4. Trace Information

Jurisdiction	Number of Recovered	Number of Successful Traces	Top Four Reasons for Unsuccessful Trace
New Orleans, 2011–2012	3,068	2,269	1. Retail or manufacturer dealer out of business or died (N=183; 26.4 percent) 2. Serial number missing, invalid, or obliterated (N=135; 19.5 percent) 3. Gun sold before recordkeeping requirements (N=99; 14.3 percent) 4. FFL paperwork unavailable (N=96; 13.9 percent)
Chicago, 2011–2013	18,455	11,248	1. Gun sold before recordkeeping requirements (N=1,978; 30.5 percent) 2. Retail or manufacturer dealer out of business or died (N=1,287; 19.8 percent) 3. FFL paperwork unavailable (N=787; 12.1 percent) 4. Serial number missing, invalid, or obliterated (N=683; 10.5 percent)
Prince George's County, 2011–2013	2,034	1,286	1. Gun sold before recordkeeping requirements (N=169; 26.5 percent) 2. Retail or manufacturer dealer out of business or died (N=154; 24.1 percent) 3. Serial number missing, invalid, or obliterated (N=100; 15.7 percent) 4. Information missing from trace request (N=67; 10.5 percent)

Source: Authors' calculations.

Table 5. Source Location of All Guns and New Guns with Short TTR

	All Guns Recovered		Guns with TTR < Two Years	
	In State	Out of State	In State	Out of State
New Orleans, 2011–2012	77.2	22.8	86.3	13.7
Chicago, 2011–2013	42.2	57.8	57.5	42.5
Prince George's County, 2012–2013	47.1	52.9	62.9	37.2

Source: Authors' calculations.
Note: Percentages were calculated using denominator 3 from table A6.

with indicators of gun trafficking or problematic firearms purchases at the highest rate. Consistent with prior research, we treated cases in which a female purchased a pistol or revolver recovered in the possession of a male as a possible indicator of a straw purchase (see Cook et al. 2015).[19] Although a 2000 ATF report on criminal investigations involving firearm traffickers indicated that this classification scheme represented only 18 percent of straw purchases, following friends (45 percent) and relatives (23 percent), it was the only category readily measurable with our trace data (ATF 2000a). We recognize that this is only one possible subset of straw purchasers, and note that the measurement of straw purchasing is in need of development.[20]

Sources of Firearms
We first examined the relative importance of different state sources in supplying firearms to our jurisdictions of interest. Firearms first purchased in a different state than where it was recovered are a potential indicator of interstate trafficking, whereby prohibited purchasers or associates may take advantage of varying state regulations to obtain firearms. We compared the proportion of firearms first purchased in the state in which they were recovered to those purchased out of state to examine the impact of neighboring state regulations on crime guns recovered in our jurisdictions of interest. We would expect based on the relatively lax regulatory environment in Louisiana, that guns recovered in New Orleans would be more likely to have been initially purchased within the same state than those recovered in Prince George's County and Chicago (given that both Maryland and Illinois have stricter laws and are bordered by states with lower regulation scores). In addition, these differences may be even greater for firearms recovered within two years of their first legal sale. We assessed the proportions of successfully traced crime guns purchased in state rather than out of state across the jurisdictions (see table 5); the results show that the proportion of successfully traced guns first purchased by individuals residing out of state in which the gun was eventually recovered is lower for New Orleans than for Chicago or Prince George's County. These findings are consistent when the firearms are restricted to guns recovered within two years of first purchase. Despite differences in source states that conformed to our expectations based on jurisdictional gun regulations, with a sample of only three jurisdictions and an inability to control for confounding factors, we are unable to attribute this difference to these regulations. However, our findings do align with a study that included a larger sample of cities and controlled for multiple confounding factors (Webster, Vernick, and Hepburn 2001). They also align with studies analyzing the effect of Virginia's one-handgun-per-month law on interstate trafficking (Braga 2017; Weil and Knox 1996).

When broken out by type of crime, firearms

---

19. Because the sex of the possessor was not available in the New Orleans trace data, and we wanted to be consistent across datasets, we estimated the sex of the purchasers and possessors using the gender package in R statistical software (https://cran.r-project.org/web/packages/gender/gender.pdf, accessed October 1, 2017).

20. Table A1 provides alternate straw purchase estimates using an array of definitions, which might be of value in future work.

Table 6. Source Locations of Successfully Traced Firearms

	In State	Out of State	Total
Violent crime			
New Orleans, 2011–2012	80.4	19.6	100, n=393
Chicago, 2011–2013	44.9	55.1	100, n=675
Prince George's County, 2012–2013	44.1	55.9	100, n=247
Property crime			
New Orleans, 2011–2012	82.8	17.2	100, n=87
Chicago, 2011–2013	68.8	31.3	100, n=48
Prince George's County, 2012–2013	53.7	46.3	100, n=54
Weapon crime			
New Orleans, 2011–2012	76.3	23.7	100, n=801
Chicago, 2011–2013	38.9	61.1	100, 9,111
Prince George's County, 2012–2013	39.5	60.5	100, n=380
Drug crime			
New Orleans, 2011–2012	79.9	20.2	100, n=546
Chicago, 2011–2013	41.5	58.5	100, n=357
Prince George's County, 2012–2013	41.0	59.0	100, n=188
Other crime			
New Orleans, 2011–2012	71.6	28.4	100, n=423
Chicago, 2011–2013	42.2	57.8	100, n=809
Prince George's County, 2012–2013	58.0	42.0	100, n=405
Overall			
New Orleans, 2011–2012	77.3	22.8	100, n=2,250
Chicago, 2011–2013	39.7	60.3	100, n=11,000
Prince George's County, 2012–2013	47.1	52.9	100, n=1,274

Source: Authors' calculations.
Note: Percentages were calculated using denominator 3 from table A6.

recovered during property crimes are more likely to originate within the state where they are recovered than out of state across all three jurisdictions (table 6). However, for the other crime types assessed (violent, weapon, drug, and "other"), the relative frequency of guns originating within or outside of the recovery state varies according to jurisdiction.[21] Furthermore, in the low regulation jurisdiction, weapons recovered in all crime types are largely from in-state purchases.[22] Again, despite being consistent with our hypotheses, other unmeasured explanations could explain this pattern.

Age of Recovered Firearms

We next examined the amount of time between first purchase and recovery, which the ATF uses as an indicator of gun trafficking (with a shorter time to recovery associated with a higher likelihood that a gun was traf-

---

21. The "other" crime category includes the remaining NCIC crime types, such as found firearms, traffic offenses, and public order offenses.

22. Prior research has noted that changes in regulations, specifically the background checks mandated under the Brady Act, have affected out-of-state gun recoveries in Chicago (Cook and Braga 2001). We replicated this analysis for our jurisdictions' recovered firearms (results available on request). Over time, firearms purchased from FFLs in-state make up a greater proportion of all recovered firearms in all three jurisdictions.

Table 7. Time to Recovery by First Purchaser Location and Crime Type

	In State	Out of State	Total
Violent crime			
New Orleans, 2011–2012	7.4	11.9	391
Chicago, 2011–2013	10.1	13.8	675
Prince George's County, 2012–2013	10.6	13.8	246
Property crime			
New Orleans, 2011–2012	5.5	7.3	87
Chicago, 2011–2013	13.0	19.6	48
Prince George's County, 2012–2013	9.2	9.6	54
Weapon crime			
New Orleans, 2011–2012	7.1	8.2	801
Chicago, 2011–2013	11.9	14.4	9,111
Prince George's County, 2012–2013	9.0	12.4	380
Drug crime			
New Orleans, 2011–2012	6.7	11.0	546
Chicago, 2011–2013	12.6	15.4	357
Prince George's County, 2012–2013	9.2	15.5	188
Other crime			
New Orleans, 2011–2012	9.0	10.9	422
Chicago, 2011–2013	11.7	14.4	809
Prince George's County, 2012–2013	9.0	14.8	405
Overall			
New Orleans, 2011–2012	7.3	9.9	2,247
Chicago, 2011–2013	11.7	14.5	11,000
Prince George's County, 2012–2013	9.3	13.7	1,273

Source: Authors' calculations.
Note: Percentages were calculated using denominator 3 from table A6.

ficked). We expected to see fewer years between first legal sale and recovery by law enforcement in New Orleans compared to Chicago or Prince George's County, because, among other factors, the less restrictive gun regulations should allow offenders to gain access to newer guns more easily. As expected, the average time to recovery for successfully traced firearms was lowest in New Orleans, followed by Prince George's County and then Chicago, and was uniformly lower for purchases within the state than for outside of the state (table 7). These findings appear to hold across crime types. Along with differences in gun regulations, the variation in the age of recovered crime guns could be due to numerous other factors, such as the prevalence of gangs across the cities, though some research suggests that gang members have a different relationship to gun use and possession than nongang members do and that their guns may be older (on the relationship, Braga 2017; on gun age, Cook et al. 2015).

First Purchaser Characteristics
To understand differences among first purchasers who either consciously or inadvertently divert guns from the legal market, we divided our purchasers into several groups: female purchasers whose pistols or revolvers were recovered in the possession of a male, same purchaser-possessor, and multiple fire-

Table 8. Purchaser Characteristics Representing Potentially Problematic Buyers

	New Orleans	Chicago	Prince George's County
	(2011–2012)	(2011–2013)	(2012–2013)
Straw purchasers[a]			
Percent	14.2	12.1	10.5
n	208	861	85
Total	1,461	7,095	813
Same purchaser possessors[b]			
Percent	19.7	15.3	27.1
n	327	1,219	242
Total	1,660	7,978	894
Multiple firearm purchasers[c]			
Percent	5.4	6.8	4.6
n	122	769	59
Total	2,269	11,248	1,286

Source: Authors' calculations.
[a] Percentages were calculated using denominator 5 from table A6.
[b] Percentages were calculated using denominator 4 from table A6.
[c] Percentages were calculated using denominator 2 from table A6.

arm purchasers.[23] These transaction types do not represent the majority of the guns recovered but are potentially informative (table 8). For example, females are less likely to have a criminal history and are more likely to be successful in purchasing a firearm legally from an FFL; when their purchased guns are recovered in possession of a male, it is therefore possible that the purchase was made on behalf of a prohibited male associate.[24] As this is likely to be especially true for pistols and revolvers, we condition our estimates on this weapon type. Cases in which the first purchaser is also the possessor at time of recovery may disproportionately represent the class of individuals who are not prohibited possessors and can legally purchase a firearm for potential misuse despite lacking a criminal record. Finally, the ATF considers multiple firearm purchases as an indicator of possible diversion into the illegal market and has instituted various programs and data collection priorities to track them.[25]

These categories are not mutually exclusive (a female first purchaser could also be the final possessor and purchase multiple handguns), but in New Orleans possible straw transactions make up 14.2 percent of all successfully traced crime guns, in Prince George's County 10.5 percent, and in Chicago 12.1 percent. The greater proportion of possible straw

---

23. We coded multiple firearm purchasers as the first purchasers of successfully traced firearms that were reported to the ATF by the FFL as being part of a multiple handgun sale. The ATF uses this code as an indicator of illegal diversion (ATF 2000b).

24. This definition of straw purchasers is drawn from Philip Cook and his colleagues (2015, 743). We realize that this definition of straw purchaser, though widely used in the firearms literature, is problematic. Obviously, not all female purchasers are straw purchasers, but given the available data this is the closest approximation we can get to measuring this type of purchaser. For that reason, we urge caution in drawing strong conclusions from this portion of our analysis.

25. The ATF cites multiple purchases as an indicator of firearms trafficking and tracks multiple purchases on the part of southern border states by requiring FFLs to report instances of multiple sales of rifles designated as semiautomatic (see ATF 2016).

Figure 1. New Orleans Purchaser Groups, 2011–2012

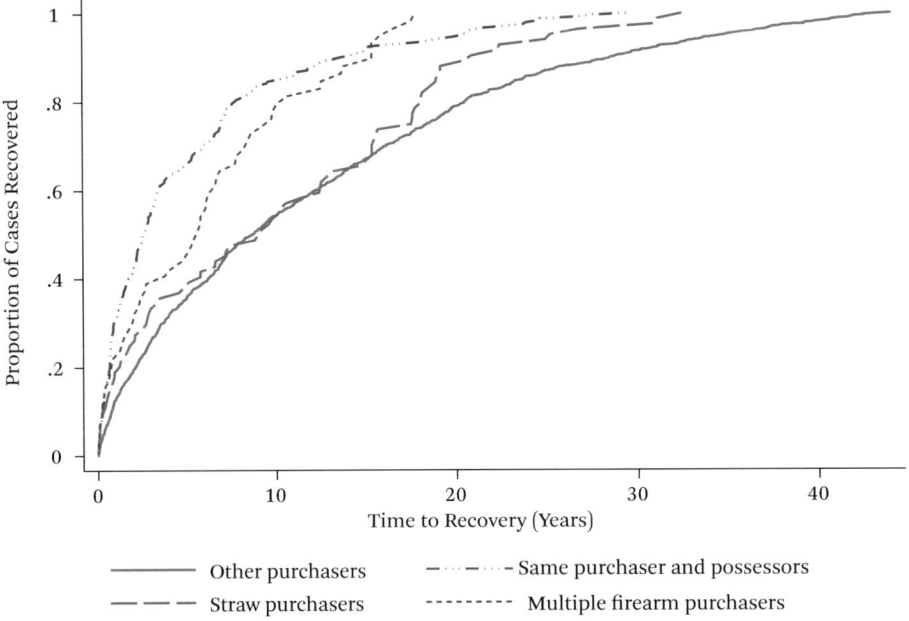

Source: Authors' tabulation.

purchases in the weakest gun regulatory area might suggest that straw purchasers perceive a greater willingness of dealers to sell to them, though we are unable to test this hypothesis with a sample of only three jurisdictions. To estimate the frequency of the same purchaser-possessor, we used a probability matching procedure to match fields with identical first name, last name, and date of birth and, as a result, may underestimate the same extent of same purchaser-possessor.[26] This purchase type is highest in Prince George's County. The mixed findings across jurisdictions make this purchaser type difficult to diagnose.

Next, we examined the average cumulative time to recovery across different purchaser groups (figures 1, 2, and 3). We hypothesized that if these purchaser types—straw purchasers, same purchaser-possessors, and multiple firearm purchasers—represent potentially dangerous or illicit buyers, then the firearm they purchased is more likely to be used in a crime and recovered by law enforcement relatively quickly. We find that in each jurisdiction, the firearms most quickly recovered from crimes are those associated with the same purchaser-possessor. The short time to recovery for this purchaser group seems to suggest that many of these individuals are purchasing the crime gun with the intent of using it. We also observe a steeper slope for the cumulative time to recovery of crime guns purchased as part of a multigun sale and by straw purchasers relative to other successfully traced purchasers. Again, although these purchaser types are only a proxy for straw purchasers or firearm diverters, the shorter time to recovery may indicate that the firearms are being turned over to individuals who intend to use them illegally. However, this claim is given some validity by the fact that multiple analyses from many other states have come to the same or similar conclusions using these proxies (Koper 2014; Pierce et al. 2004; Wright, Wintemute, and Webster 2010).

Federal Firearms Licensee Sources

Earlier we described jurisdictional differences in purchaser source states and time to recovery for recovered and successfully traced crime guns. To better understand where these guns

---

26. We used the STATA matchit command with a 75 percent probability threshold.

Figure 2. Chicago Purchaser Groups, 2011–2013

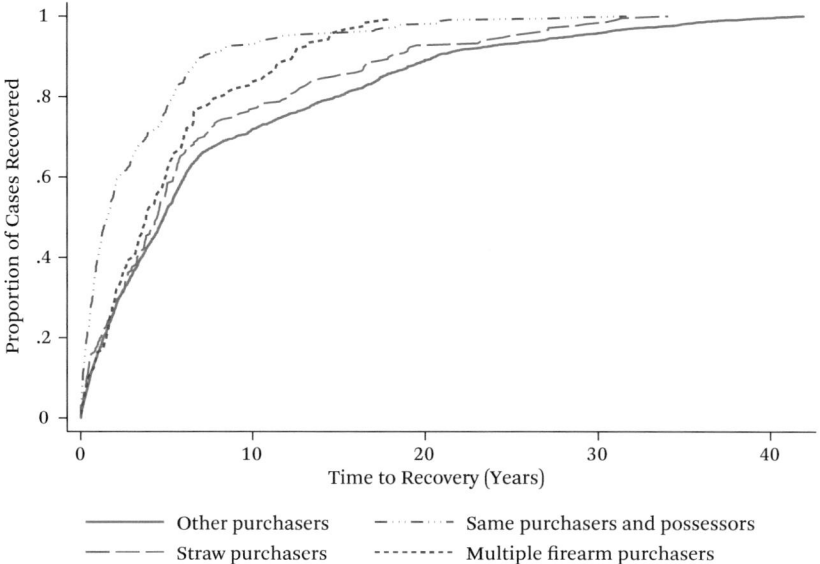

Source: Authors' tabulation.

Figure 3. Prince George's County Purchaser Groups, 2012–2013

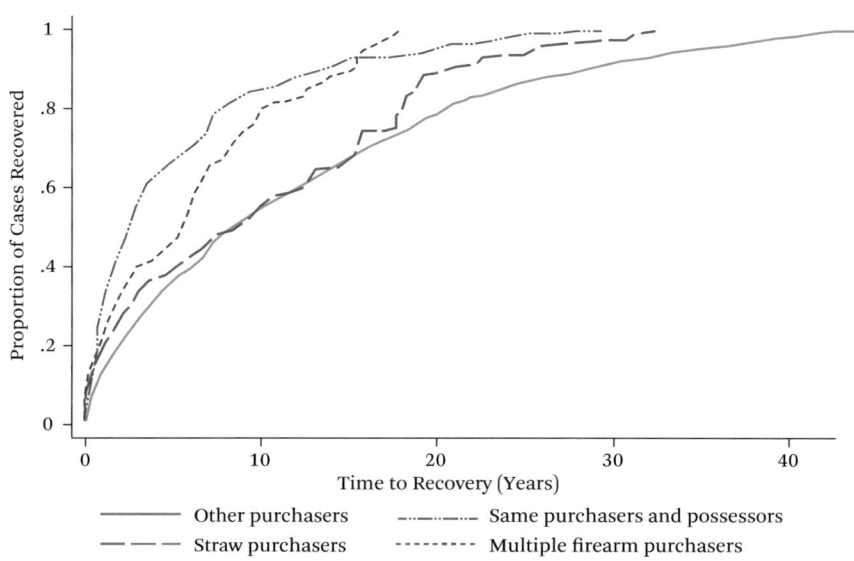

Source: Authors' tabulation.

are coming from and how they end up in offenders' hands, we examined differences in the concentration of FFLs used by the original purchasers, and probed whether straw purchasers, as we defined them, were more likely to shop at a certain few dealerships—"point sources"—than nonstraw purchasers (Cook and Braga 2001). Further, Garen Wintemute finds that FFLs with high rates of trace requests or denials were more likely to sell to women and were more likely to have attempted straw purchases within the past year than other FFLs in his multistate mail survey (2017). He also finds, in another study, that certain gun dealers in Califor-

Figure 4. Concentration of All Gun Sales Among FFL Dealers

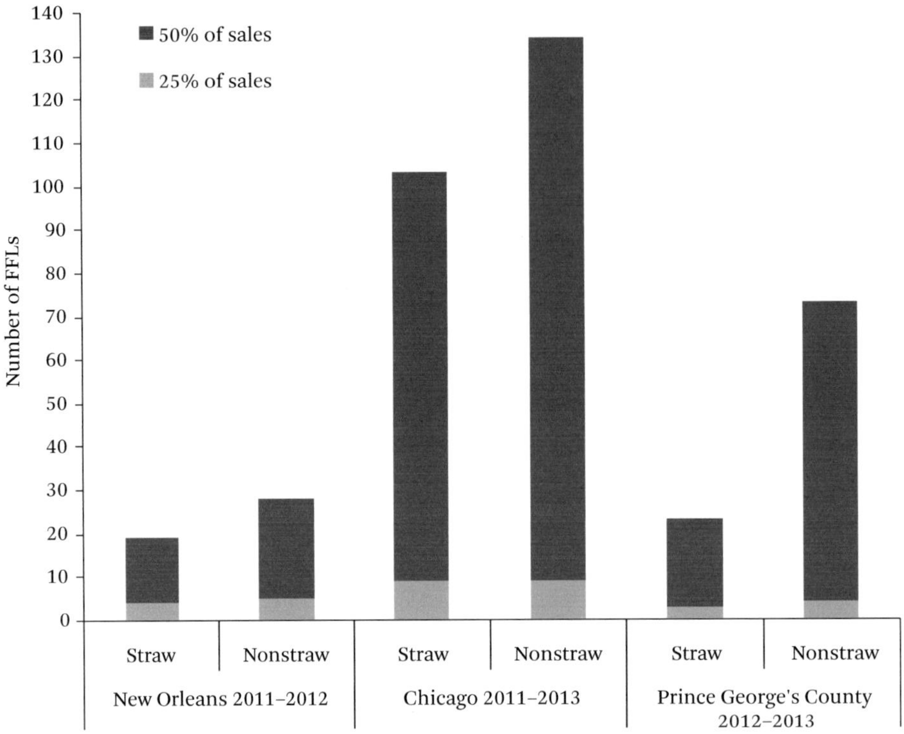

Source: Authors' tabulation.

nia were more likely to agree to sell to an explicit straw purchaser, and that their likelihood depended on the FFLs' location within the state (2010).

We sought to examine whether this variability in sales, as measured by the number of sales to our straw purchaser proxy, varied between our three jurisdictions. To do so, we assessed the proportions of dealers accounting for 25 percent and 50 percent of pistol or revolver sales, conditional on sales to straw or nonstraw purchasers, for all recovered guns and guns recovered within two years of purchase (figures 4 and 5). These figures reveal that new, recovered crime guns come from relatively few dealers, and sales to possible straw purchasers appear to be concentrated among even fewer FFLs. For example, 50 percent of all new guns sold across the three jurisdictions came from only around ten dealers. We postulate that in jurisdictions with stricter gun regulations, it may be more difficult to find a dealer willing to supply firearms to potential straw purchasers, so these individuals may be more likely to frequent more 'liberal' gun dealers. Although the findings for New Orleans and Chicago are mixed, the difference in FFL concentration between straw and nonstraw purchasers is consistently highest in Prince George's County, indicating that straw purchasers especially concentrate their purchases to a few FFLs within this jurisdiction. Future research aimed at understanding why this is the case might provide useful information for reducing the movement of guns into the illegal market.

In summary, our analysis of successful firearms traces in three jurisdictions suggests that fewer than 25 percent of all crimes committed with a gun result in gun recovery, that serious crimes such as homicide yield the highest recovery rates across jurisdictions, and that crimes with recovered guns differ from crimes where guns are used but not recovered.

Of those recovered and submitted for tracing, approximately two-thirds are successfully

Figure 5. Concentration of New Gun Sales Among FFL Dealers

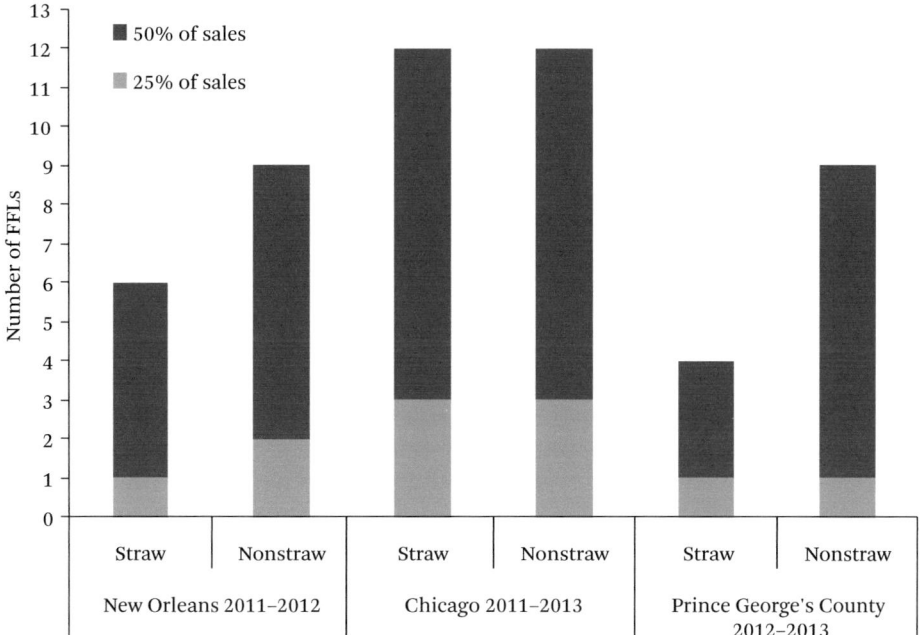

Source: Authors' tabulation.

traced. Common reasons for an unsuccessful trace across jurisdictions include the age of the gun and record-keeping requirements, difficulty obtaining records from manufacturers, dealers, and FFLs, and problems identifying the firearms' serial numbers.

In jurisdictions with fewer firearms regulations the proportion of guns purchased in the same state where they were recovered was considerably higher than in states with greater regulations; this was true for all crime types. Regardless, since 2000, recoveries of in-state purchases have been increasing across all three jurisdictions. Despite our inability to causally attribute this finding to jurisdictional differences in gun regulation, our descriptive findings are similar to those of other studies that examine a greater number of jurisdictions, include a larger number of confounders, and examine specific regulatory changes. Importantly, our findings remain descriptive.

No observed relationship is evident across our jurisdictions regarding the percent of cases where the first purchaser and the possessor at time of recovery are the same person. Approximately 15 percent of guns recovered and successfully traced involved the same purchaser and possessor.

Time to recovery was longer in jurisdictions with stricter gun regulations. Time to recovery was consistently shorter for cases with the same purchaser and possessor across jurisdictions. Again, although we do not attribute this finding solely to differences in gun regulation across the jurisdictions, our findings support previous research showing shorter time to recovery in different low regulation states.

Our proxy measure for straw purchasers provided results inconsistent with our expectations: the state with the lowest regulations had the highest proportion of individuals identified as possible straw purchasers.[27] Somewhat in line with our expectations was the finding that straw purchasing is concentrated to a

---

27. Data on state of purchase and residence are difficult to interpret without information on movement by purchasers and proximity to borders, both of which could result in assumption of out-of-state purchase that is incorrect. This applies to all analyses using state of purchaser, not just attempts to measure straw purchase.

greater extent among fewer FFLs (point sources) in Prince George's County than in New Orleans or Chicago. Future research will need to more accurately operationalize straw purchasers and parse out how much of these effects are due to gun regulations as opposed to other social or political causes.

INMATE SURVEY DATA

In each jurisdiction, we sought to determine how incarcerated individuals described how offenders acquired guns in their jurisdiction. In Louisiana, we used a random sample of 321 persons incarcerated in the state prison system for a crime of violence that they had committed in New Orleans between 2011 and 2012. These inmates were surveyed in groups of between eight and thirty-one, in seven different prisons. Responses were received from 220 (69 percent), almost all of the refusals coming at one maximum security prison in which survey conditions were very difficult. The instrument asked twelve questions about how guns were obtained, used, stored and transferred in New Orleans. Two instruments were used, one that asked the subject how they acquired guns and the other how people in their city acquired guns. In Maryland, we were able to identify 173 incarcerated offenders who had been convicted between 2010 and 2015 in Prince George's County of using a gun in a crime. Of these inmates, 149 were available for administration of the survey and sixty-eight completed the survey. This is a total response rate of 39.3 percent and an available rate of 45.6 percent. Surveys were administered to these offenders individually, or in groups of as many as twenty-one, at nine institutions using the version of the instrument that asked about gun acquisition in their jurisdiction. In both versions of the survey, inmates were asked to provide opinions based on hypothetical scenarios (for example, "Assuming someone wanted to get a weapon to use to commit a crime in New Orleans, how would they get this weapon?"). In summary, for the inmate surveys we present responses for 265 individuals (207 in New Orleans, and 58 in Prince George's County).[28] Monetary compensation was not provided to participants at the request of prison officials.[29]

In Chicago, interviews were attempted with 138 individuals who were detained in the Cook County Jail for gun possession or who had a history of gun crime involvement. Interviews were completed with ninety-nine of those sampled. The sample was not randomly selected but rather was a convenience sample of gun-involved arrestees. Those who participated received a ten-dollar phone card in their account. The interview consisted of forty open-ended questions, conducted by interviewers under the direction of Alisù Schoua-Glusburg's firm Research Support Services. Respondents were asked how they acquired guns and from whom and, hypothetically, how guns could be acquired in their neighborhood. Their responses to this more general question are used here for comparability with the questions posed to respondents in New Orleans and Prince George's County (for responses to the more specific questions, see Cook, Parker, and Pollack 2015).

In all instances, we assured respondents that their answers would not be shared with anyone outside the project and gave them ample opportunity to not participate.[30] We found respondents eager to participate. In addition, we consider the results from federal surveys of gun use reported by offenders to provide a broader source of respondents than in our surveys.

Further, we acknowledge that different sampling schemes and questions were used across sites.[31] We might expect that a random sample of violent inmates in New Orleans and Prince

---

28. In Maryland, refusals to participate primarily reflected a strong gang and no-snitch culture in the prisons.

29. Individuals who completed the instrument were informed that they could request a written letter of appreciation from the research staff, which would be placed in their file.

30. Human subject reviews were conducted for all locations.

31. In Louisiana, no differences were discernable in findings between those who were administered an instrument asking about their personal acquisition or about acquisition by those in their jurisdiction. In Chicago, responses differed depending on whether the response set was the respondent's actions or those in their neighbor-

George's County have different knowledge of gun acquisition than arrestees sampled on gun-related charges in the Cook County Jail. In any case, neither sample is ideally representative of gun assaults in any jurisdiction. However, the two populations are likely to have important knowledge, though perhaps differing levels of familiarity, of how individuals who may use guns in crime obtain guns when they are likely prohibited from doing so from a gun dealer. Many individuals in our samples who might have a prior criminal record cannot obtain guns by legal purchase the way that many individuals who possess a gun legally are able to do. They therefore must rely on either other methods or the illegal market. All responses discussed in the following section originate from questions about how respondents think guns are acquired in their jurisdiction based on their local knowledge.[32] We can obtain more information about how these markets work in terms of sources and methods of acquisition by asking those who have knowledge of how it works in their experience.

RESULTS FROM INMATE SURVEYS

We find that across jurisdictions, survey methods, and time periods, respondents are most likely to report that individuals in their jurisdiction would purchase their firearm than acquire it in any other way. In all jurisdictions, we find that respondents reported that individuals in their jurisdictions were most likely to acquire the weapon "on the street" than from other sources, followed by family or friend. In each jurisdiction, a street source is the most likely method of acquisition.

Paying to Acquire a Firearm

In all jurisdictions, the most frequent response to how individuals acquire guns was to buy one. In New Orleans, 43 percent of respondents reported that paying for a gun was the most common method of acquisition in their jurisdiction, Chicago and Prince George's County respondents reporting 82 percent and 66 percent respectively. It is possible that the different rates for buying a gun in the different markets could pertain to regulations in place in higher regulation states, though many other factors could also account for the response and this information does not permit us to draw conclusions about the differences. What is clear from our data across jurisdictions is the importance of payment in acquiring a firearm.

The source most frequently reported in their respective markets was "on the street," indicating the importance of the underground, illegal market in all jurisdictions. In New Orleans, paying for a gun in the illegal market made up 70 percent of all responses where payment was cited, or 30 percent of overall responses. In Chicago, of responses involving payment, 54 percent involved a street source, making up 44 percent of all gun transactions. In Prince George's County, of all responses involving payment, 68 percent were from a street source, totaling 45 percent of all responses tabulated. Despite the lower reported rate of overall street transactions in New Orleans, the importance of purchasing a gun in the illegal market as a source of guns to individuals who might use them in crime is common to all jurisdictions.

Payment for a firearm at gun stores was also reported across jurisdictions. What we find regarding payment for a firearm from a gun store is that though respondents report its occurrence, it is not a majority in any of the jurisdictions: 7 percent in New Orleans, 10 percent in Prince George's County, and 19 percent in Chicago. It is possible that in New Orleans the

---

hood (see tables A4 and A5). The primary difference in Chicago is in the different rates of theft and borrowing reported; individuals were more likely to borrow and less likely to report theft for their own gun acquisition than their perceptions of the market as a whole. These differences reinforce the need for a program of methodological research on surveying about guns.

32. In Chicago, responses to "how do guns come into the neighborhood?" were coded from open-ended responses to interviewer questions. In New Orleans and Prince George's County, responses to "assuming someone wanted to get a weapon to use to commit a crime, how would they get this weapon?" were coded from close-ended responses to a written survey (see table 8).

denser gun availability drives fewer individuals to a gun store, but the lower proportion could also result from lesser police enforcement, stringent dealers, or other factors beyond the scope of this article.

To a lesser extent, individuals reported purchasing firearms from family or friends. One respondent in New Orleans said that paying family or friends was a possibility, and in Prince George's County and Chicago, 13 percent and 24 percent said the same.

Theft to Acquire a Firearm

Respondents in all jurisdictions reported that gun theft was a common method of acquiring a firearm, ranking below payment in all jurisdictions and above borrowing in all jurisdictions by similar proportions. New Orleans respondents reported that 39 percent of the time, individuals would acquire their gun by theft. Prince George's County and Chicago markets were lower, 25 percent and 12 percent respectively. These rates are consistent in that gun theft is a source of guns to potentially prohibited possessors in all jurisdictions though not as primary a method of gun acquisition as paying for a gun.

Each jurisdiction is also similar with regard to the distribution among possible sources of theft—that is, from family or friend, on the street, pawn shops, gun shows, or gun shops. All respondents across all jurisdictions reported that gun theft from "the street" is the way to obtain guns in the illegal market, all jurisdictions citing at least 55 percent of guns were obtained from the illegal market. The second primary source reported, also at a similar rate of approximately 20 percent, is friends or family. Significantly, obtaining stolen guns on the street does not equate to the quantity of stolen guns in a jurisdiction but rather a single transaction a respondent reported. It is possible that gun theft is a repeated process in the course of a gun changing hands in the illegal market. Finally, few respondents thought that sources such as pawn shops or gun shows were sources from which guns could be stolen.

Borrowing to Obtain a Firearm

With regard to borrowing as a source of firearms, all jurisdictions reported that borrowing a gun is a way of acquiring a firearm, but not as important a one as either buying or stealing. In New Orleans, 17.9 percent of respondents reported that they would borrow a gun versus 6 percent in Chicago and 9 percent in Prince George's County. Because of these small numbers (n=5 and n=4), we cannot speak to the distribution of guns among the sources from which a gun could be borrowed. In New Orleans, most respondents reported that they would borrow a firearm from family and friends or on the street. What is notable overall is that the reported incidence of borrowing a gun is lower than either theft or payment in the overall sample.

Sources for Acquisition

Across methodologies, jurisdictions, and time frames, respondents reported the most likely source for acquiring a firearm is on the street (see table 9). In New Orleans, 73 percent of respondents reported that they would obtain a gun from a street source, in Prince George's County 69 percent and in Chicago 51 percent. In all jurisdictions, though with some range, more than half indicated that they would acquire a firearm from a source on the street. These transactions include borrowing, paying for, and stealing a gun, though across all jurisdictions, the most frequent method is paying for it.

All jurisdictions reported that the next most common source involves family and friends or relatives: in New Orleans 18 percent, in Prince George's County 14 percent, and in Chicago 28 percent. The third most common in Chicago and Prince George's County is gun shops, hardware stores, and mail order or ad sales.

Few respondents reported gun shows as a source for purchasing a gun. In New Orleans, none did, in Prince George's County 4 percent, and in Chicago 1 percent. It is possible that for the individuals in our samples, access to gun shows might be limited by other factors, such as transportation, and that instead relatively few individuals could traffic from gun shows, thus supplying the illegal market from gun shows. Traffickers who profitably transfer guns may not often appear in data collection of individuals in prison or in jail for gun-related or violent offenses. Acknowledging this limita-

Table 9. Methods and Sources of Gun Acquisition

	New Orleans				Prince George's County				Chicago[a]			
	Steal (%)	Borrow (%t)	Pay[b] (%)	Total	Steal (%)	Borrow (%)	Pay[b] (%)	Total	Steal (%)	Borrow (%)	Pay[b] (%)	Total
Family or friend	20.7 n=17	51.4 n=19	1.1 n=1	17.9 n=37	13.3 n=2	20.0 n=1	13.2 n=5	13.8 n=8	22.2 n=2	100.0 n=4	24.1 n=14	28.2 n=20
On the street	70.7 n=58	32.4 n=12	70.5 n=62	63.8 n=132	73.3 n=11	60.0 n=3	68.4 n=26	69.0 n=40	55.6 n=5	0.0 n=0	53.5 n=31	50.7 n=36
Pawnshop or collector	3.7 n=3	10.8 n=4	6.8 n=6	6.3 n=13	6.7 n=1	0.0 n=0	2.6 n=1	3.5 n=2	0.0 n=0	0.0 n=0	0.0 n=0	0.0 n=0
Gun show	0.0 n=0	0.0 n=0	0.0 n=0	0.0 n=0	0.0 n=0	0.0 n=0	5.3 n=2	3.5 n=2	0.0 n=0	0.0 n=0	1.7 n=1	1.4 n=1
Gun shop, hardware store, mail order, ad sale	4.9 n=4	5.4 n=2	21.6 n=19	12.1 n=25	6.7 n=1	20.0 n=1	10.5 n=4	10.3 n=6	22.2 n=2	0.0 n=0	20.7 n=12	19.7 n=14
Total	n=82	n=37	n=88	n=207	n=15	n=5	n=38	n=58	n=9	n=4	n=58	n=71

Source: Authors' calculations.

[a]Chicago's survey method was an open-ended interview; not all responses can be categorized into similar categories. Those answers excluded include responses such as "I don't know" or refusals to answer as well as "other."

[b]*Pay* is a summary measure of the responses *rent, trade,* and *buy.*

tion, we find gun shows were not reported to be a proximate source for individuals arrested or in prison.

Comparison with Existing Surveys of Gun Acquisition

We compared our survey data with existing sources to provide additional context and verification of our findings. We used federal survey data from the SISCF and SILJ to replicate the samples of prisons in New Orleans and Prince George's County along with a sample of jail arrestees to replicate Chicago's sample. We find that relative to federal survey data, the largest sources and methods of gun acquisition in our jurisdictions are largely in line with prior estimates. Federal data match the importance of paying for a gun in each jurisdiction as the most prevalent method of acquisition. Theft and borrowing are below payment, as in the jurisdiction surveys, but their rank ordering differs. In federal surveys, borrowing is more frequent than theft, unlike in the jurisdictional surveys. The largest difference is in the importance of theft. In federal surveys, respondents reported stealing the firearm used in crime in fewer than 7 percent of cases; but in jurisdictional surveys, theft accounted for at least 12 percent in Chicago and as high as 39 percent in New Orleans. Federal surveys also report borrowing firearms more frequently, at 16 to 18 percent. The importance of family and friends as sources of firearms for potentially prohibited possessors is clear in both surveys, though jurisdictional respondents all reported street sources as more prevalent (see tables A2 and A3).

The many reasons for these differences are impossible to discern from either our data or federal data and could include time frames, sampling methods, and enforcement actions, among others. It could also be that the jurisdictional differences in proportion are masked in a national sample. Several defining characteristics regarding sources and methods of gun acquisition were corroborated in federal surveys.

In summary, the survey analyses reveal several significant findings. Survey participants in New Orleans, Prince George's County, and Chicago cite the illegal or street market as the most significant potential source for crime guns. The most prevalent transaction type in all jurisdictions was purchase from a street source. Family and friends were also identified as important sources. Most respondents reported purchasing the firearm rather than stealing or borrowing it. Purchases were rarely reported to originate from either gun stores or gun shows across the survey samples. Few respondents reported gun shows as a source; no respondent in New Orleans did so. Gun stores were used in fewer than 20 percent of crime gun transactions. Purchase was the most common method of acquisition, but distribution across stealing, borrowing, and paying varied from jurisdiction to jurisdiction.

CONCLUSIONS

The results of our research, which sought to describe a significant portion of the process of how individuals acquire guns that are used in crimes, especially violent crimes, has led us to focus on the consideration of three related issues: methodological issues in doing this research; descriptive information about criminals' sources of firearms across three jurisdictions that are both similar and vary on a number of characteristics, including levels of gun regulation; and the implications these findings may have for law enforcement efforts to reduce gun violence. We consider these issues with a clear understanding of the limitations of our research but also with the goal of encouraging others to learn from the problems we encountered and our findings to advance this critical research area.

Data Acquisition and Reliability

In two of the three jurisdictions studied, we encountered substantial difficulty in gaining access to the ATF trace data even though the relevant law enforcement agencies had requested their data and supported our research. The ATF is permitted to provide its data to law enforcement agencies for law enforcement purposes, but in two of the jurisdictions they resisted and in the other the data were supplied without delay. The ATF has entered into Memoranda of Understanding with these agencies, authorizing the ATF to approve the release of an agency's data to a third party. The research community should take note of this example and help the ATF understand why researchers working with law enforcement agencies using ATF trace data can yield insights useful to those agencies, policymakers, and the public. Given that our work with these data makes clear that the ATF performs minimal data checks, that law enforcement agencies submit different data with their trace requests, and that the trace results contain errors, concerted effort to improve the quality of trace data is also needed. Greater access will help law enforcement agencies better understand the strategic value of trace results and will help improve their accuracy.

Similarly, in conducting inmate surveys, we encountered considerable difficulties in obtaining inmate cooperation in two of our three jurisdictions. Human subjects committees, the NIJ, and some of the correctional agencies discouraged offering cash incentives to inmates to participate. As a result, without substantial cooperation from correctional personnel, response rates are less than is ideal for good research.

Gun owners have many legitimate concerns about the uses of data acquired for research on guns. However, concern about accessing information that law enforcement agencies have generated for the ATF and that Congress has indicated can be provided to those agencies is not legitimate. Although no one wants to coerce inmates to engage in research that has more than minimal risk, inmates should not be deprived of rewards for participating in less than minimal risk research that would be readily available to others. Without some improvements to the quality of and access to trace data, and better ways to gain information from those engaged in gun violence, we are unlikely to significantly advance our understanding of the acquisition of guns used in crimes.

Jurisdictional Commonalities and Differences
We find numerous similarities and differences in crime gun sources, methods of acquisition, time to recovery, and purchasing patterns across our three jurisdictions. Throughout this article, we have made and examined (but not tested) hypotheses based on the levels of gun regulation across our three jurisdictions because these regulations should have some of the greatest impact on illicit gun use, which is supported by considerable research. Because we do not attempt to causally identify the effect or effects of these gun regulations, however, our findings remain descriptive and open to a number of interpretations. We must rely on future research and methods that allow for causal identification to interpret how much of the differences across jurisdictions are due to gun regulations as opposed to other social and political forces. Because the jurisdictions were selected based on their level of gun regulation, however, we present differences in that regard.

Consistent with existing research, we find that crime guns are more likely to be purchased in-state in low regulation jurisdictions; this finding is reflected in shorter times-to-recovery and probably lower monetary costs, and suggests that more lax regulation is correlated with the likelihood of purchasing guns later recovered in crime from an in-state source. Still, although the rates differ, most crime guns are purchased in-state in all of our jurisdictions.

Our research also makes it clear that most offenders report that the primary source of crime guns is from street sources where a transaction between individuals is the primary mechanism for acquiring guns later recovered. These results differ from those found in Chicago (Cook et al. 2015), reflecting the methodological differences in the sample and survey, but possibly also a greater need to understand inmate responses and behaviors as elicited in surveys. We still do not know the path of the gun from legal purchase to the street.

Implications for Law Enforcement
Law enforcement agencies are only just beginning to understand how the analysis of trace and other data on crime guns can assist them in reducing violent crime. In the three agencies we worked with, routine analysis is limited on trace data that might allow patterns of access including large volume dealers and repeat purchasers of crime guns to be identified. This situation is beginning to change. In 2008, ATF launched the Interstate Trafficking Program, which used trace data from multiple agencies to target law enforcement efforts (Lisko and

Arends 2015). This effort was evaluated by the IACP in 2013. It revealed evidence of the use of trace data but subsequent analysis was infrequent, even in gun fusion centers. The Providence Police Department has recently assigned an officer to trace all guns recovered and to use the trace results and then to track the gun from first legal owner to use in crime (Milkovits 2015). Similar efforts are under way in the Wilmington Police Department. Milwaukee launched a multiagency effort that included analysis of trace results to target enforcement (Horn 2015; Lisko and Arends 2015). These tend to be the exception. Law enforcement agencies continue to be case-focused in the use of trace data rather than strategic.

The similarities across jurisdictions suggest several important implications for law enforcement. First, the purchase of guns later recovered in crime did not often originate from gun stores in any of the jurisdictions we studied in any of our data sources.[33] The same purchaser-possessor relationships in the trace data and the infrequent reports of purchasing a gun at a gun store among inmates and arrestees surveyed suggests that enforcement against illegal gun purchases targeted at gun stores may not be the most effective route for police when other enforcement options are possible. Second, although the trace data cannot corroborate this finding, the proportion of firearms purchased from a gun show was markedly low in every jurisdiction. It is possible that gun shows and similar events play a role in arming individuals who are likely to use a gun in crime by arming not those in prison, but instead potential brokers who sell guns to others. However, the individuals sampled who were incarcerated or in jail for potentially violent offenses involving a gun had not acquired their firearms from gun shows.

Additionally, the importance of street transactions in arming individuals suggests that actions police can take to increase the difficulty of these transactions could be effective in deterring them or increasing the difficulty of their occurrence. That is, operations in which the police seek to deter transactions through purchasing illegal guns in an effort to arrest individuals who sell them would be more attuned to transactions that arm individuals who might use the gun than gun store or gun show enforcement efforts would.

Lack of police emphasis on gun trace data is unfortunate in part because we are beginning to assemble a number of programs that are effective in reducing gun violence if police understand the nature of gun violence, including gun markets, as they deploy their resources. Using these programs, Charles Wellford, Megan Collins, and Carlos Acosta developed a guide for police agencies to address gun violence that includes careful analysis of their trace data (2016). Further developments in the use of trace and survey data by police in part depends on addressing the access issue and improving the data as discussed in this article.

33. In a related project, we interviewed 181 of the original legal purchasers of the guns recovered in violent crimes in New Orleans and Prince George's County. Although our analysis of these data continues, we do note that 41 percent of respondents reported their gun had been stolen and 33 percent reported that they had sold their gun. We were unable to locate 19 percent of this group. No one objected to being interviewed about how their gun left their possession. All of the guns were purchased legally through an FFL.

APPENDIX

Table A1. Alternative Straw Purchaser Operationalizations

	New Orleans			Chicago			Prince George's County		
	Number of Cases	Traced	%	Number of Cases	Traced	%	Number of Cases	Traced	%
Female purchaser, male possessor and pistol or revolver[a]	208	1,461	14.2	862	6,388	13.5	85	813	10.5
In-state purchaser[a,b]	171	206	83.0	279	830	33.6	30	81	37.0
Out-of-state purchaser[a,b]	35	206	17.0	551	830	66.4	51	81	63.0
Less than two years TTR[a,c]	59	207	28.5	153	861	17.7	21	84	25.0
More than two years TTR[a,c]	149	207	72.0	664	861	77.1	64	84	76.2
High-caliber firearm[a,d]	73	208	35.1	183	862	21.2	27	85	31.8
Weapon offense[a,e]	102	208	49.0	688	817	84.2	43	85	50.6
Felon in possession of weapon[a,e]	47	208	22.6	92	817	11.3	N/A	N/A	N/A
Same address, different buyer[f]	N/A	N/A	N/A	170	5,981	2.8	25	832	3.0
Same last name, same address, different buyer[f,g]	N/A	N/A	N/A	92	5,981	1.5	15	832	1.8

Source: Authors' calculations.

[a]Total includes cases not missing information on purchaser or possessor gender or type of weapon.
[b]Total additionally includes cases not missing information on purchaser state.
[c]Total additionally includes cases not missing information on time to recovery.
[d]Total additionally includes cases not missing information on caliber.
[e]Total additionally includes cases not missing information on offense type.
[f]Total includes cases not missing information on purchaser and possessor address.
[g]Total additionally includes cases not missing information on purchaser and possessor last name.

Table A2. Methods of Gun Acquisition

	Violent Offenders (<Two Years Incarcerated)[a] (percentage)	Gun Offenders (<Five Years Incarcerated)[b] (percentage)
I stole it	6.3, n=14	4.7, n=38
I rented it	0.0, n=0	0.5, n=4
I borrowed it from somebody / held it for somebody	18.4, n=41	16.0, n=129
I traded something for it	4.0, n=9	3.6, n=29
I bought it	47.5, n=106	48.0, n=387
It was a gift	9.0, n=20	9.9, n=80
Other	9.4, n=21	9.3, n=75
Don't know, refused	5.4, n=12	7.9, n=64
Total responses	100, n=223	100, n=806

Source: Authors' tabulation based on the National Archive of Criminal Justice Data (Bureau of Justice Statistics 2007).
Note: Data from Survey of Inmates in State and Federal Corrections Facilities (SISCF).
[a] SISCF Sample: Offenders who reported violent offenses (V0729 =1; V0730=1; V0731=1) and who have been incarcerated for less than two years.
[b] SISCF Sample: Offenders who reported carrying a gun at the time of their crime (V1072=1 and V1073=1) who had been incarcerated for less than five years.

Table A3. Sources of Firearms

	Violent Offenders (<Two years incarcerated)[a] N (percent)	Gun Offenders (<Five years incarcerated)[b] N (percent)
From a gun shop or gun store	12.5,, n=27	8.9, n=69
From a pawnshop	2.3,, n=5	3.1, n=24
At a flea market	0.0, n=0	0.3, n=2
At a gun show	1.4, n=3	1.2, n=9
From the victim(s)	3.2, n=7	2.5, n=19
From a friend or family member	39.8, n=86	38.3, n=296
From a fence or black market source	5.1, n=11	5.0, n=39
Off the street or from a drug dealer	22.2, n=48	24.7, n=191
In a burglary	1.4, n=3	1.6, n=12
Other	6.9, n=15	7.4, n=57
Don't know or refused	5.1, n=11	7.1, n=55
Total responses	100, n=216	100, n=773

Source: Authors' tabulation based on the National Archive of Criminal Justice Data (Bureau of Justice Statistics 2007).
Note: Data from Survey of Inmates in State and Federal Corrections Facilities (SISCF).
[a] SISCF Sample: Offenders who reported violent offenses (V0729 =1; V0730=1; V0731=1) and who have been incarcerated for less than two years.
[b] SISCF Sample: Offenders who reported carrying a gun at the time of their crime (V1072=1 and V1073=1) who had been incarcerated for less than five years.

Table A4. Chicago Methods of Firearm Acquisition

Method	Percentage
Buy or trade	61.5, n=83
Borrow or hold	10.4, n=14
Gift	8.9, n=12
Share	7.4, n=10
Steal	1.5, n=2
Unclear	8.9, n=12
Refuse to answer	1.5, n=2
Total	100, n=135

Source: Cook et al. 2015.

Table A5. Chicago Sources of Firearm Acquisition

Source	Percentage
Prior relationship	44.3, n=31
Other connections	21.4, n=23
Gun store	2.9, n=2
Unclear	27.1, n=19
Refuses to answer or NA	4.3, n=3
Total	100, n=70

Source: Cook et al. 2015.

Table A6. Firearms Submitted for Tracing and Available Information

Denominator	New Orleans, 2011–2012	Chicago, 2011–2013	Prince George's County, 2012–2013
1. Total number of guns submitted for tracing	3,068	18,455	2,034
2. All successfully traced crime guns with a purchaser first name, last name, and date of birth	2,269	11,248	1,286
3. Successfully traced crime guns (Denominator 2) with state of first purchase	2,249	11,000	1,272
4. Successfully traced crime guns (Denominator 2) with possessor first name, last name	1,660	7,978	894
5. Successfully traced crime guns (Denominator 2) with possessor first and last name, and purchaser and possessor gender	1,461	7,095	813

Source: Authors' calculations.

REFERENCES

Azrael, Deborah, Phillip J. Cook, and Matthew Miller. 2004. "State and Local Prevalence of Firearms Ownership Measurement, Structure, and Trends." *Journal of Quantitative Criminology* 20(1): 43–62.

Beck, Allen, Darrell Gilliard, Lawrence Greenfeld, Caroline Harlow, Thomas Hester, Louis Jankowski, Tracy Snell, James Stephan, and Danielle Morton. 1993. "Survey of State Prison Inmates, 1991." NCJ-136949. Washington: U.S. Department of Justice, Bureau of Justice Statistics.

Braga, Anthony A. 2017. "Long-Term Trends in the Sources of Boston Crime Guns." *RSF: The Russell Sage Foundation Journal of the Social Sciences* 3(5): 76–95. DOI: 10.7758/RSF.2017.3.5.04.

Braga, Anthony A., Phillip J. Cook, David M. Kennedy, and Mark H. Moore. 2002. "The Illegal Supply of Firearms." *Crime and Justice* 29: 319–52.

Braga, Anthony A., Garen J. Wintemute, Glenn L. Pierce, Phillip J. Cook, and Greg Ridgeway. 2012. "Interpreting the Empirical Evidence on Illegal Gun Market Dynamics." *Journal of Urban Health* 89(5): 779–93.

Bureau of Alcohol, Tobacco and Firearms (ATF). 1992. "Protecting America: The Effectiveness of the Federal Armed Career Criminal Statute." Washington: U.S. Department of Justice. Accessed July 5, 2017. https://www.ncjrs.gov/pdffiles1/ Digitization/137208 NCJRS.pdf.

———. 2000a. "Following the Gun: Enforcing Federal Laws Against Firearms Traffickers." Washington: U.S. Department of Justice. Accessed July 5, 2017. https://www.atf.gov/file/11876/download.

———. 2000b. "Crime Gun Trace Reports (1999)." Washington: U.S. Department of Justice. Accessed July 5, 2017. https://www.atf.gov/resource-center/docs/ycgii-report-1999-highlightspdf-0/download.

Bureau of Alcohol, Tobacco, Firearms and Explosives (ATF). 2015. "Fact Sheet – National Tracing Center." Washington: U.S. Department of Justice. Accessed March 2016. https://www.atf.gov/resource-center/fact-sheet/fact-sheet-national-tracing-center-ntc.

———. 2016. "Fact Sheet – Multiple Firearms Sales or Other Disposition Reporting." Washington: U.S. Department of Justice. Accessed July 7, 2017. https://www.atf.gov/resource-center/fact-sheet/fact-sheet-multiple-firearms-sales-or-other-disposition-reporting.

Bureau of Justice Statistics. 2007. "Survey of Inmates in State and Federal Correctional Facilities, 2004 (ICPSR 4572)." Ann Arbor: University of Michigan, Institute for Social Research. Accessed July 15, 2017. http://www.icpsr.umich.edu/icpsrweb/NACJD/studies/4572?q=ICPSR+4572.

Centers for Disease Control and Prevention (CDC), National Center for Health Statistics. 2016. "Underlying Cause of Death 1999–2015" on CDC Wonder online database, released December 2016, from Multiple Cause of Death files, 1999–2015, Vital Statistics Cooperative Program. Accessed August 15, 2017. https://wonder.cdc.gov/ucd-icd10.html.

Cook, Philip J., and Anthony A. Braga. 2001. "Comprehensive Firearms Tracing: Strategic and Investigative Uses of New Data on Firearms Markets." *Arizona Law Review* 43: 277–309.

Cook, Phillip J., Richard J. Harris, Jens Ludwig, and Harold A. Pollack. 2015. "Some Sources of Crime Guns in Chicago: Dirty Dealers, Straw Purchasers, and Traffickers." *Journal of Criminal Law and Criminology* 104(4): 717–59.

Cook, Phillip J., and Jens Ludwig. 1996. *Guns in America: Results of a Comprehensive National Survey on Firearms Ownership and Use*. Washington, D.C.: Police Foundation.

Cook, Phillip J., Jens Ludwig, Sudhir Venkatesh, and Anthony A. Braga. 2007. "Underground Gun Markets." *Economic Journal* 117: F558–88.

Cook, Phillip J., Susan T. Parker, and Harold A. Pollack. 2015. "Sources of Guns to Dangerous People: What We Learn by Asking Them." *Preventive Medicine* 79(1): 28–36.

Cook, Philip J., and Harold A. Pollack. 2017. "Reducing Access to Guns by Violent Offenders." *RSF: The Russell Sage Foundation Journal of the Social Sciences* 3(5): 1–36. DOI: 10.7758/RSF.2017.3.5.01.

Federal Bureau of Investigation (FBI). 2011. "Crime in the United States 2010." Washington: U.S. Department of Justice. Accessed December 2015. https://www.fbi.gov/about-us/cjis/ucr/crime-in-the.u.s/2010/crime-in-the.u.s.-2010.

———. 2013. "Crime in the United States 2012." Washington: U.S. Department of Justice. Accessed July 5, 2017. https://ucr.fbi.gov/crime-in-the.u.s/2012/crime-in-the.u.s.-2012.

———. 2016. "Crime in the United States 2015." Washington: U.S. Department of Justice. Accessed December 2016. https://ucr.fbi.gov/crime-in-the.u.s/2015/crime-in-the.u.s.-2015.

Gast, Scott. 2005. "Appendix C: Judicial Scrutiny of Challenged Gun Control Regulations: The Implications of an Individual Right Interpretation of the Second Amendment." In *Firearms and Violence: A Critical Review*, ed. Charles F. Wellford, John V. Pepper, and Carol V. Petrie. Washington, D.C.: National Academies Press.

Horn, Brittany. 2015. "Semi-Automatics Key Factor in Wilmington Violence." *Delaware Online*, December 11, 2015. Accessed July 5, 2017. http://www.delawareonline.com/story/news/crime/2015/12/11/semi-automatics-key-factor-wilmington-violence/75169628/.

Kanter, Dan, and Craig Fischer, eds. 2010. "Guns and Crime: Breaking New Ground by Focusing on the Local Impact." Washington, D.C.: Police Executive Research Forum. Accessed July 5, 2017. http://www.policeforum.org/assets/docs/Critical_Issues_Series/guns%20and%20crime%20-%20breaking%20new%20ground%20by%20focusing%20on%20the%20local%20impact%202010.pdf.

Koper, Christopher S. 2014. "Crime Gun Risk Factors: Buyer, Seller, Firearm, and Transaction Characteristics Associated with Gun Trafficking and Criminal Gun Use." *Journal of Quantitative Criminology* 30(2): 285–315.

Koper, Christopher S., and Peter Reuter. 1996. "Suppressing Illegal Gun Markets: Lessons from Drug Enforcement." *Law and Contemporary Problems* 59(1): 119–46.

Law Center to Prevent Gun Violence. 2014. "Annual

Gun Law State Scorecard, 2014." Accessed July 5, 2017. http://gunlawscorecard.org.

Lisko, Richard, and Ross Arends. 2015. "The ATF iTrafficking Program: Integration of Firearms Trace/Ballistic Data into Fusion Center Intelligence Sharing." *Police Chief* 82(1): 50–55.

Mayors Against Illegal Guns. 2010. "Trace the Guns: The Link Between Gun Laws and Interstate Gun Trafficking." Accessed July 5, 2017. https://tracetheguns.org/report.pdf.

Milkovits, Amanda. 2015. "On the Trail of Guns in Providence." *Providence Journal*, November 28. Accessed July 5, 2017. http://www.providencejournal.com/article/20151128/NEWS/151129373.

Moore, Mark H. 1981. "Keeping Handguns from Criminal Offenders." *Annals of the American Academy of Political and Social Science* 455(1): 92–109.

National Institute of Justice (NIJ). 2011. *Firearms and Violence Topical Working Group Meeting Summary 2011*. NCJ 238490. Washington: U.S. Department of Justice. Accessed July 5, 2017. https://www.ncjrs.gov/pdffiles1/nij/238490.pdf.

Pierce, Glenn L., Anthony A. Braga, Raymond R. Hayatt Jr., and Christopher S. Koper. 2004. "Characteristics and Dynamics of Illegal Firearms Markets: Implications for a Supply-Side Enforcement Strategy." *Justice Quarterly* 21(2): 391–422.

Sheley, Joseph F., and James D. Wright. 1993. "Gun Acquisition and Possession in Selected Juvenile Samples." Research in Brief. Washington: U.S. Department of Justice, Office of Justice Programs, National Institute of Justice.

U.S. Census Bureau. 2010. "Profile of General Population by Housing Data." Accessed August 15, 2017. https://factfinder.census.gov/faces/tableservices/jsf/pages/productview.xhtml?src=cf.

Vittes, Katherine A., Jon S. Vernick, and Daniel W. Webster. 2012. "Legal Status and Source of Offenders' Firearms in States with the Least Stringent Criteria for Gun Ownership." *Injury Prevention* 19(1): 26–31.

Wachtel, Julius. 1998. "Sources of Crime Guns in Los Angeles, California." *Policing: An International Journal of Police Strategies & Management* 21(2): 220–39.

Webster, Daniel W., Lorraine H. Freed, Shannon Frattaroli, and Modena H. Wilson. 2002. "How Delinquent Youths Acquire Guns: Initial Versus Most Recent Gun Acquisitions." *Journal of Urban Health* 79(1): 60–69.

Webster, Daniel W., Jon S Vernick, and Lisa M. Hepburn. 2001. "Relationship Between Licensing, Registration, and Other Gun Sales Laws and the Source State of Crime Guns." *Injury Prevention* 7(3): 184–89.

Weil, Douglas S., and Rebecca C. Knox. 2016. "Effects of Limiting Handgun Purchases on Interstate Transfer of Firearms." *Journal of the American Medical Association* 275(22): 1759–61.

Wellford, Charles F., Megan E. Collins, and Carlos F. Acosta. 2016. "Policing Gun Violence: What Works?" *Police Chief Magazine,* May. Accessed July 5, 2017. http://www.policechiefmagazine.org/policing-gun-violence-what-works/.

Wellford, Charles F., John Pepper, and Carol Petrie, eds. 2005. *Firearms and Violence: A Critical Review*. Committee to Improve Research and Information on Firearms. Washington, D.C.: National Academies Press.

Wintemute, Garen. 2010. "Firearm Retailers' Willingness to Participate in an Illegal Gun Purchase." *Journal of Urban Health* 87(5): 865–78.

———. 2017. "Firearms Licensee Characteristics Associated with Sales of Crime-Involved Firearms and Denied Sales: Findings from the Firearms Licensee Survey." *RSF: The Russell Sage Foundation Journal of the Social Sciences* 3(5): 58–74. DOI: 10.7758/RSF.2017.3.5.03.

Wright, James D., and Peter H. Rossi. 1994. *Armed and Considered Dangerous: A Survey of Felons and their Firearms*. Hawthorne, N.Y.: Aldine de Gruyter.

Wright, Mona A., Garen J. Wintemute, and Daniel W. Webster. 2010. "Factors Affecting a Recently Purchased Handgun's Risk for Use in Crime Under Circumstances That Suggest Gun Trafficking." *Journal of Urban Health* 87(3): 352–64.

The Initial Impact of Maryland's Firearm Safety Act of 2013 on the Supply of Crime Handguns in Baltimore

CASSANDRA K. CRIFASI, SHANI A.L. BUGGS, SEEMA CHOKSY, AND DANIEL W. WEBSTER

This study assesses the impact of Maryland's Firearm Safety Act (FSA) of 2013 on indicators of diversion of handguns to prohibited persons. Interrupted time-series analyses were conducted, and the findings were supplemented by results from a survey of men on parole and probation regarding Baltimore's underground gun market. The FSA was associated with an 82 percent reduction in police recovery of handguns with strong indicators of diversion (IRR=0.18, p=.005). Forty-one percent of survey respondents reported having more difficulty getting a handgun after the FSA because of increased cost, lack of trusted sources, or people less willing to engage in straw purchases on their behalf. These findings are consistent with the theory that the FSA reduces the diversion of handguns into the underground market.

Keywords: underground market, gun policy, diversion

The potential effectiveness of gun sales laws rests not only on individuals at high risk of committing harm with guns being prohibited from purchasing or possessing guns, but also on how well the laws prevent the diversion of guns to prohibited persons. Various laws have been put in place to prevent the diversion of guns to prohibited persons. The foundation of these laws includes requirements that purchasers pass background checks and sellers maintain records of purchaser information, dates of sale, and the specifics of the guns, including serial numbers. These requirements allow law enforcement to trace guns they recover from criminal suspects or crime scenes to the original retail sale and, in some cases, even subsequent sales.

Research demonstrates that laws designed to prevent such diversion by increasing the accountability of gun sellers and buyers are as-

Cassandra K. Crifasi is assistant professor of health policy and management at the Johns Hopkins Bloomberg School of Public Health and a core faculty member in the Center for Gun Policy and Research. **Shani A.L. Buggs** is a doctoral candidate in the Department of Health Policy and Management at the Johns Hopkins Bloomberg School of Public Health. **Seema Choksy** was senior research program coordinator for the Johns Hopkins Center for Gun Policy and Research. **Daniel W. Webster** is professor of health policy and management at the Johns Hopkins Bloomberg School of Public Health and director of the Center for Gun Policy and Research.

© 2017 Russell Sage Foundation. Crifasi, Cassandra K., Shani A.L. Buggs, Seema Choksy, and Daniel W. Webster. 2017. "The Initial Impact of Maryland's Firearm Safety Act of 2013 on the Supply of Crime Handguns in Baltimore." *RSF: The Russell Sage Foundation Journal of the Social Sciences* 3(5): 128–40. DOI: 10.7758 /RSF.2017.3.5.06. Funding for this research was provided by grants from the Raab Foundation and Everytown for Gun Safety to the Johns Hopkins Center for Gun Policy and Research. Direct correspondence to: Cassandra K. Crifasi at crifasi@jhu.edu, 624 N Broadway, Rm 593, Baltimore, MD 21205; Shani A.L. Buggs at sbuggs1@jhu .edu, 624 N Broadway, Rm 586, Baltimore, MD 21205; Seema Choksy at schoksy1@jhu.edu, 624 N Broadway, Baltimore, MD 21205; and Daniel W. Webster at dwebster@jhu.edu, 624 N Broadway, Rm 580, Baltimore, MD 21205.

sociated with lower levels of guns diverted to prohibited persons in cross-sectional studies. These laws include permit-to-purchase (PTP) laws for handguns, the extension of background check requirements to gun transfers between private parties, mandatory reporting of lost or stolen guns by owners, and strong regulation and oversight of licensed gun dealers (Webster, Vernick, and Bulzacchelli 2009; Webster et al. 2013; Pierce, Braga, and Wintemute 2015).

Current federal laws include many weaknesses that allow guns to be diverted to prohibited persons with relatively little risk to sellers (Webster and Wintemute 2015). Many states have passed laws that attempt to address deficiencies in federal law by extending background checks and record-keeping requirements—and in some cases gun theft reporting requirements—to transfers made by private gun owners. Nine states and the District of Columbia also have some form of licensing system for handgun purchasers that outlaws the transfer of a handgun to anyone who does not have a valid PTP. Because scofflaw retail gun dealers can potentially divert large quantities of guns to criminals over time, and federal law and oversight are somewhat weak, some states also have their own regulation of licensed gun dealers.

Studies of the diversion of guns for criminal use necessarily rely on crime gun trace data from the Bureau of Alcohol, Tobacco, Firearms and Explosives (ATF). These data provide information on the state of retail sale, state of crime involvement, whether the retail purchaser and the criminal possessor were the same person, and the dates the guns were first sold and then recovered by law enforcement. These dates allow ATF to generate a time-to-crime (TTC) for traced guns. The national average TTC for traced guns in 2015 was 10.48 years; Maryland's was 12.39 years (ATF 2016a). A gun recovered within one year of retail sale indicates to law enforcement that the gun was likely purchased with the intent of diverting that gun to a prohibited person (ATF 2002). The use of crime gun trace data to evaluate the diversion of guns to prohibited persons has gained increasing research support and validity, and supply-side constraints, such as requiring a PTP for handgun purchasers, are associated with reduced likelihood of the diversion of guns (Braga et al. 2012; Webster, Vernick, and Hepburn 2001).

Because most of the relevant laws have been in place for decades and few cities consistently traced the origins of the guns they recovered in crime before the late 1990s, opportunities to examine whether changes in these laws result in changes in indicators of diversion of guns for criminal use have been limited. Recent studies of changes in PTP handgun laws in Connecticut, which implemented its law along with universal background check requirements in 1995, and Missouri, which repealed its PTP law in 2007, provide evidence that these laws reduced criminal access to guns and homicides committed with guns. Using analytic methods to create so-called synthetic controls for Connecticut's gun and nongun homicide rates to estimate counterfactuals for the first ten years following the implementation of the law requiring background checks and PTP for all handgun purchases, researchers estimated that the law was associated with a 40 percent reduction in gun homicide rates over the first ten years it was in place (Rudolph et al. 2015). A separate study estimated that Missouri's repeal of its PTP law was associated with a 14 percent increase in murders during the first five full years after the law's repeal, with the effects specific to events involving guns (Webster, Crifasi, and Vernick 2014). Missouri's repeal of its PTP handgun law was also followed by a twofold increase in the percentage of crime guns with very short intervals between retail sale and crime involvement and a large increase in the share of crime guns from sales originating within Missouri versus other states (Webster et al. 2013). Another study provides evidence that the repeal was associated with increased risk of law enforcement officers being shot in the line of duty in ways consistent with PTP laws being protective against criminal gun use (Crifasi, Pollack, and Webster 2015).

In 1996, Maryland enacted a law that made all handgun transfers, including those made by a private seller, contingent on the purchaser passing a background check. In 2013, Maryland lawmakers enacted the Firearm Safety Act (FSA), which has multiple components that could potentially reduce diversion of guns into the hands of prohibited persons. These include requiring a PTP for anyone purchasing a handgun from either a licensed gun dealer or a private owner, expanding authority for state police to act against gun dealers found to have violated state gun sales laws (such as fines or license suspension or revocation), and mandating that gun owners report within seventy-two hours any theft or loss of a regulated gun. Additionally, the FSA bans the sale of assault rifles, limits magazine size to ten rounds, and bars persons who receive probation before judgment for violent crimes from possessing guns.

The PTP provision requires prospective purchasers to obtain a license issued by Maryland State Police, contingent on their passing a background check and completing a four-hour safety training course conducted by an approved and registered instructor. Individuals who were registered handgun owners before the FSA went into effect are exempt from the safety training requirement. Applicants for the license must also be fingerprinted during the application process by certified vendors that submit digital images of the prints to the Maryland State Police.

This article assesses the impact of Maryland's FSA of 2013 on the underground gun market in Baltimore. We analyzed data from handguns recovered by police and submitted for tracing to assess whether the new law was associated with fewer crime handguns recovered shortly after a retail sale from someone other than the retail purchaser, and an increase in the number of recovered crime handguns initially purchased in other states. To assess the perceived impact of the FSA on the underground gun market, we supplemented the analysis of crime handgun trace data with a qualitative evaluation of knowledge of the FSA and the perception among individuals prohibited from purchasing or possessing guns—Baltimore City residents currently on parole or probation—of changes in gun accessibility following the implementation of the FSA.

METHODS

Data on guns recovered by police and submitted for tracing were obtained from the Baltimore Police Department (BPD) for the period from January 1, 2007, through September 30, 2015. When a gun trace was successful, the data included information on original sale date and purchaser, recovery date, possessor, and the type of incident in which the gun was recovered. Gun trace data were excluded from our analyses if the incident in which the gun was recovered was recorded as "found/recovered property" or as "safe-keeping/turn in/buyback." Such weapons were excluded so that only guns recovered in a crime were included in the dependent variable, making the analysis as specific as possible in testing the law's effect on the diversion of guns to criminals. Additionally, because most guns used in crime are handguns, and the FSA specifically licenses handgun purchasers, analyses were restricted to handguns.

We obtained data from Maryland State Police by month and year on the number of gun registration applications approved during the study period to have a proxy measure for the number of handguns also at risk for diversion to the underground gun market during the month and year a crime handgun was sold.

Because of legal restrictions on the sharing of crime gun trace data, simply no data are available at this granular level to generate an appropriate city-level comparison. The only available data are state-level reports of crime gun recoveries published by ATF; these reports, however, do not distinguish between types of guns (handgun or long gun), and they do not provide information on source state for short TTC guns, on whether the criminal possessor was the original purchaser, or in what month the gun was sold. These data elements are key to evaluating the effect of the FSA on the diversion of guns into the underground market. Thus, though we do present some state-level descriptive data, our time-series analyses are restricted to crime handguns recovered by police in Baltimore City and submitted for tracing.

Analytic Methods

We used an interrupted time-series design to test whether any changes were significant in key indicators of handgun trafficking or diversion of handguns for criminal purposes coincident with the implementation of the FSA on October 1, 2013. Similar to studies on gun trafficking or diversions of guns to individuals who used those guns in crime, ours examined two trafficking indicators—short TTC following a retail sale and the percentage of crime guns initially sold by out-of-state retailers.

We used four outcomes with monthly time series: the number of handguns originally sold in Maryland with a TTC of less than one year; the number of handguns originally sold in Maryland with a TTC of less than one year and the criminal possessors were not the purchasers of record; the number of handguns originally sold by out-of-state gun dealers; and the number of handguns originally sold by out-of-state gun dealers and the criminal possessors were not the purchasers of record.

For the less than one year TTC outcomes, observations were based on the month the handgun was sold, which enabled us to categorize whether a handgun used in crime had been sold under FSA rules. Measures that involved handguns recovered from someone other than the lawful purchaser allowed for a direct assessment of the FSA's effect on the diversion of handguns for criminal purposes. Our hypothesis was that the FSA would be associated with reductions in measures of guns that originated in Maryland. If that proved true, we hypothesized a modest increase in measures of guns originating outside of Maryland as individuals seeking handguns for criminal use pursued alternatives to new handguns originating from retail sales in Maryland.

Interrupted time-series analyses were performed on crime handgun trace data to discern whether the implementation of the FSA was associated with changes in the outcomes described above. Negative binomial regression models were used due to overdispersion in the data (likelihood ratio test of alpha=0, $p<.05$). We controlled for baseline trends in the outcome variables in two ways, with year fixed effects and a linear trend term. Indicator variables for calendar month were evaluated for inclusion to adjust for potential seasonality in the outcome variables.

The number of less than one year TTC handguns recovered by police may be influenced by policing practices that vary over time with respect to the degree to which arrests for illegal gun possession are prioritized. Therefore, we controlled for variation in the mean number of all handguns recovered by the BPD during the twelve months following a sales month observation, t. Because of the short observation period following the law's implementation and the truncated follow-up period such that handguns sold after October 1, 2014, have less than one year in which they would be at risk of recovery by the BPD, we included a covariate to measure exposure for the number of months a handgun was at risk of being recovered in a crime.

Because of the limited control variables available, and the lack of an appropriate comparison jurisdiction with the same granular-level crime gun trace data, we evaluated our data's pre-intervention stationarity using autoregressive integrated moving average modeling. The autoregressive component to our outcome variables was significant; however, the inclusion of monthly gun recoveries accounted for the lack of stationarity and made the autoregressive component nonsignificant. We were therefore confident in our use of an interrupted time-series model with negative binomial regression controlling for monthly crime gun recoveries.

We also ran the models with and without a control for the number of gun registration applications approved during the month of a crime handgun's sale that originated in Maryland. An argument can be made for excluding approved gun applications from the regression models because it could partly mediate the effect of the FSA on handguns diverted for criminal use and bias estimates of the full effect of the new policies. We therefore present findings with and without controls for changes in the volume of gun purchase applications.

The estimated effects from the interrupted time-series analyses are presented as incident rate ratios (IRR) with 95 percent confidence intervals. Analyses were conducted using Stata IC version 14.2 (StataCorp 2015).

Survey Methods

To assess awareness and perceived impact of the FSA among persons legally prohibited from purchasing or possessing guns, we included four FSA-specific questions in a multipart survey designed to appraise gun availability in the underground gun market in Baltimore. Using a convenience sampling methodology, we administered the survey in May and June 2016 to 195 men on parole or probation in Baltimore. The selection was to identify persons with recent interaction with the criminal justice system that would prohibit them from purchasing or possessing a gun under Maryland state law.

Survey respondents were recruited outside parole and probation offices in Baltimore. Men who asserted that they were over the age of eighteen, currently on parole or probation, and Baltimore residents were invited to complete the survey after eligibility was determined via screening questions. All participants were anonymous volunteers. If an individual met the eligibility criteria and was interested in participating, research assistants escorted him to a semiprivate location where he received additional information and specific instructions about the study.

Both the informed consent process and the survey were self-administered using a closed-ended computerized survey instrument with audio assistance to ensure confidentiality and prevent issues of low literacy from affecting participation. This methodology allowed for uniform and anonymous collection of data related to the underground gun market that would be otherwise difficult to obtain. Research assistants, who were trained in participant recruitment, supervised the survey completion and provided technical assistance when needed. The survey process took approximately thirty minutes. The four survey items specifically related to the FSA asked whether respondents perceived that the new law affected the following factors:

- the difficulty of obtaining a gun generally,
- the cost of a gun,
- the willingness of another individual to buy a gun on the respondent's behalf (a straw purchaser), and
- the ease of finding a trusted source that would sell a gun to the respondent.

A respondent who answered yes, to indicate that the law made it more difficult to obtain a gun, was presented with a narrative text box to provide detail on how the law made obtaining a gun more difficult. This study was approved by the Johns Hopkins Institutional Review Board.

RESULTS
The results are comprised of an analysis of BPD's crime gun trace data and surveys of prohibited purchasers in Baltimore City.

Crime Gun Trace Data
Over the study period, BPD submitted 21,546 guns for tracing. Of these, 6,520 were found guns or guns turned in by citizens and 5,476 were rifles or shotguns; these categories were excluded from the analysis. Data for 11,462 handguns that were connected to a criminal suspect, crime scene, or criminal investigation were submitted for tracing. More than half (55.6 percent) of the handguns were recovered in arrests for illegal handgun possession; 20.3 percent were recovered in drug-related arrests; and 17.8 percent were connected to some type of violent crime (see table 1).

Table 2 shows, by year, the total crime handguns recovered by BPD as well as the number and percentage that could be traced to the state of original retail sale. The number of handguns recovered and submitted for tracing declined through the study period. The proportion of handguns recovered by BPD that originated in Maryland hovered around 45 percent from 2007 to 2012, but declined gradually starting in 2013.

During the study period, Maryland State Police processed and approved 441,882 gun registration applications. Figure 1 presents the trend for the number of approved applications per month. A sharp increase occurred in late 2012, followed by a huge spike in purchase applications just before FSA implementation.

Figure 2 depicts a three-month moving average of the number of handguns that originated in Maryland and were recovered within one year of retail sale when the purchaser was someone other than the criminal possessor. The monthly count of crime handguns diverted within a year of retail sale hovered around a mean of two from 2009 through the first half of 2013 and then spiked in the third quarter of 2013, just before the FSA went into effect. The indicator then fell to less than one

Table 1. Handguns Recovered, January 2007 to September 2015

Crime Category	Number (n=11,462)	Percentage with Offense Type Listed (n=11,131)
Assault	910	8.2
Carjacking	48	0.4
Illegal discharge of firearm	67	0.6
Discharge (police involved)	15	0.1
Domestic assault	15	0.1
Drug related	2,252	20.3
Handgun violation	6,191	55.6
Homicide or attempted homicide	289	2.6
Homicide or attempt (police involved)	33	0.3
Nonfatal shooting/attempt	584	5.2
Nonfatal shooting or attempt (police involved)	97	0.9
Property crime	106	1.0
Questionable death	49	0.4
Rape/sex offense	15	0.1
Other	166	1.5
Missing	331	

Source: Authors' calculations based on Baltimore Police Department crime gun trace data.

Table 2. Crime-Involved Handguns Recovered, January 2007 to September 2015

Year	Total Recovered: n	Traced to State of Retail Sale: n (percent)
2007	1,527	1,193 (78)
2008	1,383	1,046 (76)
2009	1,370	1,082 (79)
2010	1,308	1,027 (79)
2011	1,243	976 (79)
2012	1,202	1,012 (84)
2013	1,162	915 (79)
2014	1,238	929 (75)
2015[a]	1,029	845 (82)
Total	11,462	9,025

Source: Authors' calculations based on Baltimore Police Department crime gun trace data.
[a] Data through September 2015.

per month after the FSA went into effect on October 1, 2013 (see figure 2). Overall, the mean number of handguns per month with TTC of less than one year for the retail sales period before the FSA was 6.0 (SD=3.31), dropped to 2.58 (SD=1.08) during the first twelve months the FSA was in effect, and then increased to 4.25 (SD=2.25) for the period between October 2014 and September 2015.

The results from the regression analyses are consistent with the hypothesis that the FSA would be protective against the diversion of guns into the underground market for criminal use (see table 3). For all handguns originally sold in Maryland that were recovered within one year of retail sale, the IRR for the FSA is 0.33 ($p=.001$), which translates to a 67 percent decline in this outcome. The FSA was associ-

Figure 1. Firearm Registration Applications Approved in Maryland

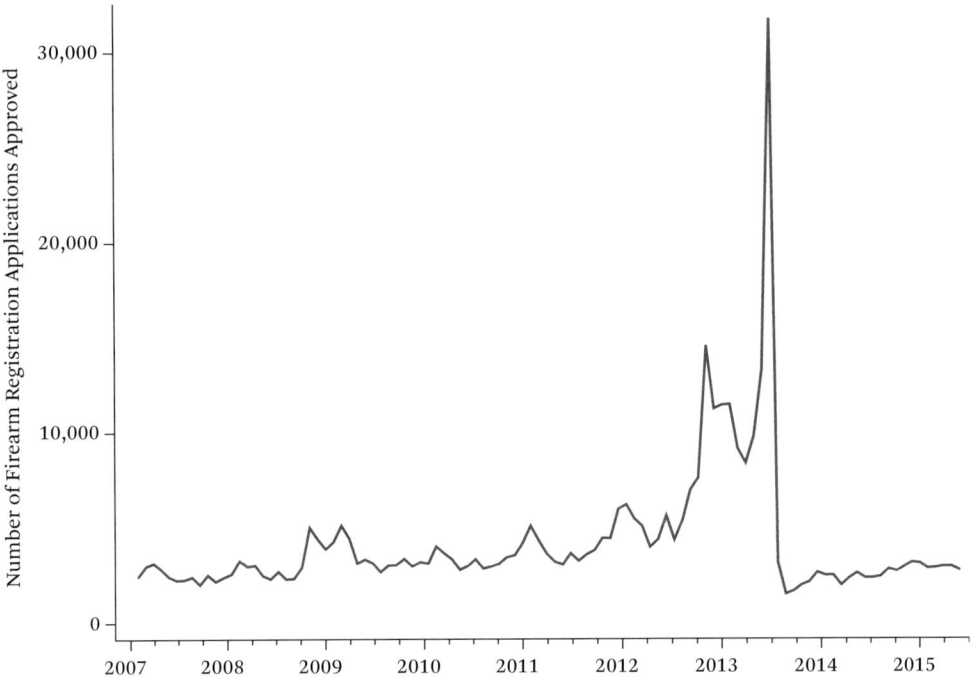

Source: Authors' calculations based on Baltimore Police Department crime gun trace data.

Figure 2. Handguns Sold in Maryland and Recovered in Criminal Incidents

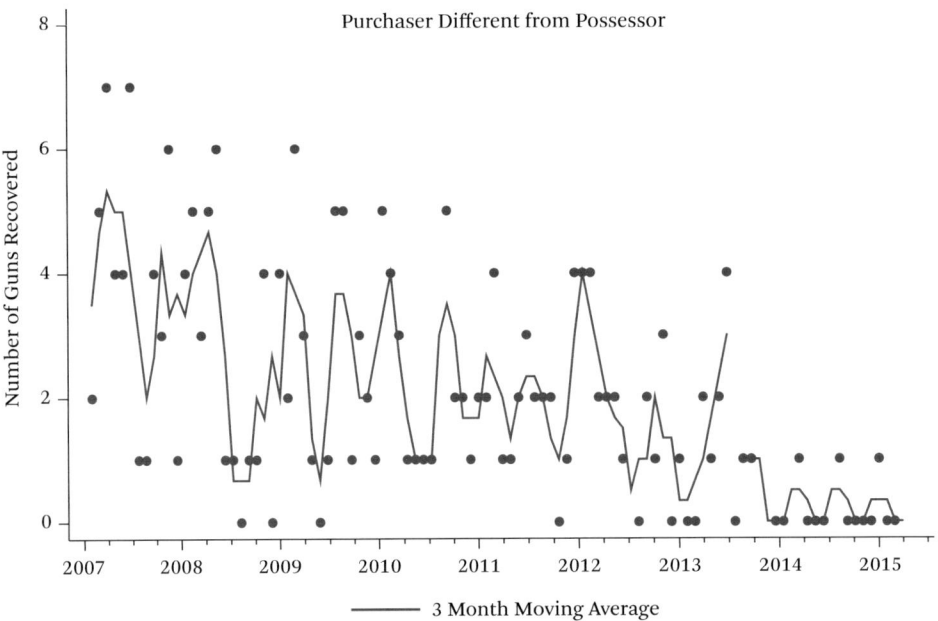

Source: Authors' calculations based on Baltimore Police Department crime gun trace data.
Note: Within one year of retail sale, purchaser different from possessor.

Table 3. Estimated Effects of Maryland's Firearm Safety Act

Dependent Variable	FSA IRR (95 percent CI)	Overall Crime Gun Recoveries IRR (95 percent CI)	Linear Trend IRR (95 percent CI)
Guns sold in Maryland and recovered within one year of retail sale	0.33* (0.17 to 0.64)	1.03* (1.00 to 1.05)	1.00 (0.99 to 1.01)
Guns sold in Maryland and recovered within one year of retail sale and purchaser different from possessor	0.18* (0.05 to 0.60)	1.02 (0.99 to 1.06)	0.99 (0.98 to 1.01)
Guns sold outside Maryland	1.20 (0.61 to 2.37)	0.996* (0.99 to 1.00)	Year fixed effects used
Guns sold outside Maryland and purchaser different from possessor	1.13 (0.53 to 2.45)	0.996* (0.99 to 1.00)	Year fixed effects used

Source: Authors' calculations based on Baltimore Police Department crime gun trace data.
*$p < .05$

Table 4. Estimated Effects of Maryland's Firearm Safety Act, Controlling for Volume

Dependent Variable	FSA IRR (95 percent CI, p)	Overall Crime Gun Recoveries IRR (95 percent CI, p)	Total MD Firearm Registration Applications Approved IRR (95 percent CI, p)	Linear Trend IRR 95 percent CI, p)
Guns sold in Maryland and recovered within one year of retail sale	0.41* (0.20 to 0.82)	1.02 (1.00 to 1.05)	1.00 (1.00 to 1.00)	0.99 (0.98 to 1.00)
Guns sold in Maryland and recovered within one year of retail sale and purchaser different from possessor	0.24* (0.069 to 0.84)	1.02 (0.98 to 1.05)	1.00 (1.00 to 1.00)	0.99 (0.97 to 1.00)

Source: Authors' calculations based on Baltimore Police Department crime gun trace data.
*$p < .05$

ated with an 82 percent reduction in the number of handguns originally sold in Maryland that were recovered within one year of retail sale and the purchaser was not the same as the possessor (IRR=.18, p=.005); this is a key indicator that a gun was purchased with the intent of diverting it for criminal use.

Controlling for the volume of gun registration applications approved in the month of a crime gun's sale (that is, how many handguns were at risk of being diverted for criminal purposes at the time a crime handgun was sold) did not remarkably affect the magnitude or significance of the estimates for the FSA (see table 4). After controlling for pre-FSA trend, the estimated increase in the number of handguns recovered by police that were originally sold outside of Maryland was 20 percent but was not statistically significant (see table 3).

Figure 3 depicts the percent of guns (includes handguns and long guns) recovered in crime within one year of retail sale that were

Figure 3. In-State Crime Guns Sold Within Year of Crime

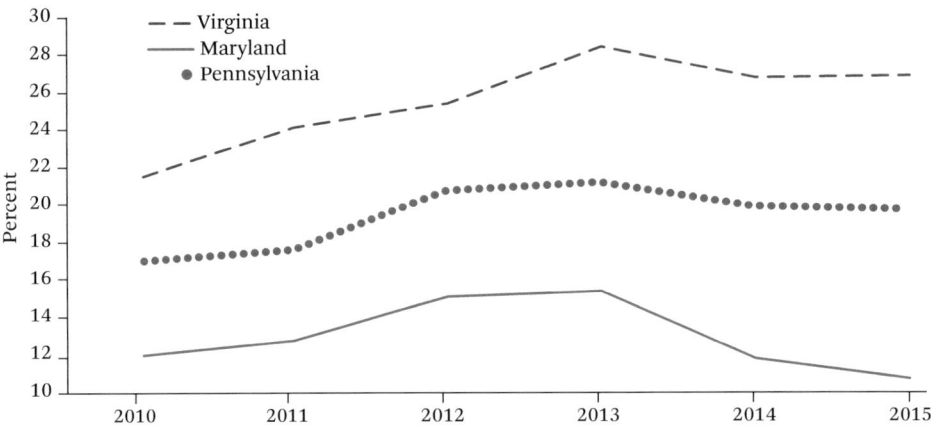

Source: Authors' calculations based on ATF 2016a.

originally sold in the state of recovery for Maryland, Pennsylvania, and Virginia. These numbers are not to the same granular level as that of the time series for Baltimore City. The state-level data do not differentiate between type of gun and do not contain information on whether the purchaser was the criminal possessor or the month of sale. All three states were on an upward trajectory for the percentage of in-state crime guns with a TTC of less than one year. However, after 2013, although the indicators for Pennsylvania and Virginia leveled off, Maryland saw a 30 percent decline (see figure 3). This data provides further support to the hypothesis that the FSA reduced the diversion of guns into the underground market.

Parolee-Probationer Surveys
In May and June 2016, we fielded an audio-assisted computer-based survey of men on parole and probation in Baltimore. Our research teams approached 448 men and screened 251 for eligibility (55 percent). Of those who were screened, 216 were eligible to participate and 195 completed the survey on their experiences with the underground gun market in Baltimore (91 percent).

Individuals completing the survey reported significant experiences with gun violence and the underground gun market. Sixty-three percent had been shot at one or more times in their lives, 48 percent had been shot at multiple times. Of the 122 men who had been shot at, 43 percent had suffered gunshot wounds (see table 5). The most common reasons respondents had been most recently jailed were related to violence (32 percent) or drugs (28 percent).

Of the 195 respondents, 41 percent stated that it was more difficult to obtain a gun after the passage of the FSA (see table 6). Forty percent perceived that the new gun law affected the cost of guns in the underground market. In referencing how the FSA affected cost, respondents stated that, for instance, the law "made guns more expensive." The law was also perceived to have affected access to individuals willing to purchase guns on behalf of the survey respondents (34 percent) and access to a trusted source who would sell guns to the respondents (25 percent) (see table 6). Respondents made comments related to the difficulty of finding trusted sources such as "u [sic] have to have a permit" or "cause you don't always know the person thats [sic] selling the gun."

DISCUSSION
Several components of Maryland's Firearm Safety Act of 2013—a handgun purchaser licensing requirement, mandatory lost or stolen gun reporting by gun owners, and stronger regulation of retail gun dealers—were designed principally to prevent the diversion of handguns to prohibited persons and those seeking to acquire guns for criminal purposes. Findings from the analysis of handguns recov-

Table 5. Demographic Characteristics of Survey Respondents

Demographics	N=195	Percent
Age (mean [range])	38.7 (19–69)	
Race (n=179)		
African American	144	80
White	23	13
Multiracial	12	7
Relationship status (n=192)		
Never married	153	80
Married	19	10
Previously married	20	10
Currently employed (n=192)		
No	142	74
Yes	50	26
Education (n=191)		
Middle school	17	9
High school	95	49
GED	42	22
Some college	29	15
Associate's degree or higher	8	4
Ever shot at (n=192)		
Never	70	37
Once	28	15
Multiple times	91	48
Ever hit when shot at (n=122)		
Yes	53	43
No	69	57
Last six months, ever carried or used a gun		
Did not carry or use a gun	130	67
Carried but not used	34	17
Pointed or shown gun	6	3
Fired in the air	7	4
Fired at an individual	6	3
Other	12	6

Source: Authors' calculations based on underground gun market survey.

ered by Baltimore police are consistent with the theory that the FSA suppressed diversions of guns for criminal use. Indeed, the FSA was associated with an 82 percent reduction in the risk of a handgun being recovered from a criminal possessor who was not the retail purchaser less than twelve months after its retail sale in Maryland. The data suggest that the new legislation, most probably the licensing requirement for handgun purchasers, may have also contributed to a reduction in the number of legal purchasers subsequently involved in a crime with the gun. In further support of the theory that the FSA reduced diversion of handguns into the underground gun market, Maryland saw a 30 percent reduction in in-state handguns recovered in crime less than a year after retail sale. Pennsylvania and Virginia,

Table 6. Baltimore Underground Gun Market Survey Respondents' Perceptions of the Impact of Maryland's Firearm Safety Act.

Survey Question	N=192	Percent
Have the new laws made it more difficult to get a gun?		
Yes	79	41
No	104	54
Don't know	6	3
Refuse to answer	3	2
Have the laws affected the cost?		
Yes	77	40
No	102	53
Don't know	9	5
Refuse to answer	4	2
Have the laws affected the willingness of someone to buy a gun on your behalf?		
Yes	66	34
No	106	55
Don't know	15	8
Refuse to answer	5	3
Have the laws affected how easy it is to find someone you trust to sell you a gun? (n=191)		
Yes	48	25
No	129	68
Don't know	11	6
Refuse to answer	3	2

Source: Authors' calculations based on underground gun market survey.

neighboring states that did not change their laws, did not see a similar decline.

Forty percent of the survey respondents, who were prohibited under Maryland law from legally purchasing or possessing guns, reported that the new law made it more difficult to get guns. More than 30 percent indicated that the law affected the willingness of other individuals to purchase guns on behalf of the respondents. Additionally, 25 percent reported that the law affected the ease of finding a trusted source who would sell guns to the respondents. This is an important factor in the underground gun market. The ability to find a trusted source, or to continue trusting a previously used source, can greatly influence a prohibited individual's ability to acquire a gun (Cook, Parker, and Pollack 2015). Respondents in our survey, when asked how the law made it more difficult to find a trusted source, said that they did not know whether they could trust the person or they were wary that the gun might have been stolen. Additionally, when asked how the law affected the willingness of a person to purchase a gun on the respondent's behalf, several respondents stated that purchasers now must have a permit and that laws are in place against straw purchases. These survey data, in conjunction with the analysis of the crime gun trace data, suggest that Maryland's FSA is reducing the diversion of guns to persons prohibited from legally acquiring or possessing them.

Although survey results indicate a possible deterrent effect of Maryland's FSA on access to guns among the prohibited persons interviewed, it is not possible from this study to statistically estimate an impact of the law on overall prohibited access to and use of guns. A shift toward a greater share of crime handguns from out of state following enactment of the FSA, however, might signal some degree of scarcity of handguns from local sources in Baltimore's underground market. As an example, federal and local law enforcement announced the arrest of a gun trafficking ring in December 2015 that was allegedly bringing thirty guns per week from Tennessee, where gun sales laws are much weaker than in Maryland, to gangs in Baltimore (Anderson 2015).

Additionally, the share of Baltimore crime handguns from states other than Maryland did increase steadily each year from 55 percent in 2012 (last full year before the FSA) to 64 percent through the first three quarters of 2015. The point estimate from our regression analysis indicated a 20 percent increase in out-of-state crime handguns recovered in Baltimore coincident with the FSA, but the change was not statistically significant. However, the nearly two-thirds of crime handguns in Baltimore traced to original out-of-state retail sales in 2015 further support the existence of notable constraints in the local supply lines to Baltimore's underground gun market (ATF 2016a).

The limited crime gun trace data publicly released by ATF greatly hampers the ability to draw conclusions about the effects of gun sales regulations, especially when juxtaposed against what our research team could do with the granular crime gun data used for this study, as well as in studies by other researchers using gun-level crime gun trace data supplied by local police (Cook et al. 2007; Cook et al. 2014). Discussions of the restrictions Congress has placed on access to ATF's crime gun trace data often focus on limiting law enforcement access and accountability of gun sellers, but these restrictions also hinder research that can inform gun policy decisions and enforcement efforts (Webster et al. 2012).

Although our analyses controlled for the overall number of crime guns being recovered by BPD and general baseline trends in the outcomes, as well as monthly gun registration application approvals before and after passage of the FSA, we did not have monthly handgun sales data to accurately measure and control for exposure risk for the number of handguns sold in each month. However, one way the FSA provisions may affect the rate of crime involvement of handguns sold in Maryland is in decreasing sales volume.

An important historical confounder we could not control for was the uprising and civil unrest in April 2015 following the death of Freddie Gray, who died of injuries sustained in a BPD van after being arrested. The unrest was followed initially by a decrease in arrests, including a decline in handgun violations, and a historically steep rise in homicides and nonfatal shootings. Weapon arrests subsequently increased and the rate of increase of homicides and shootings slowed (Morgan and Pally 2016). These events likely influenced Baltimore residents' purchases of handguns and the probability that police would arrest someone for illegally carrying or using a handgun during the last five months of the study period, which could influence the relationship between the FSA and recovery of crime guns. Additionally, although this is a longitudinal study, the lack of an appropriate comparison group limits our ability to draw causal inference regarding the effect of the FSA on Baltimore's underground gun market.

In the future, additional years of post-FSA data should be examined to assess whether the ratio of in-state to out-of-state source crime guns continues to trend toward more out-of-state crime guns. When Missouri repealed its handgun purchaser licensing law in 2007, the share of in-state to out-of-state crime guns shifted gradually but steadily over time, such that in-state crime guns rose from 56 percent during 2006 to 74 percent in 2014 (ATF 2016b). This increase coincided with an increase in gun homicide rates and police officers shot in the line of duty, suggesting that laws somewhat similar to the FSA affect criminal access to and use of guns (on rate change, Webster et al. 2014; on officers killed, Crifasi, Pollack, and Webster 2015).

This study offers an evaluation of the impact of the FSA both on indicators of diversion of handguns for criminal purposes and perceptions of the law's impact on the underground market by those prohibited from purchasing or possessing guns. The FSA appears to have constrained the local supply of illegal handguns in Baltimore. Fewer handguns were being recovered with indicators of diversion (short TTC and a different purchaser and possessor), and prohibited purchasers in Baltimore (men on parole or probation) reported increased difficulty in obtaining guns. These findings are consistent with previous literature evaluating the effect of state laws designed to reduce diversion of guns to criminals.

REFERENCES

Anderson, Jessica. 2015. "Authorities Announce Arrests in Illegal Gun Operation Between Tennessee and Baltimore." *Baltimore Sun*, December 22.

Braga, Anthony A., Garen J. Wintemute, Glenn L. Pierce, Philip J. Cook, and Greg Ridgeway. 2012. "Interpreting the Empirical Evidence on Illegal Gun Market Dynamics." *Journal of Urban Health* 89(5): 779–93.

Bureau of Alcohol, Tobacco and Firearms (ATF). 2002. "Crime Gun Trace Analysis - 2000." Washington: U.S. Department of Justice.

Bureau of Alcohol, Tobacco, Firearms and Explosives (ATF). 2016a. "Firearms Trace Data - 2015: Maryland." Washington: U.S. Department of Justice. Accessed July 6, 2017. https://www.atf.gov/about/firearms-trace-data-2015.

———. 2016b. "Firearms Tracing System." Washington: U.S. Department of Justice.

Cook, Philip J., Richard J. Harris, Jens Ludwig, and Harold A. Pollack. 2014. "Some Sources of Crime Guns in Chicago: Dirty Dealers, Straw Purchasers, and Traffickers." *Journal of Criminal Law & Criminology* 104(4): 717.

Cook, Philip J., Jens Ludwig, Sudhir Venkatesh, and Anthony A. Braga. 2007. "Underground Gun Markets." *Economic Journal* 117(524): F588–618.

Cook, Philip J., Susan T. Parker, and Harold A. Pollack. 2015. "Sources of Guns to Dangerous People: What We Learn by Asking Them." *Preventive Medicine* 79 (October): 28–36.

Crifasi, Cassandra K., Keshia M. Pollack, and Daniel W. Webster. 2015. "Effects of State-Level Policy Changes on Homicide and Nonfatal Shootings of Law Enforcement Officers." *Injury Prevention* 22(4): 274–78.

Morgan, Stephen L., and Joel A. Pally. 2016. "Ferguson, Gray, and Davis: An Analysis of Recorded Crime Incidents and Arrests in Baltimore City March 2010 through December 2015." A 21st Century Cities Initiative report. Baltimore, Md.: Johns Hopkins University Press.

Pierce, Glenn L., Anthony A. Braga, and Garen J. Wintemute. 2015. "Impact of California Firearms Sales Laws and Dealer Regulations on the Illegal Diversion of Guns." *Injury Prevention* 21(3): 179–84.

Rudolph, Kara E., Elizabeth A. Stuart, Jon S. Vernick, and Daniel W. Webster. 2015. "Association Between Connecticut's Permit-to-Purchase Handgun Law and Homicides." *American Journal of Public Health* 105(8): e49–54.

StataCorp. 2015. *Stata Statistical Software: Release 14*. College Station, Tex.: StataCorp LP.

Webster, Daniel W., Cassandra K. Crifasi, and Jon S. Vernick. 2014. "Effects of the Repeal of Missouri's Handgun Purchaser Licensing Law on Homicides." *Journal of Urban Health* 91(3): 293–302.

Webster, Daniel W., Jon S. Vernick, and Maria T. Bulzacchelli. 2009. "Effects of State-Level Firearm Seller Accountability Policies on Firearm Trafficking." *Journal of Urban Health* 86(4): 525–37.

Webster, Daniel W., Jon S. Vernick, Maria T. Bulzacchelli, and Katherine A. Vittes. 2012. "Temporal Association Between Federal Gun Laws and the Diversion of Guns to Criminals in Milwaukee." *Journal of Urban Health* 89(1): 87–97.

Webster, Daniel W., Jon S. Vernick, and Lisa M. Hepburn. 2001. "Relationship Between Licensing, Registration, and Other Gun Sales Laws and the Source State of Crime Guns." *Injury Prevention* 7(3): 184–89.

Webster, Daniel W., Jon S. Vernick, Emma Elizabeth McGinty, Katherine A. Vittes, and Ted Alcorn. 2013. "Preventing the Diversion of Guns to Criminals through Effective Firearm Sales Laws." In *Reducing Gun Violence in America: Informing Policy with Evidence and Analysis*, ed. Daniel W. Webster and Jon S. Vernick. Baltimore: Johns Hopkins University Press.

Webster, Daniel W., and Garen J. Wintemute. 2015. "Effects of Policies Designed to Keep Firearms from High-Risk Individuals." *Annual Review of Public Health* 36(1): 21–37.

Prohibited Possessors and the Law: How Inmates in Los Angeles Jails Understand Firearm and Ammunition Regulations

MELISSA BARRAGAN, KELSIE Y. CHESNUT, JASON GRAVEL, NATALIE A. PIFER, KERAMET REITER, NICOLE SHERMAN, AND GEORGE TITA

Using data from 140 interviews with individuals detained in the Los Angeles County Jail system, this article examines what gun offenders know about gun and ammunition regulation in California. Though most respondents had a consistent, albeit general, understanding of the regulations limiting gun acquisition and possession, analysis suggests that their understanding of ammunition restrictions was more limited. Our sample's awareness of firearms law is especially important to consider given that they are the very population targeted by firearms regulations and prohibitions at the local, state, and federal level. By examining what detained offenders know about firearms laws, we can better theorize about individual gaps in legal knowledge and the realistic expectations for how understanding of the law can affect behavior.

Keywords: firearms policy, guns, ammunition, deterrence, legal knowledge

California and its municipalities—especially Los Angeles (LA)—have some of the most restrictive laws in the United States regulating gun and ammunition sale, possession, and use. Some research has investigated the effectiveness of certain gun policies within the state (Pierce, Braga, Wintemute 2015; Wintemute 2013; Wintemute et al. 1998), yet no study has

---

Melissa Barragan is a doctoral candidate in the Department of Criminology, Law, and Society at the University of California, Irvine. **Kelsie Y. Chesnut** is a doctoral candidate in the Department of Criminology, Law, and Society at the University of California, Irvine. **Jason Gravel** is a doctoral candidate in the Department of Criminology, Law, and Society at the University of California, Irvine. **Natalie A. Pifer** is assistant professor in the Department of Criminology and Criminal Justice at the University of Rhode Island. **Keramet Reiter** is assistant professor in the Department of Criminology, Law, and Society at the University of California, Irvine. **Nicole Sherman** is assistant professor in the Department of Political Science and Criminal Justice at California State University, Chico. **George Tita** is professor in the Department of Criminology, Law, and Society at the University of California, Irvine.

© 2017 Russell Sage Foundation. Barragan, Melissa, Kelsie Y. Chesnut, Jason Gravel, Natalie A. Pifer, Keramet Reiter, Nicole Sherman, and George Tita. 2017. "Prohibited Possessors and the Law: How Inmates in Los Angeles Jails Understand Firearm and Ammunition Regulations." *RSF: The Russell Sage Foundation Journal of the Social Sciences* 3(5): 141–63. DOI: 10.7758/RSF.2017.3.5.07. This research was supported by an award from the California Wellness Foundation (2013-054) and the University of Chicago Crime Lab (FP054392). The opinions, findings, and conclusions presented herein reflect those of the authors and not necessarily those of the foundation or the lab. We would also like to thank our participants and the Los Angeles County Sheriff's Department, without whom this research would not have been possible. Direct correspondence to: Melissa Barragan at barragm1@uci.edu, Department of Criminology, Law, and Society, 3304 Social Ecology II, Irvine, CA 92697; Kelsie Y. Chesnut at kchesnut@uci.edu; Jason Gravel at jgravel@uci.edu; Natalie Pifer at npifer@uri.edu; Nicole Sherman at nmsherman@csuchico.edu; Keramet Reiter at reiterk@uci.edu; and George E. Tita at gtita@uc.edu.

examined what California firearms users *actually* know about state or citywide gun and ammunition laws. As has been demonstrated in other regulatory contexts, like the welfare system (see, for example, Gustafson 2011; Kidwell and Gottlober 1999), such legal knowledge is critical to understanding the process by which restrictive regulations might work to discourage illegal behavior. Given the array and complexity of California's laws governing guns and ammunition, few firearms users could be expected to have complete knowledge of such regulations. However, such laws are based, at least partially, on the twofold premise that individuals are aware of the general existence of laws along with the consequent sanctions, and that the threat of sanctions will affect an individual's behavior. Indeed, basic awareness of the law is a fundamental principle of general deterrence theory—in order for people to be discouraged from violating laws, they need to know both that the law exists and that there is a risk of being sanctioned.

Using data from 140 in-depth, qualitative interviews, this article takes a bottom-up approach to examining gun law by asking what individuals detained on gun-related charges in the Los Angeles County Jail system know about the legal landscape of gun and, especially, ammunition regulation in California. Particularly, we ask how participants understand the gun and ammunition laws that regulate and punish their behavior. Although this preliminary analysis cannot temporally establish legal knowledge as to who would have been deterred, it does raise important questions about how messaging of law might be improved. Specifically, we relate our findings to deterrence theory and discuss how the legal knowledge (or lack of it) among gun users can inform firearm regulations and prohibitions, especially those designed to restrict access to ammunition, a particular focus of this article, and an area where the knowledge of our interview subjects was comparatively limited. Further, our findings pertaining to respondents' legal knowledge warrants future study across different categories of gun and ammunition users, including both prohibited and nonprohibited users.

General deterrence theory assumes that individuals are aware of what constitutes unlawful behavior, the risks of apprehension, and the severity of punishment (Cook 1980; Gibbs 1975; Nagin 1998; Paternoster 1987; Zimring and Hawkins 1973). But in the case of ammunition regulations, assumptions may be more tenuous than those regarding firearm regulations. Those familiar with the Boston Gun Project and the similar programs it spawned, such as the federally funded Project Safe Neighborhoods program, know the story of Freddie Cardoza, a notorious career criminal and gang member from Boston who was suspected of being the trigger man on multiple shootings (Kennedy, Braga, and Piehl 2001, 14, 37). Though the state lacked the cooperation of witnesses and victims needed to bring a case against Cardoza, the police caught a break when Cardoza incriminated himself in the presence of two officers of the Boston Police Department. On the basis of a single offense, he was ultimately sentenced to nineteen years and seven months in federal custody. What serious offense was it that led to Cardoza's arrest and incarceration? Cardoza was casually flipping a single .45 caliber bullet. Given that the broad legal definition of *firearm* applies to ammunition as well as to guns, Cardoza might as well have been found in possession of a pistol. Indeed, the broad definition gave the Boston police the discretion to interpret and apply the law in a way that apparently surprised Cardoza.

It is difficult to believe that Cardoza, or any other prohibited possessor, would have treated a pistol as cavalierly, essentially pulling it out and emulating the gun slingers of the wild-west by spinning a firearm on his fingers while taunting the local sheriff. But if one reads the federal complaint, this is exactly what he is said to have done. As he was approached by two police officers, he removed the bullet and began flipping it in the air and catching it as one might do with a coin. Although we do not know what exactly motivated Cardoza in this case, we do know that the law failed to deter his illegal behavior. Because he had been able to successfully evade punishment for more serious offenses prior to this incident, we can infer that the law failed because Cardoza was simply unaware of the ammunition prohibition to begin with, and that by extension of this gap in knowledge, was unaware of both the risk of apprehension and punishment. As we discuss later, this lack of knowledge should not be surprising given the incongruence between the policies and regulations in place to ensure that firearms remain out of the hands of prohibited possessors and the efforts to monitor and control ammunition purchases.

In the instant study, we interviewed those most likely to have some knowledge of firearms regulations and sanctions—individuals with known firearms-related charges—to better understand what they knew about the law as they faced legal sanctioning. Our sample's awareness of firearms law is especially important to consider given that they are the very population targeted by many of the firearms regulations and prohibitions at the local, state, and federal level. By examining what detained offenders know about firearms laws, we can begin to theorize about both gaps in legal knowledge and the realistic expectations for how legal knowledge will affect behavior.

The central finding discussed in this article is that though most respondents had a consistent, albeit general, understanding of the regulations limiting gun acquisition and possession, their understanding of ammunition restrictions was far more limited.

FEDERAL REGULATION OF FIREARMS AND AMMUNITION

Most of the federal laws governing the sale, purchase, and possession of firearms and ammunition set forth with the passage of the Gun Control Act of 1968 treated firearms and ammunition similarly. Anyone falling into the class of prohibited possessor was restricted from purchasing or possessing either, age restrictions applied equally, and interstate commerce was banned for both firearm and ammunition sales. As with firearms sales, a license was required to manufacture, import, or distribute ammunition. Dealers were also required to maintain basic sales information on ammunition transactions. However, most of these regulations, especially those governing ammunition, were repealed with the passage of the Firearm Owners Protection Act of 1986. Licenses were only required for the manufacture or importation of ammunition and not the sale of ammunition. Furthermore, dealers were no longer required to keep data on ammunition transactions, and the interstate ban was lifted. Still, at the federal level, the age restriction remains, and those prohibited from possessing firearms are also prohibited from purchasing and possessing ammunition.

The one aspect of regulation that distinguishes firearm from ammunition transactions at the federal (and state) levels also helps put the Freddie Cardoza case into perspective: no mechanisms are in place to ensure that prohibited possessors cannot access ammunition. Whereas the Brady Act of 1994 required federally licensed firearm dealers, more accurately federal firearms licensees (FFLs), to conduct background checks to complete the sale of a firearm, the sale of ammunition carries no such requirement at the federal level. At the time of this study, only four states had created licensing requirements for firearm purchases that also extended to ammunition purchases: Connecticut, Illinois, Massachusetts, and New Jersey. New York State had also adopted an instant background check requirement for ammunition purchase to supplement their existing regulations, but as James Jacobs and Zoe Fuhr discuss in a recent analysis, implementation has been uneven and inconsistent due to financial and technical obstacles (2016). Local jurisdictions, including Los Angeles, have also adopted more restrictive policies meant to dissuade prohibited possessors from purchasing and possessing ammunition.

FIREARM AND AMMUNITION LAWS IN CALIFORNIA

California has some of the most stringent state regulations relating to gun purchase, possession, and sale. In fact, according to the Law Center to Prevent Gun Violence (LCPGV), California has been consistently rated as the most restrictive state since 2010 (Law Center to Prevent Gun Violence 2013, 2015). Table 1 uses LCPGV data to compare select firearm regulations for the ten most restrictive states as well as for the three states bordering California. When compared with other highly regulated states, California's regulatory landscape is distinguishable in three key ways: it is notably *more* restrictive in limiting the number of firearms that can be purchased and in imposing

Table 1. State Laws Regulating Transactions of Guns and Ammunitions

		California	Connecticut	New Jersey	Maryland	New York	Massachusetts	Hawaii	Illinois	Rhode Island	Delaware	Arizona	Nevada	Oregon
					Most Restrictive States							Borders California		
Sales or transfer regulations	Dealer licences	✓	✓	✓	✓	✓	✓	✓	✗	✓	✓	✗	✗	✗
	Records of sales	✓	✓	✓	✓	✓	✓	✓	✓	✗	✗	✗	✗	✗
	Multiple firearms per month	✓	✗	✓	✓	✗	✗	✗	✗	✗	✗	✗	✗	✗
	Waiting periods	✓	✗	✓	✓	✗	✗	✓	✓	✓	✗	✗	✗	✗
Background check regulations on non-FFL dealers	Any regulated background check	✓	✓	✓	✓	✓	✗	✓	✓	✓	✓	✗	✓	✓
	Specific background checks	✓	✓	✗	✓	✓	✓	✓	✓	✓	✓	✗	✗	✓
	All dealers	✓	✓	✗	✗	✓	✗	✗	✗	✓	✓	✗	✗	✓
	Select firearms and gun shows	✗	✗	✗	✓	✗	✓	✗	✓	✗	✗	✗	✗	✓
	Thirty-day permit to purchase	✗	✗	✗	✗	✗	✓	✓	✗	✗	✗	✗	✗	✗
Guns and ammunitions restrictions	Assault weapons	✓	✓	✓	✓	✓	✓	✓	✗	✗	✗	✗	✗	✗
	Large capacity	✓	✓	✓	✓	✓	✓	✓	✗	✗	✗	✗	✗	✗
	50 caliber rifle	✓	✓	✗	✓	✗	✓	✗	✗	✗	✗	✗	✗	✗
	License to sell ammunition	✗	✓	✓	✓	✓	✓	✗	✓	✗	✗	✗	✗	✗

Source: Authors' tabulation based on data from Law Center to Prevent Gun Violence (2013).

Table 2. Gun-Related Enhancement Laws and Dispositions

Crimes	Additional Sentence
Gang crime while carrying a firearm (12021.5(a)PC)	1, 2, or 3 years
Gang crime while carrying a firearm and detacheable magazine (12021.5(b)PC)	2, 3, or 4 years
Felony while armed with firearm (12022(a)1PC)	1 year
Felony while armed with assault weapon, machine gun or .50 caliber rifle (12022(a)2PC)	3 years
Possession of narcotics with a firearm (12022(C)PC)	3, 4, or 5 years
Co-offender of possessor of narcotic with a firearm (12022(d)PC)	1, 2, or 3 years
Felony while armed with firearm with metal or armor piercing ammunition (12022.2(a)PC)	3, 4, or 10 years
Sexual offense using firearm (12022.3(a)PC)	3, 4, or 10 years
Sexual offense armed with firearm (12022.3(b)PC)	1, 2, or 5 years
Furnish a firearm to another person during commission of felony (12022.4(a)PC)	1, 2, or 3 years
Use of firearm during felony (12022.5(a)PC)	3, 4, or 10 years
Use of an assault weapon or machine gun during felony (12022.5(b)PC)	5, 6, or 10 years
Assault with a firearm used from a vehicle (12022.5(d)PC)	3, 4, or 10 years
Assault with an assault weapon or machine gun from vehicle (12022.5(d) PC)	5, 6, or 10 years
Use of firearm during murder, mayhem, kidnapping, robbery, carjacking, assault with intent to commit a felony, assault with a firearm on a peace officer or firefighter, rape, sodomy, lewd act on a child, oral copulation, sexual penetration, assault by a prisoner, holding a hostage by a prisoner, and any felony punishable by death or prison for life (12022.53(b)PC)	10 years
If firearm discharged (12022.53(C)PC)	20 years
If causes death or great bodily injury (12022.53(d)PC)	25 years to life
Discharge a firearm from a vehicle causing death or great bodily harm during felony (12022.55PC)	5, 6, or 10 years

Source: Authors' tabulation based on Sentence Enhancements, Cal. Penal Code § 12201-12022.95 (2014).

restrictions on high-powered rifles (earning the state its "high regulation" reputation), but notably *less* so on ammunition sales than other similarly restrictive states.[1] Other than these few differences, California gun laws appear to be comparable in their restrictiveness to many of the largest northeastern states. Note, however, that firearm and ammunition regulations in the states surrounding California are some of the least restrictive.

California laws also impose sentencing enhancements related to the use of firearms during the commission of different offenses. Table 2 presents specific enhancements related to firearm possession and use along with the potential additional sentencing dispositions associated with each action. These enhancements are designed to deter individuals (prohibited or not) from using, or even carrying, a firearm during the commission of an offense.

City and county governments, like state governments, have considerable leeway in regulating gun transactions within their jurisdictions, producing further variation within and across

---

1. At the time of data collection, Proposition 63—which creates a background check requirement for ammunition purchase across the state—had not yet been passed. Since passage of this law, California has become one of the most restrictive states on ammunition laws.

Table 3. Gun Regulations in the City of Los Angeles and Surrounding Large Cities

	Long Beach	Glendale	Santa Clarita	Pomona	Torrance	Pasadena	El Monte	Downey	Inglewood
Firearms									
Sales or transfers									
Permit to sell	✓					✓	✓		
No sales of ultracompact firearms-accessories									
No "swap meet" sales or purchases of firearms									
Posession or use									
Reporting of theft or loss to police within forty-eight hours									
No disposing in trash or public place									
No gun parts in airports									
No false or secret compartments in vehicles									
Safe storage (locked container or trigger lock) or within close proximity and control of owner									
Ammunition									
Sales or transfers									
Permit to sell									
No retail sales seven days prior and on January 1 and July 4									✓
No sales of ammunition clips									✓
No sales of .50 caliber ammunition									
Reporting requirements for purchase									
Date, name, address, date of birth				✓					✓
State ID number				✓					✓
Signature				✓					✓
Fingerprint									✓
Records maintained onsite for two years				✓					✓
Records transferred electronically to police department within five days									
Possession or use									
No possession of large-capacity magazines									
No disposing in trash or public place									
Property abatement against unlawful weapons	✓								

Source: Authors' tabulation based on city municipal codes as of March 2016.

state lines. For instance, Los Angeles County includes eighty-eight cities, many of which have their own laws regarding the sale, purchase, and possession of firearms and ammunition. The City of Los Angeles (LA) imposes a broad range of restrictions that go beyond those enacted either elsewhere in the county or elsewhere in the state.[2] Table 3 presents LA municipal code laws regarding firearms and ammunition that go beyond state and county regulations and also compares these laws to the municipal codes of several surrounding large cities. This comparison highlights both the restrictiveness of LA municipal codes and

2. "LA" refers to the City of Los Angeles and not other cities within Los Angeles county bounds.

Figure 1. Geographical Distribution of Restrictiveness of Ammunition Sales Regulations

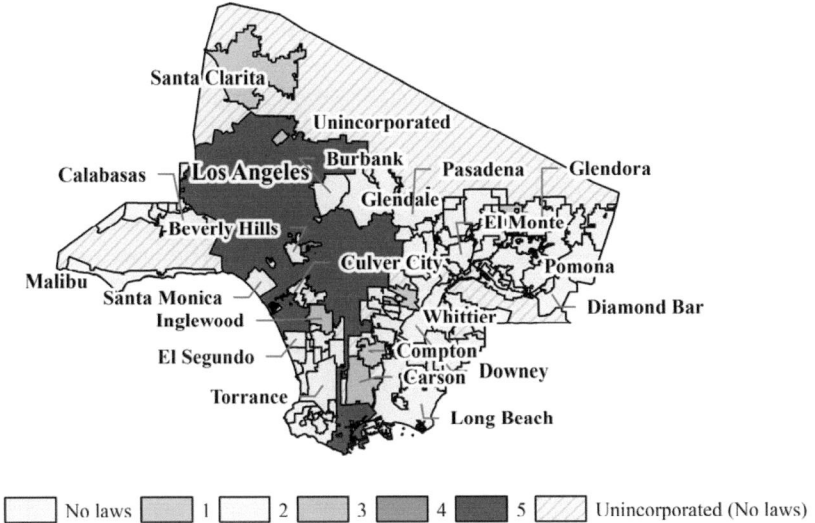

Source: Authors' calculations from city municipal codes.
Notes: Not shown on the map are the cities of Lancaster and Palmdale situated northeast of Santa Clarita. Scores reflect the number out of five categories of ammunition regulations each city has implemented. The categories are: permits to sell ammunition, sale period and/or type of ammunition restrictions, ammunition logs, fingerprint requirement for ammunition sales, and electronic transfer of ammunition logs to the police department.

the variability of gun restrictions at the local level.

LA is especially restrictive regarding the purchase of ammunition. In the city, ammunition sellers must possess a license, and purchasers are required to provide a valid state ID and leave a fingerprint impression. The seller must also maintain a record of all transactions including the purchaser's personal information (name, date of birth, gender, address, and ID number) as well as the type of and quantity of ammunition purchased. Information on each transaction is entered into an electronic database that is transferred to the police department within five days. The city also imposes restrictions on the sales of certain types of ammunition and prohibits ammunition sales for the week leading up to both the Fourth of July and New Year's Eve.

Figure 1 contextualizes these city regulations within the context of the variety of ammunition laws across Los Angeles County. Each city was given a score from 0 to 5, 0 indicating that the city did not have laws that went beyond that of the state or federal regulations on ammunition. A municipality's score was increased by one point for each of the following requirements: license to sell ammunition, restriction of sales during particular times of the year, ammunition sales log, fingerprints taken at the time of purchase, and electronic transfer of records to local law enforcement.

The unevenness of the legal landscape at the local level can have potentially serious implications for the effectiveness of even the clearest, most restrictive, and best enforced laws. For instance, restrictive regulations in one area can be undermined when a prohibited possessor is able to cross into a neighboring municipality with less restrictive laws in order to purchase ammunition. This assumes, of course, that those targeted by local laws are aware both that their status as a prohibited possessor applies to ammunition purchase and possession and that there are local variations in laws regulating the purchase of ammunition. However, as we discuss later, our respondents seemed to have limited knowledge of ammunition law overall, be it federal, state, or local law.

METHODS

The data presented in this article were collected as part of a multicity project focused on examining the contours of the illegal firearms market from the perspective of detained gun offenders. Interviews were conducted at four Los Angeles County jails between January and October of 2014, including a first phase of eleven pilot interviews. Based on a sampling criteria of eighteen offenses associated with firearm possession, the LA County sheriff generated rosters of all individuals currently detained on at least one of the qualifying charges (see table A1).

Rosters were generated on a biweekly basis, and potential interview participants were randomly selected from these lists, provided they were above the age of eighteen and did not have a mental health designation. In total, the research team sampled 215 detainees and interviewed 140, yielding a refusal rate of 34.9 percent. In terms of race/ethnicity, our sample was overwhelmingly male and of color. Black respondents were slightly overrepresented relative to the jail population (45 percent). Overall, however, our sample is reflective of the general LA County jail population, which is 31 percent black, 49 percent Hispanic, 15 percent white, and 3 percent Asian (Austin et al. 2012; for additional demographics, see table A2).

Interviews were conducted by a trained team of five doctoral students, were audio recorded, and lasted between 45 and 120 minutes. Respondents were given a $10 jail-issued vending card for their participation, regardless of whether the interview was completed. Interviewers asked respondents to discuss their perceptions of and experiences with: gun access and illegal gun acquisition in their community; community safety and gun violence; gangs; law enforcement; and gun and ammunition laws. Anonymity was of paramount concern because of the respondents' legal vulnerability as an (often pretrial) incarcerated population. Respondents were therefore not asked to provide specific details about their most recent case, nor did the LA County Sheriff's Department provide such individualized data. Any information recorded about a participant's current legal status or charge was provided voluntarily and not corroborated with official data; we cannot therefore provide a detailed analysis of how charges varied across the entire sample.

However, we were able to obtain self-report information on a majority of respondents' prohibited possessor status. In all, 82.86 percent (n=116) of respondents reported that they could not legally possess a gun because of a prior felony or other legal restrictions, 7.14 percent (n=10) reported that they were legally able to possess a gun, and 10 percent (n=14) of respondents provided no information or unclear information relevant to their status. In comparison, approximately 96 percent of possible respondents in our sampling frame were charged with at least one violation related to being a prohibited possessor. The vast majority of respondents, therefore, should technically have some baseline knowledge about being prohibited from both guns and ammunition given their legal status. However, the level and depth of understanding of the regulations varies among respondents—particularly when it comes to ammunition.

All interviews were transcribed verbatim and analyzed with TAMS Analyzer Software. The team took a modified grounded theory approach to develop analytic codes inductively from the data (Abbott 2004; Charmaz 2008; Strauss and Corbin 1990). After the initial pilot phase of interviewing, members of the research team refined and added questions to the interview instrument based on emergent findings and observations from the field. After conducting interviews, the team then broadly coded transcripts of participants' interviews thematically. Key areas of interest for the instant analysis included respondents' knowledge of gun and ammunition laws, knowledge of sanctions associated with violating gun and ammunition laws, and experiences with gun and ammunition laws and sanctions. Subsequent analysis focused on the specific types of regulations noted by respondents, the frequency with which respondents mentioned each type of regulation, and the varied types of punishments that might be imposed for violations of regulations (for sample questions, see table A3). The specificity of respondents' legal knowledge varied considerably by the type of law and its related punishments.

FINDINGS: PATTERNS OF LEGAL KNOWLEDGE

Our interviews reveal different patterns of knowledge within three sub-categories of firearm-related laws: gun regulations, ammunition regulations, and punishments for violating these regulations. The legal knowledge our respondents articulated was based on both their lived and vicarious experience with the law, which might have included: legal gun or ammunition purchases, interactions with police and the courts, prior gun-related convictions, being arrested, and serving time in jail. A majority of respondents had a general understanding of state and federal restrictions on gun purchase and possession. However, respondents' knowledge of more local-level regulations and sanctions, especially local ammunition regulations, was both more limited and less consistent. Respondents also perceived punishment for violating gun regulations—but not for violating ammunition regulations—as a relatively certain and relatively severe outcome. Moreover, their knowledge of the sentences likely to be imposed for violating gun possession and use regulations was generally accurate; again, however, they knew little about the potential sentences likely to be imposed for ammunition violations.

General Understandings of Gun Regulations

Our respondents revealed a basic, but relatively imprecise knowledge of gun acquisition and possession regulations. Of our 140 respondents, nearly 86 percent (n=120) openly discussed at least one aspect of law that regulated gun possession and ownership. Among the remaining twenty respondents, the interviewer did not raise this question during early pretests (n=11), and the remaining nine respondents declined to discuss the subject. All the percentages in this section therefore reflect the population of 120 respondents who indicated some knowledge of gun regulations, not the total sampled group. Among these 120 respondents, we coded knowledge of twelve aspects of gun regulations (listed in table 4 in descending order of their overall frequency).

Prohibition of acquisition and possession, based on an existing criminal record, was by far the most common regulation mentioned and described by respondents: 80.8 percent (n=97) indicated some knowledge of this prohibition. Their knowledge was accurate, if fairly generalized. For instance, one respondent said: "I know you can buy it in the shop but you've got to . . . have a clean record" (Respondent 59). In another interview, a respondent explained, "I know you can't have a record; I know that. You've got to be eighteen and this and that. That's all I really know" (Respondent 95). That respondents in jail on firearms-related charges were aware of prohibited possessor regulations is perhaps unsurprising, given that prohibited possession was the regulation most likely associated with their arrest and one that would continue to affect them postincarceration (for a list of sampled charges, see table A1).

The second most common regulation mentioned was the requirement for licensure, permit, or registration to legally possess a gun (n=37, or 30.8 percent). Additionally, 17.5 percent (n=21) of respondents discussed parole or probation status—as distinct from having a criminal record—as prohibiting legal firearm purchase or possession. Fewer than 5 percent of respondents discussed either the minimum age required for gun purchase, waiting periods, skills tests, or other valid identification requirements for legal gun purchase or possession in California.

Though these findings suggest that respondents are aware of their prohibited status for gun acquisition and possession, there was less consistent reporting of other gun laws. This abbreviated legal knowledge may imply that respondents' knowledge of the law stops once their status as illegal possessors is made known to them. The notion that respondents only refer to laws on a need-to-know basis is reinforced by our analysis of ammunition regulations.

(Non-)Specific Knowledge of Ammunition Regulations

Although the majority of respondents (69 percent) were able to discuss some aspect of the federal, state, and local laws regulating the pur-

Table 4. Aspects of California Gun Laws Discussed by Respondents

	Frequency	Percentage[a]
Criminal record restricts legal gun purchase or possession	97	80.83
License, permit, registration, or paperwork required for legal purchase or possession	37	30.83
Parole or probation restricts legal gun purchase or possession	21	17.50
Specific retail stores named for available legal gun purchase	7	5.83
Minimum age requirement for legal gun purchase	5	4.17
Gang member or injunction restricts legal purchase or possession	4	3.33
Waiting period required for legal gun purchase	3	2.50
Skills test, classes, training required for legal gun purchase	2	1.67
Identification required at time of gun purchase	2	1.67
Background check required at time of gun purchase	1	0.83
Fingerprinting required at purchase	1	0.83
Legal gun purchase available ordering online	1	0.83

Source: Authors' calculations.
[a] Respondents who discussed California gun law (n=120). Not cumulative because respondents often cited multiple aspects of law

chase or possession of guns, they were generally less familiar with ammunition regulations (56 percent, n=79). Importantly, those who did discuss ammunition regulations revealed fewer and less consistently accurate details about those regulations than those who discussed gun regulations. There are, of course, a few possible explanations for these substantive differences in knowledge.

First, research has described the relative ease with which prohibited possessors can access firearms in LA's illicit gun market (Chesnut et al. 2016). This might render the need to access the legal ammunition market unnecessary and explain respondents' lack of familiarity with ammunition regulations. On the other hand, that there are fewer legal mechanisms restricting ammunition purchase than gun purchase might actually increase the likelihood that a prohibited possessor would attempt to access the legal market.

Second, our respondents might have only known about the implications of the crimes with which they were charged, and, as mentioned, our data does not allow us to determine which of our respondents were caught and charged with gun possession versus ammunition possession, or both. On the other hand, based on self-reported areas of residence, we do know that 55.7 percent of our respondents lived within LA city limits before their incarceration (n= 78), and 37.9 percent (n=53) lived outside the city, so they were subject to a variety of possible ammunition regulations. Given that ammunition regulations vary across Los Angeles County, we indicate where relevant whether respondent knowledge of these laws is consistent with those corresponding to their place of residence. In asking respondents about both ammunition and gun regulations, we sought to analyze these potential explanations of comparative knowledge and better understand prohibited possessors' knowledge of local ammunition laws.

The most noticeable distinction between respondents' descriptions of guns and of ammunition was relative availability and accessibility. Whereas respondents rarely identified specific retail sources where guns could be obtained legally, they described ammunition as readily obtainable from legitimate retailers. One respondent said, for example, "You can go buy bullets from Wal-Mart. Or what's it called, Big 5, or whatever. [You can] buy bullets anywhere" (Respondent 10). Table 5 lists the locations respondents identified as available legal sources in order of the frequency with which the location was mentioned. Respondents most commonly reported the retailers Big 5 Sporting Goods and Wal-Mart (though not all

Table 5. Locations Where Ammunition Can Be Purchased

	Frequency	Percentage[a]
Big 5 Sporting Goods	31	39.24
Wal-Mart (department store)	14	17.72
Gun store (not specified)	8	10.13
Turner's Outdoorsman (sporting goods)	4	5.06
Sporting goods store (not specified)	4	5.06
Gun show	2	2.53
Big Lots (department store)	1	1.27
Online	1	1.27
Target (department store)	1	1.27

Source: Authors' calculations.
[a]Respondents who discussed California gun law (n=120). Not cumulative because respondents often cited multiple aspects of law.

Wal-Mart stores in Southern California actually sell ammunition). Interestingly, Turners Outdoorsman—the only chain retailer in Los Angeles County that focuses on firearm sales—was named by a comparatively small portion of respondents (5 percent versus 39 percent for Big 5 Sporting Goods). Respondents also reported generic sources such as gun stores, sporting goods stores, and gun shows. However, these were reported much less frequently than chain retailers.

Respondents' characterizations of ammunition as widely legally available contrasted sharply with those of guns as simply not legally available to them, primarily because of their known legal status as a prohibited possessor. Indeed, many respondents signaled that "It's easier to get ammunition than it is weapons" (Respondent 57), with one even stating that getting ammunition is the "easiest thing in the world" (Respondent 104). One factor that might have contributed to this facility of access, at least in the eyes of Respondent 104, was that he could walk into his local Wal-Mart, show his ID, and walk out with a box of bullets, no questions asked. In fact, despite understanding that he could not legally possess a gun, this respondent stated that he only bought ammunition *legally*, thus showing how the comparatively lax regulations in his local area (Lancaster) did not affect his willingness to illegally possess ammunition. On the other hand, for some, going through a legitimate retailer was seen as unnecessary, because of the perception that "ammo is passed out, like candy" on the streets (Respondent 39). This finding of ammunition as easy to procure is essentially the opposite from what researchers recently found among jailed gun offenders in Chicago, where bullets are apparently much more difficult to acquire than guns (Cook, Parker, and Pollack 2015).

Among those seventy-nine respondents who discussed some aspect of ammunition law, only nine kinds of regulations were mentioned. These are listed, in order of frequency, in table 6. The only one mentioned with some consistency (n=40, 50.6 percent) is the requirement that a current form of photo identification be presented at the time of purchase. Three respondents (3.8 percent), however, incorrectly stated that identification was *not* required to purchase ammunition. For instance, one said confidently that anyone could go in and buy ammunition because "[gun store owners] already thinking that you got that gun, so [they] gonna give it to you without having to do that fingerprinting, all that stuff" (Respondent 47). Indeed, he went even further to say that "all you need is money." As a resident of the City of LA, this respondent was wrong not only about the lack of any official identification requirement, but also about the fingerprinting requirement.

Some of the respondents understated the restrictions on ammunition purchases. Others overstated them. Fourteen (17.7 percent) erroneously reported that purchasing ammunition

Table 6. Aspects of California Ammunition Laws Discussed by Respondents

	Frequency	Percentage[a]
Identification requirement		
ID required at time of purchase	40	50.63
No ID required at time of purchase	3	3.80
Criminal record, background check requirements		
Criminal record restriction	14	17.72
No background check at purchase	5	6.33
Age requirement		
Minimum eighteen years old	9	11.39
Minimum twenty-one years old	2	2.53
"Old enough" (minimum age)	1	1.27
No minimum age	1	1.27
License or permit requirements		
None required at purchase	3	3.80
Required at purchase	2	2.53
Ammunition logs		
Ammunition purchase recorded	3	3.80
No record of ammunition purchase or untraceable	2	2.53
Ammunition amount restrictions		
Restriction on amount purchased at once	2	2.53
No restriction on amount purchased at once	1	1.27
Miscellaneous		
Possession of ammunition not illegal or not a weapon	3	3.80
No waiting period to purchase	2	2.53
Restriction on type purchased at once	1	1.27

Source: Authors' calculations.
[a]Respondents who discussed California ammunition law (n=79). Not cumulative because respondents often cited multiple aspects of law.

required a background check. Respondent 37, for example, explained that "you can't have no record because they're going to look up to see if you got a record. If you got any type of robbery records or shooting records they're not going to sell you nothing. They're not going to give you a break. They might call the police on you." It could very well be that this respondent's knowledge of gun regulations led him to this conclusion, but he ultimately misrepresented the ammunition regulations operating in his immediate community: although one must show proper identification and leave behind a thumbprint when purchasing ammunition within city boundaries, retailers do not run Brady background checks or call the police. Only a few respondents (6.3 percent, n=5) were accurate in their understanding, reporting that an individual with a criminal record could technically purchase ammunition because background checks are not required.

Several other ammunition regulations were noted, though with much less frequency. As indicated in table 6, 15.2 percent (n=12) of respondents reporting any knowledge of ammunition regulations indicated that there was an age requirement for ammunition purchases, with age limits ranging from "old enough" to eighteen to twenty-one. Respondents also mentioned miscellaneous laws on ammunition purchases, some of which were valid and some of which were not. For example, several correctly noted that retailers maintain ammunition purchase records and that there are restrictions on the types of ammunition that one can purchase at a store. However, some also incorrectly believed that a permit or license was needed for ammunition purchase, that the amount of ammunition a person can buy is limited, and that waiting periods apply.

Overall, our respondents' understanding of ammunition laws varied, reflecting an inaccurate or incomplete view of the law. Whereas it might not be surprising that members of a sample consisting primarily of prohibited possessors are aware that they cannot acquire firearms legally, it is noteworthy that these same individuals appear to be relatively uninformed about ammunition regulations. Nowhere in the United States is it legal for a prohibited possessor to purchase ammunition. Therefore, the variability in the restrictiveness of local regulations *should* be irrelevant because prohibited possessors should arguably be aware of their status restriction. However, our findings suggest that respondents perceive gun and ammunition restrictions as two distinct issues even if the law, for all intents and purposes, does not treat them as such.

Understandings of the Law That Punishes

Our respondents were able to describe in specific (if not always accurate) terms the punishment they would experience if the police caught them with a gun. Their knowledge of the punishment they might encounter was, in fact, more detailed than that of the underlying gun (and ammunition) regulations for which they might be punished. Respondents' descriptions of legal consequences included knowledge of the specific charges they might face, possible sentencing enhancements, precise sentence lengths, and even the percentage of sentenced time they would likely serve.

The majority of respondents (80.7 percent, n=113) were aware of the consequences of being caught with a gun by the police (see table 7). Only six indicated not knowing what would happen. Information from twenty-one is coded as "missing." Of the 113 respondents who were aware of the potential consequences of being caught with a gun, nearly all (86.7 percent, n=98) identified incarceration as the conse-

Table 7. Consequences Reported of Being Caught with a Gun by Police

	Frequency	Percentage[a]
Incarceration	98	86.73
Arrested or charged	6	5.31
Shot by police	6	5.31
Missing	3	2.65

Source: Authors' calculations.
[a]Respondents who discussed consequences of being caught with a gun (n=113).

quence. Other consequences respondents cited included being arrested or criminally charged (5.3 percent, n=6) and being "shot by the police" (5.3 percent, n=6), which Respondent 114 described as follows:

> More than likely . . . they're going to take you to jail. They aren't going to let you go. They are going to take you to jail because they feel like you are a threat, and they might shoot you, the police, depending on how they feel about it.

Respondents who reported incarceration as the expected consequence of police apprehension were also asked whether they knew any additional information, such as the specific charge or the amount of time they might serve. Among the subgroup who both self-reported having criminal records and described incarceration as the consequence of police catching them with a gun (n=72), more than two-thirds described detailed knowledge of possible criminal charges or duration of associated sentences (69.4 percent, n=50). Respondents like Number 56 described the ways that being caught with a gun could translate into a particular punishment:

> Possession of a firearm, a CCW [carrying a concealed weapon] the law stipulates that if you didn't use that gun to commit a crime, you were just in possession of it, sixteen, two, and three. For sixteen months will add two and a half or three and a half, three being the max, sixteen being the least. So you're looking at the most eighteen months in prison or in the county jail.

But, as Respondent 56 continues, final sentencing length is contingent on additional factors such as the defendant's specific criminal history:

> Some people who get caught with a gun . . . get probation. Some people who get caught with a gun will get like a county lick. So it varies but if you have a strike on your record and you get caught with a gun that's sixteen, two and three, doubles up to a thirty-two and eighty-four or eighty-five or six with eighty-five. Doubles up.

He then continued to identify the spectrum of possible sentence enhancements that might be imposed on a person in possession of an illegal gun:

> Then you got gun enhancements—just certain type of gun enhancements, like you got a ten-year gun enhancement, fifteen-year gun enhancement. Then if you use a gun for a crime and it's loaded like it's not loaded like a full clip like one in the brain, ready to squeeze that's like ten years automatically, fifteen years automatically, ain't no way around it. So it all depends.

In sum, respondents described punishment as individualized—imposing, as Respondent 56 characterized it, "different strokes for different folks." Indeed, under state and federal laws, sentences can vary according to offense type, offense history, and one's assumed propensity for committing future harm, as Respondent 48 explained: "It would [d]epend on . . . how bad my record is, if they think I need to stay in because I'm a menace to society . . . if you're fighting or stabbing people, [versus] you know raping them." Taken together, respondents' knowledge of the law suggested that punishment—consisting of multiple years of incarceration—was relatively certain should they be apprehended.

This articulation of the multiple forms that their punishments might take contrasts sharply with discussions of regulatory laws, generally described as binary categories pivoting on whether the purchase of guns or ammunition was legal or illegal (depending on the respondents' status as a prohibited possessor). However, in both California and the City of Los Angeles, the laws governing gun, and especially ammunition, purchases are far more detailed than respondents described. Given that our respondents were either awaiting sentencing or had recently completed the sentencing process, it is perhaps unsurprising that they had more robust knowledge of the punishments they might face, having broken the law, than of the laws they had broken in the first place.

When it came to the punishments associated with ammunition possession, however, respondents' reported both a lack of knowledge concerning ammunition law and an overall astonishment at the severity of sanctions they experienced specific to ammunition law. For instance, Respondent 79 described his shock that, after being caught with five rifle bullets in his pocket, he was facing prison time for a charge of "felon in possession of ammunition":

> Not only did I get arrested, but they hit me with a very severe sentence, and I'm now for the first time in my life going to prison. . . . It really shocked me, really surprised me. . . . I got stopped by the cops. . . . It was gonna be just a routine check. It wasn't gonna be a problem, issue at all, and now it'll be [nineteen months] before I'm free.

Even after his arrest, the scope of the consequences for possessing ammunition as a prohibited possessor was not entirely clear to this respondent: "People kept telling me, 'Oh, it's not a big deal. It's not a big deal. You didn't have a gun.' Even one of the cops told me, 'Ah, it's not a big deal.' Then it turned out to be a big deal." Reminiscent of the Cardoza case, this respondent's lack of knowledge of ammunition restrictions meant that he did not realize he was engaging in a prohibited behavior, and so was alarmed by the consequences of his actions. (Even his description of police officers' reactions reveals the potential discretion at play in enforcing the law, again similar to the Cardoza case.) This respondent's surprise suggests that, had he known both that the ammunition regulations existed and had consequences, he might have behaved differently.

In a similar situation, another respondent described his experience of unknowingly violating his probation *or* parole, due to the seizure of a decorative bullet during a routine home search:

> The charge I have is a possession of ammunition. It was just one bullet that I had in my house that when the police came to search my house, they decided to charge me for it, because I'm not supposed to have it I guess but that's something I've had for like the past five years, it was sitting up on my wall as decoration. (Respondent 25).

Although it is not clear whether this respondent was prohibited because of prior felony convictions or other legal restrictions (such as probation, parole, or restraining order), what is clear is that he was unaware that he could not legally possess ammunition. One could argue that had he known, he would have gotten rid of the bullet, or at the very least removed it from plain view, so that it would not immediately implicate him during a police search.

Unaware of the potential serious consequences of storing ammunition in his home beforehand, one respondent disclosed the circumstances of his current case to us:

> They searched my townhouse. I have no furniture—nothing. For two hours. They find a bullet. I have no weapons charges on my record. Never been to prison for a gun. Never been, you know, nothing. I went to court. It was a charge of possession of a firearm—ex-felon with a firearm because since I have a bullet I must have a gun. They never found one. . . . They want to give me six years, eight months for a bullet. . . . I'd been out five years, and it's like in a way I feel like well I thought I was doing right, you know? Getting, you know, myself together, and everything that I worked for in these last five years has been taken away from me—was taken away from me overnight. . . .
>
> So, it's mine though. But I'm like—I'm trying to figure out what crime did I commit? Well, possession of ammunition. Well, I didn't have possession. You guys found it. You know, but anyways, because me personally possession means they found it on my person. So, that's what I'm here for. It's just, once again, it just all falls on the fact that I'm an ex-felon. I have a history, you know, but no gun charges. (Respondent 112)

As in the previous examples, this respondent knew the bullet was present, yet was unaware of the associated consequence. In this instance, he believed his particular history as a nongun offender should exclude him from any ammunition sanctioning. He also disagreed with the severity of the sanction he was facing, given the actual ammunition offense: "six years, eight months for a bullet." Further, he goes on to criticize the punishment levied against him by contesting the meaning of possession and describing the charges against him as a proxy for status, not offense. Although we do not know how many individuals in our sample experienced predicaments like those of the previous respondents, these examples poignantly reveal how a lack of legal knowledge can undermine the effectiveness of firearms regulations, moot the potential deterrent effects of legal sanctions, and even compromise an individual's perceived legitimacy of the law.

DISCUSSION

As David Kennedy puts it, "while criminal justice agencies are very much in the business of, as the phrase goes, 'sending signals,' they in practice often send those signals in obscure, incoherent, ineffective, and even self-defeating ways" (1996, 463). These signals come in the shape of new enforcement strategies and sentencing policies that are often complex, inconsistently enforced, and sometimes simply implausible in their stated goals (such as "zero-tolerance" policies). Together, these signals and policies decrease the likelihood that any specific offender will be deterred. Theorists have had seemingly endless debates about how to manipulate both the elements of deterrence theory—certainty, severity, and celerity—and the dosage of these elements in order to ensure compliance with the law (Kennedy 2009). As elusive as answers to these debates have been, there is one fundamental principle of deterrence theory that seems rather immutable, and perhaps as a result is often taken for granted:

"That which is not known simply cannot deter" (479).

This article examines what firearm offenders do and do not know, detailing how they understand and navigate California's complex layering of gun and ammunition restrictions and sanctions. Specifically, we were interested in understanding the breadth and depth of our respondents' knowledge of gun and ammunition law. The study's use of detained gun offenders may not allow us to reach broad conclusions about the potential deterrent effect of these laws in the general population. However, we do believe that our findings have important implications for firearms law by focusing on the critical first stage of deterrence: awareness of the law. Additionally, by sampling from an often underreached population (jail detainees), this study provides a baseline understanding of firearm legal knowledge among a group that by definition should have accurate, standardized information of firearms law, given their recent apprehension and adjudication. Yet as our findings suggest, knowledge about gun and ammunition law is incomplete even among a population that should arguably know. This central finding should generate pause among scholars and policymakers because awareness of the law is a key tenet of deterrence-based policies. That is, how can we expect individuals—and prohibited possessors in particular—to be deterred from illegally possessing guns and ammunition if they are not aware of the laws to begin with? Additional studies are needed to assess whether and how specific and general knowledge of firearms law factors into an individual's decision to illegally possess ammunition or guns, but the present analysis provides an important first step by examining gun and ammunition law from the perspective of those who were not deterred.[3]

However, as a result of our sampling among jail detainees, we have no way of knowing whether our respondents' knowledge about the law predates their current incarceration or is a result of their most recent experience with the law. Their knowledge, then, may be significantly greater than that of those who have not been arrested, charged, and incarcerated for violations related to guns and ammunition, if only because of the direct (as opposed to vicarious) and recent nature of their experiences with the law. In this context, that most of our respondents were well aware of the gun restriction associated with their status as prohibited possessors is not entirely shocking.

On the other hand, significant gaps remained in respondents' knowledge of gun regulations in California (such as age requirements, licensing, and the like). Again, this may simply be related to the nature of our sample, dominated by prohibited possessors. After all, all you need to know once you are prohibited is that you are prohibited. Future studies should therefore examine the extent to which general gun regulations are understood among those who are not prohibited possessors, particularly in a place like California, where gun owners must navigate a complicated web of restrictions.

One of the most significant gaps in our respondents' knowledge was about ammunition laws. Our sample, although aware that they were excluded from buying or possessing guns, knew very little about the restrictions regarding ammunition, in either Los Angeles County broadly, or within the high regulation jurisdiction of the City of LA. Respondents' lack of awareness of ammunition regulations, especially relative to gun regulations, can be explained in a number of ways. First, because we have no way of verifying whether offenders were charged with gun or ammunition violations, it could be that the unevenness in knowledge is an artifact of differential ex post facto experience—if you have not been caught violating ammunition law, you may have less knowledge of the regulations. Second, it could be that the high geographic variability in ammu-

---

3. This is especially relevant given existing research suggesting that gun violence tends to involve a relatively small number of known offenders within any given neighborhood (Papachristos, Braga, and Hureau, 2012; Papachristos and Kirk 2015; Papachristos, Meares, and Fagan 2007; Papachristos and Wildeman 2012); in other words, understanding those who know the law but are not deterred is important to designing (more) effective regulations.

nition law in Los Angeles County impeded our respondents' abilities to obtain full and accurate information about the law. In some jurisdictions, such as the City of LA, ammunition transactions are, short of a background check and waiting period, treated almost as restrictively as gun transactions. But in neighboring jurisdictions, ammunition can be found and readily purchased in most sporting goods stores, and even in superstores like Wal-Mart. The unevenness of regulations in such geographically proximate areas may reinforce the idea that possessing ammunition is "not a big deal," as Respondent 79 noted.

Third, lax enforcement of ammunition regulation may also explain the lack of awareness about these regulations. Until 2015, ammunition transactions in the City of LA were recorded on paper forms, which is how other jurisdictions that mandate the use of ammunition logs continue to maintain their records. According to the Los Angeles Police Department (LAPD) gun unit officers, the archaic paper system meant that officers would need to periodically drive to the various FFLs that sell ammunition and collect the forms. For the logs to be useful, the officers in the "gun unit" would need to manually run each individual purchaser to determine whether they were a prohibited possessor and then decide whether to seek a warrant or arrest those who had violated the laws.[4] Although research has demonstrated that prohibited possessors continue to purchase ammunition (Tita et al. 2006), the personnel hours needed to run every single purchaser is beyond the thinly stretched resources of the LAPD.

In April 2015, the collection of the ammunition log format moved from paper to digital. However, the only savings realized in this transition is that officers no longer need to drive to the stores to collect the logs, as they are now electronically submitted. To determine whether a particular transaction involved a prohibited possessor, the members of the gun unit must still manually run the criminal history of the purchaser. According to preliminary data the LAPD shared with our research team, as of the end of January 2016, more than fifty-five thousand ammunition transactions had been recorded, but background checks had been run on less than 1 percent of the ammunition purchases. The inconsistent regulations across Los Angeles County, in combination with the lax enforcement of ammunition restrictions, may well influence how prohibited possessors perceive the availability of ammunition and the likelihood of getting caught buying it. In sum, it could well be that ammo laws are being enforced less than gun laws, and so people are both at less risk of experiencing them (low certainty of enforcement) and know less about them, thus limiting their deterrent effect. More analysis of what police are doing—and not just what prohibited possessors know and experience—could be an important topic for future research.

Although limitations in our data prevent us from disentangling when and from where respondents acquired their legal knowledge, our findings have important implications for the theory of deterrence, individual experiences of punishment, and the practical implementation of firearm regulations. Deterrence theory assumes that people who violate the law have accurate information about the law and the subsequent consequences, thereby equipping them to make a rational decision. However, our data reveal that individuals often have no, incomplete, or inaccurate information about firearms law, particularly ammunition law—even after having been punished for firearm-related offenses.

For gun laws, unlike for ammunition laws, the prerequisites for deterrence to operate effectively did appear to be present: participants in our study—especially those whose criminal records rendered them prohibited possessors—had enough information about the law to

---

4. Jacobs and Fuhr point out that one of the major problems with applying background checks to ammunition is that federal law prohibits the use of the National Instant Criminal Background Check System to check whether one is disqualified from being able to purchase (2016). Therefore, states interested in applying such a requirement must create their own database of those prohibited from buying ammunition. Also, it is not possible to electronically check the criminal backgrounds of lists of individuals electronically. Instead of batch checking, each individual must be entered individually.

know that they could not legally purchase, possess, or carry a firearm and that, should they be caught violating those laws, the punishment imposed would be certain and often severe. However, given that our sample was constructed from those members of the jail population who were there for firearms-related charges, their knowledge of the laws and consequences did not appear to dissuade them from unlawfully possessing a gun.

It is unclear from our data whether respondents' legal knowledge about gun laws was acquired before or after their most recent gun charge. What we do know is that our respondents discussed multiple experiences with the criminal justice system over time, as well as knowledge of multiple regulations and multiple punishment possibilities, suggesting that their knowledge was not based solely on the charge they were facing when we spoke with them. Moreover, results from prior analyses using the same data suggest that respondents both knew about gun laws prior to being arrested, going to jail, and participating in an interview with us and were not deterred from violating these laws, in spite of their knowledge. Findings from that analysis also suggest that extralegal factors, such as direct and indirect experience with gun victimization, as well as fear of violence from both police and gang members, weighed more heavily than legal factors in respondents' cost-benefit analysis (Barragan et al. 2016). Thus, when considered in this context, deterrence-related factors, like certainty and severity, might have only a marginal, if not negligible, impact on decision making.

RESEARCH AND POLICY IMPLICATIONS

Acknowledging the importance of both legal knowledge and the context within which decisions to violate the law are made, we offer several research and policy recommendations. To start, to better understand which deterrence-related components are more or less consequential for gun offending behavior, studies should examine whether and how much the certainty and severity of punishment works to deter potential offenders. These studies should also consider how other contextual factors, like police interactions, police legitimacy, and experiences with gun victimization, might mediate the impact of legal knowledge of certainty and severity of punishment for individual gun behavior. Additionally, studies should examine how detained offender perceptions of gun law compare with perceptions of gun law among nondetained populations, thus allowing for a more complete assessment of how the law does or does not deter illicit gun behavior in different contexts. If such studies replicate our findings that offenders are not aware of the regulations in the first place (ammunition regulations), or are aware of the regulations and the punishments, yet violate the law anyway (gun regulations), then alternative interventions deserve further consideration.

We also suggest that ammunition law warrants increased attention in the firearms literature. An important aspect of deterrence theory is that, for a policy to deter criminal behavior, it must first alter individual perceptions of risks of engaging in that behavior through effective communication of the threat of punishment, visibility of actors responsible for enforcing the law, and evidence of the actual enforcement of the law (see, for example, Apel 2013; Nagin 1998; Waldo and Chiricos 1972). Moreover, perceptions of the risk of sanctions are likely to be influenced by extensive media coverage and vicarious experiences of punishment by peers and family members (Apel 2013; Stafford and Warr 1993). The lax regulations on the sale of ammunition in the Los Angeles area, and the variability from one jurisdiction to the next, could potentially undercut the deterrent effect of firearms laws. The inconsistency of the law may lead to both misunderstandings and the creation of loopholes, which enable individuals to circumvent the law. Perhaps more important, the high variability of laws may cause those targeted by the laws to perceive arbitrariness in regulation and enforcement. This study provides a preliminary window into understanding these issues, but further research is warranted to more thoroughly disentangle how the unevenness of ammunition regulation and enforcement impacts knowledge of firearms law and illicit gun behavior both within California and beyond.

An obvious policy solution would be to implement laws and enforcement tools that rival those used for gun sales and to ensure that those laws would be the same for all jurisdictions. At the time of this study, California legislators had attempted to adopt ammunition purchase regulations similar to those in Los Angeles, which are arguably some of the most stringent in the state. Legal disputes impeded statewide passage of such regulations. However, in November 2016, the state approved Proposition 63, a comprehensive ammunitions regulation measure requiring all federally licensed dealers to perform background checks on individuals purchasing ammunition. Although the state's new ammunition regulatory measures will take one to two years to go into effect, our findings suggest a need to investigate how greater uniformity in ammunition law might affect both individual knowledge about ammunition regulation and gun-related behaviors among California residents. Yet such studies also have implications beyond the ammunition context because they can help inform scholarly and policy understandings on the benefits and limitations of policies that standardize previously disparate legal landscapes.

Last, our data suggest that ammunition regulations may have an untapped deterrent value worthy of further study. Prior policy efforts have suggested that directly "retailing" a regulation and punishment message to prohibited possessors might effectively deter high-risk individuals from possessing firearms (Braga and Weisburd 2012; Braga et al. 2001; Kennedy 1996; Tita et al. 2004; Wallace et al. 2016). Although additional study of the specific mechanism by which "retailing the message" to a specific few leads to widespread deterrence is necessary (Gravel and Tita 2015), including ammunition laws in this emergent conversation about preventative strategies may be especially fruitful. First there is the potential that universal background checks could prevent gun violence by stopping a purchase, which in turn prevents an imminent use. Second, messaging could lead to a better general understanding of both who can legally purchase and possess ammunition and what the legal ramifications are of being found unlawfully possessing either. Enforcement of ammunition regulations will not keep all motivated prohibited possessors from accessing ammunition, but as one of a menu of policies and regulations, it could contribute to the goal of reducing gun violence.

Limitations

Several limitations about participants' knowledge of the law in the present study warrant discussion. First, because laws in California can vary by jurisdiction (city, county, state), it is possible that individuals have incomplete knowledge about the laws governing their immediate neighborhood (a more restrictive city area versus a less restrictive county area, for instance). We also do not have exact address information from the participants (because we prioritized protecting their anonymity), so we cannot determine whether the information they provided is indeed accurate and reflective of the laws governing the communities where they lived before incarceration. Thus it is nearly impossible to determine whether respondents' understandings—or lack thereof—of gun and ammunition laws are the result of having specific knowledge of local laws, or of a more general understanding of local, state, and federal laws governing firearms.

Furthermore, respondents' comparatively limited knowledge of the laws regulating the purchase of ammunition may be explained by their unfamiliarity with the ammunition purchase process. Several respondents indicated that the guns they had purchased in the underground market came with ammunition, and others described the bullets as readily available in their communities. Together, these realties may render the need to purchase ammunition through regulated channels moot, which, in turn, decreases the need to understand the set of laws that govern this behavior. It is therefore perhaps of little surprise that respondents demonstrated the least understanding of ammunition laws.

Yet, unlike guns, which respondents knew they could not walk into a store to buy, respondents correctly identified the range of local stores where ammunition could be readily purchased. We take this to mean that regardless of their actual experiences, respondents in general perceived that regulation of the purchase of ammunition is far less restrictive than regulation of guns themselves—and that there are comparatively fewer ways to violate these laws and to trigger the associated punishments.

CONCLUSION

Overall, the findings presented here provide an important first step in grasping how offenders who have been subject to arrest and punishment make sense of a complicated web of gun and ammunition regulations within their communities. Our findings suggest that inconsistent regulations across jurisdictions, a lack of knowledge of some laws, and a willingness to violate them in spite of a perception that the punishment will be certain and severe compromise the practical implementation of deterrence-based firearms prohibitions. As state, local, and national conversations about firearm regulations move forward, it is important for policymakers and scholars to thoughtfully consider the role that legal knowledge plays in deterring illicit gun behavior, both among prohibited and nonprohibited possessors. Absent such study, it is incredibly difficult to know whether firearms restrictions are indeed effective at impacting individual behavior.

APPENDIX

Table A1. Current Charges of Sampled Participants

	Percentage
Felon with firearm 29800(A)(1)PC; 12021PC; 12021(A)1PC; 12021(C)1PC; 12021(E)PC	96.51%
Concealed carry firearm 12025(A)1PC; 12025(A)2PC	41.00
Prohibited possessor with ammunition 30305(A)1PC	14.80
Assault with firearm 245(A)(2)PC	14.50
Assault with semiautomatic firearm 245(B)PC	2.80
Carrying loaded firearm 12031(A)1PC	2.60
Carrying firearm 12020(A)PC	2.30
Possession short-barreled rifle or shotgun 33215PC	1.20
Armed during felony 12022.2PC	0.10
Prohibited transaction 12072(D)PC	0.10

Source: Authors' calculation from data provided by the Los Angeles County Sheriff's Office.
Note: Per our agreement with the Institutional Review Board, we had to delete any identifying information, including booking numbers, once a potential participant was approached to participate in the study. As a result, this table includes information of participants that were randomly sampled but not interviewed. It was not possible to differentiate between our participants and those who could not be approached or refused without access to their booking numbers. The California Penal Code sections referenced in this table were taken from the information provided to us for sampling purposes. Firearm related penal code sections were moved to a different section in 2012 and therefore some of the sections in the current table reflect sections used prior to these changes.

Table A2. Demographics of Respondents

	Male (n=129)		Female (n=11)		Total (n=140)	
	Frequency	Percentage	Frequency	Percentage	Frequency	Percentage
Age (years)						
≤ 20	12	9.30	3	27.27	15	10.95
21–30	69	53.49	4	36.36	73	52.14
31–40	33	25.58	2	18.18	35	25.00
41–50	9	6.98	1	9.09	10	7.14
≥ 51	4	3.10	—	—	4	2.86
Missing	2	1.55	1	9.09	3	2.14
Range	19–66		18–44		18–66	
Median age	26		27.5		27	
Mean age	29.21		28		29.12	
Race-ethnicity						
Black	62	48.06	2	18.18	64	45.71
Hispanic or Latino/a	44	34.11	6	54.55	50	35.71
White	4	3.10	1	9.09	5	3.57
Multiracial	7	5.43	1	9.09	8	5.71
Other	6	4.65	—	—	6	4.29
No response	6	4.65	1	9.09	7	5.00
Education						
High school not completed	42	32.56	3	27.27	45	32.14
High school diploma or GED	49	37.98	6	54.55	55	39.29
Some college	35	27.13	1	9.09	36	25.71
College degree	1	0.78	—	—	1	0.71
Missing	2	1.55	1	9.09	3	2.14
Gang affiliated?						
Yes	61	47.49	4	36.36	65	46.43
Have been shot at?						
Yes	52	40.31	3	2.73	55	39.29
Know someone shot at?						
Yes	68	52.71	7	63.64	75	53.57

Source: Authors' calculations.

Table A3. Sample Interview Questions

Question Category	Sample Questions
Guns	How might someone get a gun in your community? What if someone can't go to the store? How did you get this gun?
Ammunition	How about ammo? If you go to the store, what do you need to do in order to buy ammo? How did you get ammunition for this gun?
Punishment	Before this arrest, were you allowed to carry a gun? Why or why not? What happens if the police catch you with a gun? What would you get charged with? How much time will you get? What does this depend on?

Source: Authors' tabulation.

REFERENCES

Abbott, Andrew D. 2004. *Methods of Discovery: Heuristics for the Social Sciences*. New York: W. W. Norton & Co.

Apel, Robert. 2013. "Sanctions, Perceptions, and Crime: Implications for Criminal Deterrence." *Journal of Quantitative Criminology* 29(1): 67–101.

Austin, James, Wendy Naro-Ware, Roger Ocker, Robert Harris, and Robin Allen. 2012. *Evaluation of the Current and Future Los Angeles County Jail Population*. Denver, Colo.: The JFA Institute.

Barragan, Melissa, Nicole Sherman, Keramet Reiter, and George E. Tita. 2016. "'Damned if You Do, Damned if You Don't': Perceptions of Guns, Safety, and Legitimacy Among Detained Gun Offenders." *Criminal Justice and Behavior* 43(1): 140–55.

Braga, Anthony A., David M. Kennedy, Elin J. Waring, and Anne Morrison Piehl. 2001. "Problem-Oriented Policing, Deterrence, and Youth Violence: An Evaluation of Boston's Operation Ceasefire." *Journal of Research in Crime and Delinquency* 38(3): 195–225.

Braga, Anthony A., and David L. Weisburd. 2012. "The Effects of Focused Deterrence Strategies on Crime: A Systematic Review and Meta-Analysis of the Empirical Evidence." *Journal of Research in Crime and Delinquency* 49(3): 323–58.

Charmaz, Kathy. 2008. "Reconstructing Grounded Theory." In *The SAGE Handbook of Social Research Methods*, edited by Pertti Alasuutari, Leonard Bickman, and Julia Brannen. Thousand Oaks, Calif.: Sage Publications.

Chesnut, Kelsie Y., Melissa Barragan, Jason Gravel, Natalie Pifer, Nicole Sherman, Keramet Reiter, and George E. Tita. 2016. "Not an 'Iron Pipeline,' but Many Capillaries: Regulating Passive Transactions in Los Angeles' Secondary, Illegal Gun Market." *Injury Prevention*. Published online October 6, 2106. DOI: 10.1136/injuryprev-2016-042088.

Cook, Philip J. 1980. "Research in Criminal Deterrence: Laying the Groundwork for the Second Decade." *Crime and Justice* 2: 211–68.

Cook, Philip J., Susan T. Parker, and Harold A. Pollack. 2015. "Sources of Guns to Dangerous People: What We Learn by Asking Them." *Preventive Medicine* 79: 28–36.

Gibbs, Jack P. 1975. *Crime, Punishment, and Deterrence*. New York: Elsevier.

Gravel, Jason, and George E. Tita. 2015. "With Great Methods Come Great Responsibilities: Social Network Analysis in the Implementation and Evaluation of Gang Programs." *Criminology & Public Policy* 14(3): 559–72.

Gustafson, Karen S. 2011. *Cheating Welfare: Public Assistance and the Criminalization of Poverty*. New York: NYU Press.

Jacobs, James B., and Zoe A. Fuhr. 2016. "Universal

Background Checking—New York's SAFE Act." *Albany Law Review* 79(4): 101–28.

Kennedy, David M. 1996. "Pulling Levers: Chronic Offenders, High-Crime Settings, and a Theory of Prevention." *Valparaiso University Law Review* 31: 449–84.

———. 2009. *Deterrence and Crime Prevention: Reconsidering the Prospect of Sanction.* New York: Routledge.

Kennedy, David M., Anthony A. Braga, and Anne M. Piehl. 2001. "Reducing Gun Violence: The Boston Gun Project's Operation Ceasefire." NCJ 188741. Washington: U.S. Department of Justice.

Kidwell, Kaye D. and Paul A. Gottlober. 1999. *Temporary Assistance for Needy Families: Improving the Effectiveness and Efficiency of Client Sanctions.* Washington: Office of Inspector General, Department of Health and Human Services.

Law Center to Prevent Gun Violence. 2013. "2013 State Scorecard: Why Gun Laws Matter." San Francisco: Law Center to Prevent Gun Violence.

———. 2015. "2015 Gun Law State Scorecard." San Francisco: Law Center to Prevent Gun Violence.

Nagin, Daniel S. 1998. "Criminal Deterrence Research at the Outset of the Twenty-First Century." *Crime and Justice* 23(1): 1–42.

Papachristos, Andrew V., Anthony A Braga, and David Hureau. 2012. "Social Networks and the Risk of Gunshot Injury." *Journal of Urban Health* 89(6): 992–1003.

Papachristos, Andrew V., and David S. Kirk. 2015. "Changing the Street Dynamic: Evaluating Chicago's Group Violence Reduction Strategy." *Criminology & Public Policy* 14(3): 525–58.

Papachristos, Andrew V., Tracey L. Meares, and Jeffrey Fagan. 2007. "Attention Felons: Evaluating Project Safe Neighborhoods in Chicago." *Journal of Empirical Legal Studies* 4(2): 223–72.

Papachristos, Andrew V., and Christopher Wildeman. 2014. "Network Exposure and Homicide Victimization in an African American Community." *American Journal of Public Health* 104(1): 143–50.

Paternoster, Raymond. 1987. "The Deterrent Effect of the Perceived Certainty and Severity of Punishment: A Review of the Evidence and Issues." *Justice Quarterly* 4(2): 173–217.

Pierce, Glenn L., Anthony A. Braga, and Garen J. Wintemute. 2015. "Impact of California Firearms Sales Laws and Dealer Regulations on the Illegal Diversion of Guns." *Injury Prevention* 21(3): 179–84.

Stafford, Mark C., and Mark Warr. 1993. "A Reconceptualization of General and Specific Deterrence." *Journal of Research in Crime and Delinquency* 30(2): 123–35.

Strauss, Anselm, and Juliet Corbin. 1990. *Basics of Qualitative Research.* Newbury Park, Calif.: Sage Publications.

Tita, George E., Anthony A. Braga, Greg Ridgeway, and Glenn L. Pierce. 2006. "The Criminal Purchase of Firearm Ammunition." *Injury Prevention* 12(5): 308–11.

Tita, George E., K. Jack Riley, Greg Ridgeway, Clifford A. Grammich, and Allan Abrahamse. 2004. *Reducing Gun Violence: Results From an Intervention in East Los Angeles.* Santa Monica, Calif.: Rand Corporation.

Tittle, Charles R. 1980. *Sanctions and Social Deviance: The Question of Deterrence.* New York: Praeger.

Waldo, Gordon P., and Theodore G. Chiricos. 1972. "Perceived Penal Sanction and Self-Reported Criminality: A Neglected Approach to Deterrence Research." *Social Problems* 19(4): 522–40.

Wallace, Danielle, Andrew V. Papachristos, Tracey Meares, and Jeffrey Fagan. 2016. "Desistance and Legitimacy: The Impact of Offender Notification Meetings on High-Risk Offenders." *Justice Quarterly* 33(7): 1237–64.

Wintemute, Garen J. 2013. "Broadening Denial Criteria for the Purchase and Possession of Firearms: Need, Feasibility, and Effectiveness." In *Reducing Gun Violence in America: Informing Policy with Evidence and Analysis*, edited by Daniel W. Webster and Jon S. Vernick. Baltimore, Md.: Johns Hopkins University Press.

Wintemute, Garen J., Christiana M. Drake, James J. Beaumont, Mona A. Wright, and Carrie A. Parham. 1998. "Prior Misdemeanor Convictions as a Risk Factor for Later Violent and Firearm-Related Criminal Activity Among Authorized Purchasers of Handguns." *Journal of the American Medical Association* 280(24): 2083–87.

Zimring, Franklin E., and Gordon Hawkins. 1973. *Deterrence: The Legal Threat in Crime Control.* Chicago: University of Chicago Press.